THE BEEKEEPER'S FIELD GUIDE

Everything you need to know,
from honey to the hive

WILLIAM COLLINS

William Collins
An imprint of HarperCollinsPublishers
1 London Bridge Street
London SE1 9GF

WilliamCollinsBooks.com

HarperCollins*Publishers*
Macken House, 39/40 Mayor Street Upper,
Dublin 1, D01 C9W8, Ireland

First published by William Collins in 2024

10 9 8 7 6 5 4 3 2 1

Written by Meredith May, Claire Jones, Anne Rowberry and Margaret Murdin

A catalogue record for this book is available from the British Library.

ISBN 978-0-00-867291-1

Design by Eleanor Ridsdale Colussi
Picture research by Sophie Hartley

Printed and bound in Malaysia

DISCLAIMER:
The publishers urge readers to be responsible beekeepers. Please refer to the *Responsible Beekeeping*
chapter for details on the rules, safety and etiquette of beekeeping. Additionally, please familiarise
yourself with local and national restrictions and safety measures.

THE BEEKEEPER'S FIELD GUIDE

Everything you need to know,
from honey to the hive

Meredith May, Claire Jones, Anne Rowberry
and Margaret Murdin

Contents

INTRODUCTION

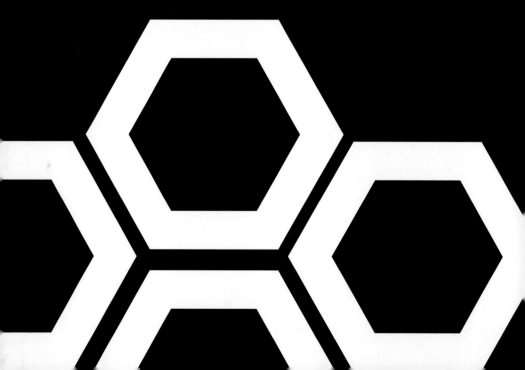

Introduction

History of beekeeping

Honey bees are among the first domesticated creatures, yet they remain fiercely independent to this day, refusing to be completely tamed. Any beekeeper knows that their bee colonies remain inside constructed hives strictly by choice; the minute the bees decide somewhere else is better, they will disappear back to the wild where they will thrive just fine without their human hosts. Maybe that's why the allure of beekeeping has withstood the test of time. It's a relationship riddle that can't be solved, but the ongoing desire to be close to these socially intelligent insects that model a harmonious society keeps us hooked.

First human–bee contacts

The oldest proof of contact between humans and honey bees comes from cave paintings in southern France, eastern Spain, and southern Africa. These ancient artworks depicted honey hunters raiding bee nests in the wild. The first to be discovered was a rock art painting done around 7,000 years ago inside the Cuevas de la Araña (Spider Caves) in Valencia, Spain. Discovered in 1917, it shows a figure who has climbed long, swaying roots, or vines, or perhaps ropes dangling from a steep cliff. The person is thrusting their right arm into a honey bee nest to grab the honeycomb as giant bees swirl around the hunter's head. In their other hand, the figure holds a basket for their plunder. Several rungs below, a second person is climbing with a honey basket.

Another, more intricate rock painting found in Spain, in the province of Castellón, depicts the perils of honey hunting. In this rendering, a dozen people plus a small animal that could be a goat wait at the bottom of a tall ladder running up a cliff to a honey bee nest. Bees swirl in the air as five honey hunters make the climb, and the unlucky person third from the top is tumbling off the ladder, limbs flailing as they fall. The fifth hunter closest to the ground appears to be jumping off, perhaps rethinking the merits of the expedition.

The perilous honey hunt was a risk worth taking for early civilizations that prized honey as one of the few sources of sugar carbohydrates needed for energy. Hunters went to great lengths to get it, withstanding multiple stings as they scaled perilous heights to reach the honeycomb. The basic methods used by these

Previous page: This rock carving from the Cuevas de la Araña, Spain, dating to ca. 5000 BCE, shows the perils of early honey hunting.

Top left: A Gurung honey hunter collects wild honey in the Nepalese foothills of the Himalayas.

Top right: A Mayan incense burner (ca. 1250–1527 CE) depicting Ah-Muzen-Cab, the god of bees and honey.

prehistoric honey hunters are still practised in some indigenous communities today, mainly the Bedouin in the Syrian desert, the Vedda of Sri Lanka, the Gurung in Nepal, and the Kattunayakan tribes in India.

Honey, which is 75 per cent sugar, was not only an important source of energy, but it was also used in wound healing, as a skin cosmetic, and to embalm the dead. Honey is a natural preservative because it absorbs water and is antimicrobial. When applied to animal tissue, it slowly releases hydrogen peroxide, which in turn inhibits bacterial growth. Egyptian and Arabic mourners in the second century CE would often seal bodies in beeswax and bury them in honey to embalm them.

Wax and honey were also used to preserve food. Both have anaerobic and drying properties that helped lengthen the shelf life of food.

Fermented honey was also used to create one of the first alcoholic drinks – mead. Water sweetened with honey and allowed to ferment was quaffed by gods, royalty, and commoners, according to the cave paintings, scrolls, and drinking horns they left behind. The oracle of Delphi insisted she couldn't predict the future without drinking honey wine first, and her priestesses were known as *mellisae*, which translates to bees. The love goddess Aphrodite was said to take bribes of mead in return for helping amorous ladies of the Greek upper class find their soulmates. Odin, the king of the Norse gods, drank mead to give him poetic prowess, and Roman warriors drank mead to get pumped up for battle.

Beeswax was also a vital resource, used to seal jars and to make glue. Egyptian cosmetologists added wax to facial creams and used it to sheen their curls. While Persians and Egyptians used beeswax to embalm their dead, Greek doctors prescribed melted wax diluted with water for dysentery. Beeswax candles brought light to homes and churches in medieval times.

Given how many of life's pleasures – sugar, alcohol, beauty cream, light – came from the beehive, early civilizations ascribed honey bees with all sorts of mystical origins and powers.

Egyptians believed that bees grew out of the falling tears of the sun god Ra, and the ancient Greeks linked the sound of buzzing bees to spirits emerging from the underworld, believing that bees could travel between the two realms and carry messages to the dead. Some Celtic peoples believed bees embodied human souls, and the Maya worshipped Ah-Muzen-Cab, the god of bees and honey. In British folklore, bees are thought to be miniature messengers of God. The Romans believed that honey bees would spring from the body of a dead ox.

The Greeks said that, if a swarm landed on an infant's mouth, the child was destined to be a great orator. Plato, Sophocles and Xenophon were all thought to have received such a visitation, as was St. Ambrose, a patron saint of beekeepers, according to Roman legend. According to the story, when Ambrose was a boy, a swarm of bees landed on his lips as he slept. Not only did they not sting him, but they also left honey behind as a gift. This was seen as the reason why Ambrose gave powerful sermons, rising to become bishop of Milan by the age of 34.

The first hives

Honey bees were universally beloved and worshipped, but it's widely believed that the first people to attempt to contain honey bees in manufactured hives were the Egyptians. The earliest known evidence of organized beekeeping dates back 4,500 years and was discovered about 16 km (10 miles) south of Cairo. There, inside the temple to the sun god Ra, built by the pharaoh Nyuserre Ini, an artist created a detailed stone bas-relief of beekeepers harvesting honey from vessels. The carving, now on display in the Neues

Museum in Berlin, shows a kneeling man blowing smoke on a stack of nine tapered, tubular beehives. Behind him, another man crouches to hold a tall urn steady as another man pours honey from a smaller saucepan into it. Another panel depicts a man tying a seal on a honey container. Above him is a shelf with two similar sealed containers, as well as an image of a honey bee.

It's believed the beehives depicted in the temple carving were made of Nile river mud or a type of clay, and a more recent discovery seems to back this up. In 2007, archaeologists in Tel Rehov in northern Israel unearthed the remains of up to 200 ancient beehives made of unfired clay. The hives were tapered cylinders, stacked up like firewood, each with a small bee entrance of less than 4 cm (less than 2 inches) on one end. Carbon dating of spilled grain found near the hives indicates that the apiary was active 3,000 years ago. Beekeepers in the Middle East today still configure their apiaries this way, stacking clay cylinders into mud walls, poking a small hole in one end for the bees, and a larger one in the opposite end to remove the honeycomb.

Roman beekeepers in the first century CE also stacked their hives in walled apiaries, according to the writings of farmer Lucius Junius Moderatus Columella of Rome, who wrote a 12-book treatise on agriculture, including one book devoted to beekeeping. He advised his readers to fashion hives from cork tree bark because of its insulating properties.

In medieval Germany, Poland, the Baltic region and Russia, where forests were plentiful, organized beekeeping began when honey gatherers began making small modifications to nests in the wild.

A man pours honey into a jar in an ancient Egyptian painted bas-relief from the tomb of Pabasa, in the Theban Necropolis. For the ancient Egyptians, honey symbolized rebirth.

They would find a honey bee colony nesting in a tree trunk, and they might make small modifications to the hole, widening the entrance or expanding the space inside. Sometimes they would hang a plank on a rope over the hollow to protect the colony from predators, leaving a small opening for the bees to come and go. They used ropes and a pulley system to lift themselves up to reach the nest to harvest honeycomb.

As the art of beekeeping spread, so did the art of making containers to hold bees. Early beekeepers used what they had on hand to make beehives. In less forested regions – such as the Netherlands, Ireland, the United Kingdom and France – beehives were not that much more than a basket of coiled rope, a bunch of reeds, coiled grass or straw woven into a small dome called a skep (from *skeppa*, a Norse word meaning 'big basket'). Skeps were often plastered with dung and mud. Other beekeepers turned clay pots upside down on the ground and made a crack near the base for a bee entrance – or hung small sections of hollow logs from tree branches.

These early beekeepers didn't have a way to open their makeshift hives and inspect what was going on inside, and the bees simply attached their wax combs to the interior walls, making it impossible to remove the honeycomb without tearing the nest apart. These early hives were an improvement over honey hunting because they allowed the beekeeper to keep the bees nearby so they could get to the honey more readily. However, beekeepers often killed the bees so they could remove the honey without getting stung. Some beekeepers lit the flammable rope or straw skeps on fire. Others put their hives in a sack and drowned the bees in water. After removing the honeycomb, if the hive vessel was still intact, they would coat the inside with honey and bang pots and pans, believing the sound would attract a new swarm of wild bees.

During most of the seventeenth century and into the eighteenth, beekeepers around the world continued to experiment with hundreds of hive designs, trying to come up with a configuration that pleased the bees yet also gave beekeepers a way to harvest honey without destroying the brood nest. Beekeepers in Germany and Japan both developed a system of stacking wooden boxes, with removable horizontal bars that rested inside the tops of the boxes. The bees built natural sheets of honeycomb suspended from the bars in the uppermost box and extended their nest downward into the lower boxes. Each individual honeycomb could be lifted out for inspection by grasping the horizontal top bar. These early designs became what is now known as the Warré hive, named for the French beekeeper Émile Warré (1867–1951) who wanted a

The movable frame hive designed by François Huber in 1789. The wooden leaves carrying the honeycomb could be flipped like the pages of a book. This example was made in 1792.

natural beehive that could be manipulated by the beekeeper.

Another beehive variation that was developed at this time is the Kenyan top-bar hive, which is still in wide use throughout Africa today. Rather than stacking wooden boxes vertically, the Kenyan top-bar hive is just one long, horizontal box with a row of bars resting inside. The two longer sides of the box slope inwards towards one another, which prevents the bees from attaching honeycomb to the inside walls.

A major revolution in beehive design came in 1789, when Swiss naturalist François Huber (1750–1831) introduced the concept of a wooden frame to enclose individual honeycombs on four sides. This would be the first step towards modern-day beekeeping. Huber, who was blind, wanted a safer way to pry apart the honey bee nest so he could study their behaviour up close. He built a hive that consisted of a dozen slender wooden boxes that were hinged together so they opened like book pages; and each 'page' held an individual sheet of honey comb. He called it the 'leaf', or 'book', hive.

Working with a sighted assistant – and his own amplified senses of touch, hearing and scent to study honey bees – Huber and his colleague used his leaf hive to make several important breakthroughs in our understanding of the honey bee's inner world, including that the queen mates outside the hive, that drones are expelled in winter, and that honey bees communicate with their antennae.

While his innovation created a better way to study honey bee behaviour and led to major advances in bee science, ultimately his design was an obstacle to practical beekeeping. It turned out to be cumbersome and difficult to build, and the bees kept building wax bridges between the 'pages', sticking them together.

The development of modern-day beekeeping

Over half a century later, Huber's scientific writings inspired another inventor to create what is essentially today's modern beehive. A pastor in Philadelphia named Lorenzo Lorraine Langstroth (1810–95) was piqued by Huber's creation of removable honeycomb frames and wanted to figure out a new way to make them work.

The 38-year-old Reverend Langstroth had turned to beekeeping after spending his youth training to be a Congregationalist pastor, only to discover he was terrified of public speaking. He suffered from debilitating depression and anxiety, sometimes unable to speak for months at a time. The dispirited pastor retreated from church leadership to recuperate in his garden, where he returned to his childhood fascination with insects and decided to become a commercial beekeeper.

He began keeping bees in basic wooden boxes with top bars, but the bees kept sticking their combs to the interior walls and gluing the hive cover down with propolis – a sticky, resinous crack filler bees make from tree sap. Every time Langstroth wanted to inspect the hive, he had to destroy part of the honeycomb nest to do so.

Langstroth became determined to improve on Huber's hive design. He built a rectangular hive box with an interior lip on the opposite, shorter sides – to hold a row of hanging wooden frames – a concept much like today's office filing cabinets, with their 'hanging' files.

He experimented with the spacing between the wooden frames, what's now referred to as 'bee space', and settled on slightly less than 1 cm (or three-eighths of an inch) as the ideal gap. Any wider, and the bees would fuse the frames together with wax. Any narrower, and the bees couldn't pass freely. When there was just under a centimetre of air space between the honeycomb frames, he could always lift them out of the hive easily. He tried adding, removing and rearranging the frames – and no matter what he changed, if he maintained the one-centimetre spacing between frames, the bees adjusted to his changes.

Langstroth had built a better beehive. Although Polish beekeeper Johann Dzierzon (1811–1906) was close to the same discovery, in 1852 Langstroth got the patent first. With the great assistance of his wife, who deciphered his near-illegible handwriting, in 1853 Langstroth published her transcription of his notes as *Langstroth on the Hive and the Honey-Bee: A Bee Keeper's Manual.*

Top left: The Reverend Lorenzo Langstroth, inventor of the 'Langstroth' hive still in use today, sits for his portrait with his revolutionary invention beside him. In the background we can see a whole apiary of working Langstroth hives.

Top right: Inside a modern-day Langstroth hive, showing the wax-covered frames.

Langstroth's design took the guesswork out of beekeeping, allowing beekeepers for the first time to carefully unpack a beehive and inspect all the parts. His creation of suspended, removable honeycomb frames allowed beekeepers to remove individual sheets of honeycomb safely, without having to destroy the brood nest, injure bees or waste honey to inspect the colony. Suddenly, beekeepers had access to the honey bee colony's private world. They could monitor the hive for egg, honey and pollen production, and catch diseases or dwindling populations in time to make changes, giving beekeepers a greater sense of control over a colony's destiny. With this new knowledge, beekeepers could produce much more surplus honey per colony than ever before. The shy reverend had changed beekeeping for ever – creating a potential for beekeeping to expand from a pastime for hobbyists and small farmers to a full-scale honey production business.

The Langstroth hive was easily replicated and reinterpreted across the world, yet Langstroth never became rich off his invention. Others tweaked his central idea and created the WBC hive, named after its British designer, William Broughton Carr (1836–1909); the Dadant, after its French American builder, Charles Dadant (1817–1902); and the National, Britain's version of the Langstroth, introduced in the 1920s. However, the general principle of stacked boxes with suspended, movable frames inside has remained fundamentally unchanged since Langstroth first conceived of it – and is the most common hive structure used in modern beekeeping today.

A burgeoning pursuit

Langstroth probably never envisioned his beehive would be universally used nearly two centuries later. From backyard gardens, schools, churches, and hotel and restaurant rooftops to large-scale industrial farms, even to airports and prisons, beehives are popping up everywhere. Today, it seems everyone knows someone who knows someone who is a beekeeper. Beekeeping courses are making their way into university curriculums, and many not-for-profit organizations that work with survivors of war, domestic violence, and human trafficking are incorporating beekeeping programmes because of the calm it brings to the people they serve. Beekeeping is being used to create entrepreneurship in the Global South, and it's also a celebrity hobby: President Barack Obama kept hives at the White House, actor Morgan Freeman built a massive bee sanctuary at his Mississippi ranch, businesswoman Martha Stewart keeps bees, as do rockers including Flea from the Red Hot Chili Peppers and Metallica front man James Hetfield.

Globally, the number of beehives has risen 26 per cent in the last decade, from 80 million to 120 million, according to the Food and Agriculture Organization of the United Nations. Most of the beekeepers tending those hives are hobbyists, with a few hives on their property that they keep for the joy and wonder of it.

There are many ways to be a beekeeper. Backyard beekeepers who want to hone their craft can benefit from becoming a Master Beekeeper. Many states, universities and beekeeping associations offer certificated master programmes, which offer classes and apprenticeships to deepen beekeeping knowledge in such fields as biology, hive management and queen rearing. Students must pass written and field exams in order to receive their certificate.

City dwellers can join the growing movement of urban rooftop beekeepers, as local authorities ease restrictions on beekeeping to address concerns over pollinator decline. Surprisingly, while it may seem counterintuitive, honey bees thrive in most cities. Urban areas offer plenty of forage from all the imported plants in city parks, community gardens and high-rise green spaces that bloom throughout the year. Unlike their country counterparts, that must compete for an annual bloom that dies out in the autumn, city bees have the luxury of a long-lasting, diverse foodscape. They also have access to water in gutters, fountains and sprinklers. Honey bees living atop urban rooftops are less likely to encounter agricultural pesticides, predators or vandals. Their isolation mimics the seclusion they prefer in the wild – out of sight, high up in a tree cavity or the crevice of a clifftop wall.

Beekeeping can also be a good business, as customers become more aware of adulterated, imported honey and seek out pure honey from local beekeepers. Furthermore, as the popularity of beekeeping increases, there's a rising market for selling starter bee colonies and mated queens. Some beekeepers make money rescuing swarms from trees or cutting them out of walls, others rent their hives to farmers for pollination, and migratory beekeepers truck thousands of hives every year to large agricultural farms following the blooming season.

In addition, there is the growing natural beekeeping movement for those whose aim is to create honey bee sanctuaries with as little disturbance to the colonies as possible. Natural beekeepers are the radical dissenters of apiculture, who eschew traditional beekeeping practices such as using chemical mite treatments, synthetic foundation frames to make bees construct neat honeycombs, clipping the queen's wings to prevent swarming, and importing queens from other parts of the world.

Natural beekeepers defer to the bees and believe that human intervention is the root of honey bee decline. They gather swarms rather than purchasing bees from outside their local area and keep them in conditions that closely resemble tree cavities. They don't harvest the honey and prefer to let overcrowded colonies swarm naturally. They let weak colonies fail so the stronger ones contribute to the gene pool.

However you decide to share your life with honey bees, beekeeping is a joyful commitment to keeping the creatures alive that hold up our food system. Nearly 75 per cent of the world's crops depend on pollinators, and honey bees alone are responsible for pollinating one-third of the fruits and vegetables we eat. That circle of care is what keeps many a beekeeper sweating in their bee suits in the hot summers, worrying and fussing over their bees, making sure they have everything they need.

Being a beekeeper means constantly monitoring the weather, planning for the changing seasons, and spending a lot of time looking at flowering plants. A beekeeper learns to see the world the way a honey bee does, and in doing so becomes more attached to the natural world.

The following chapters offer ways to become more acquainted with the history, evolution and biology of the honey bee, as well as the art, practice and business of beekeeping. Whether you are a newbie or a pro, *The Beekeeper's Field Guide* is a comprehensive tool for anybody who seeks to deepen their bond with honey bees.

A GUIDE TO
HONEY BEES
AND THE HIVE

A Guide to Honey Bees and the Hive

Honey bee origins

Bees were flying during the time of dinosaurs. They descended from a carnivorous wasp more than 100 million years ago, during the Cretaceous period. Their original home was on Gondwana, the giant southern landmass from which the continents of Africa, South America, Australia and Antarctica pulled apart.

One of these prehistoric bees flew into a glob of tree resin 99 million years ago and was preserved, later to be discovered in a piece of fossilized amber by scientists in Myanmar (Burma) in 2020. That same year, in Patagonia, scientists unearthed bee burrows fossilized in volcanic ash, determined to be 100 million years old.

Fossils, however, are just hints of history, and bees are possibly even older still. Subsequent studies of the similarities in DNA sequences of wasps and bees suggest that their lineages first diverged closer to 130 million years ago.

These primitive bees were not like modern honey bees: they did not live in complex societies with a queen and build wax honeycomb to stockpile honey. They were nomads, more like today's native bees – solitary insects that dug their own nest tunnels underground, or into plants, and took care of just themselves and perhaps a handful of offspring. The construction of large nests came much later.

Nor were these early bees interested in eating nectar or pollen like today's honey bees. They visited flowers solely to prey on other insects drawn to the blooms. This was a time in history when plants were just beginning to develop flowers, adapting to the insects that made more reliable pollinators than wind. They began transforming their lacklustre brown and green flowers into different shapes, petal colours and patterns in a competition to attract flying insects they could count on to co-mingle their pollen. One of these showy flowers must have caught the attention of some primitive bees, enticing them to try a taste of pollen. This was their first evolutionary step towards becoming honey bees.

No one knows exactly when that first bite was taken. But we do know, from the ancient specimens that contain physical characteristics of both wasp and bee, what sort of body changes occurred. Wasps developed thick hairs, making them start to look

Previous page: A honey bee harvesting pollen.

A fossilized bee, dating to 50 million years ago, found at the Green River Formation – an important Eocene fossil site located in western Colorado, eastern Utah, and southwestern Wyoming, USA.

more like the fuzzy honey bees we know today. The new hairs allowed pollen grains to stick to their bodies, making them more adept at transferring pollen between flowers. Their tongues also started to elongate, allowing them to reach the nectar deep within a bloom.

This new symbiotic relationship was a win-win for both bees and flowers. It spurred an all-out blossom competition, as flowers grew ever more fanciful and nectar-rich to attract bees. The increasing abundance of food was good for bees, who learnt that it is much easier to hunt things that don't move versus other bugs that flee. The prehistoric bees gave up eating insects and became vegetarian, sealing their future as a keystone species in the ecosystem.

At first, these early bees were happy going solo, much like today's solitary bees. When they started living in large, interdependent social groups is a bit of an educated guess – but there are clues. A stingless bee, like the highly social species that live in vast colonies today in South America, was fossilized in an 80-million-year-old piece of amber found in New Jersey. Although stingless bees are not true honey bees, they are a stepping stone and are placed in the same family, *Apidae*, along with bumble bees.

Stingless bees make wax and store smaller amounts of honey in little egg-shaped wax pots.

The first appearance of fossils resembling modern honey bees dates back to the end of the Eocene epoch, some 34 million years ago. The honey bee genus *Apis* includes as many as a dozen species, which occur mainly in Southeast Asia, India and China. The only honey bee species found in Europe is the western honey bee, *Apis mellifera*, from which beekeeping developed.

There is a long-standing debate about where contemporary honey bees originated. Bee scientists looking at thousands of fossils and archives of bee DNA sequences have drawn different conclusions. Whereas one long-held belief is that honey bees evolved in sub-Saharan Africa before spreading to Europe and Asia, other researchers pin their origin to Asia. Most recently, studies of the mitochondrial DNA of honey bees by a biologist in Newfoundland, Canada, have flipped the story, putting the origin of honey bees first in northern and southeastern Europe before their emigration through the Middle and Near East into Africa.

No matter where they started, or which way they flew, honey bees have always found a home. They have adapted to tropical jungles and Mediterranean climates, thrived near deserts and in high-altitude mountain ranges.

By the early 1600s, honey bees had made their way to the western hemisphere, Australia and the Pacific Islands. European settlers fleeing war, poverty or religious persecution brought beehives on board as they sailed towards new lives elsewhere. Some of these first imported bees migrated with the Spanish beekeepers who were moving to Mexico, or with English and Swedish colonists setting up new homesteads in Massachusetts, Delaware, Virginia and Connecticut. Most settlers travelled with dark European honey bees, named for their jet-black colour. The bees were well adapted to the relatively cool summers and long, cold winters in forested regions of Austria and Germany, which made for a particularly easy adjustment to their new lives on the temperate east coast of North America.

As these new colonies grew and divided by swarming, they rapidly colonized their host countries. The prolific *Apis mellifera* is now the most domesticated bee worldwide and can be found on every continent except Antarctica.

Clockwise from top left: A bee preserved in a piece of Mexican amber; solitary bees of the *Osmia bicornis* species flying into their nest; close-up of a stingless bee (tribe *Meliponini*) in its nest; a fossilized imprint of a bee.

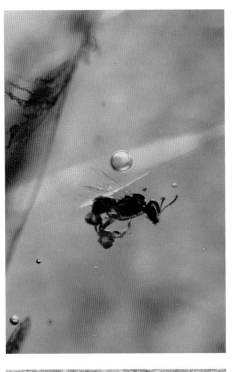

A female western honey bee (*Apis mellifera*) nectars at the flowers of a New Mexico locust tree (*Robinia neomexicana*) in the USA.

Honey bee species and identification

There are at least 20,000 known species of bee in the world, with an estimated 5,000–10,000 yet to be discovered. They can be divided into four broad categories: solitary, stingless, bumble bees and honey bees.

Almost all of these species don't store honey. Most bees are loners who prefer solitary life to a bustling colony, excavating their own small nest underground or tunnelling into trees and plants. They forage for their own nectar and pollen, preferring the peace of a quiet home. These solitary, native bees are single working mothers who care for themselves and a small number of offspring.

Approximately 250 bee species are bumble bees, 600 are stingless bees, fewer than a dozen are honey bees, and all of the rest – some 19,000 species – are solitary bees.

The extroverts are the honey bees, whose distinguishing characteristic is their highly social lifestyle, living and working cooperatively in large, complex societies under one queen, dividing labour and sharing resources. Typically, they build permanent nests high off the ground, in tree hollows, rock crevices, or dangling from branches, raising generation after generation in the same spot. These bee families build sheets of wax honeycomb and provision them with honey and pollen to get themselves through periods of shortage and cold weather.

Depending on which entomologist you ask, there are seven, or nine, or a dozen honey bee species. The discrepancy is taxonomic; opinions vary whether certain types of Asian honey bees warrant full and distinct species status or should be demoted to a subspecies, leading to different species counts.

Whichever way you map it, honey bees make up just a tiny fraction of all bees on the planet, yet they get most of the attention in both science and popular culture. Interestingly, among just the relatively few honey bee species, only two have historically been removed from the wild for modern-day beekeeping: the western honey bee and the Asian honey bee.

All honey bees are members of the genus *Apis* – the Latin word for bee – following a classification created in 1758 by Swedish botanist Carl Linnaeus (1707–78) who was the first to devise the scientific binomial system to name plants and animals we still use today. The first honey bee he described taxonomically in his *Systema Naturae* (1735) is the dark European honey bee, and his specimen is kept on a pin at the Natural History Museum in London, where it remains a useful prototype for scientists to this day.

Linnaeus's honey bee genus *Apis* is further divided into three major sub-groups based on how honey bees nest:

Megapis: giant honey bees that build massive, open-air nests;
Micrapis: dwarf honey bees that nest outside on one small sheet of honeycomb;
Apis: western honey bees and Asian honey bees that nest inside cavities.

Western and Asian honey bees are both known as 'beekeepers' bees', as they are the only two types of honey bee used in domestic and commercial beekeeping.

Western honey bee

Of the two species, the western honey bee (*Apis mellifera*) is the most widely managed honey bee throughout the world. It's the best known of all bee species, the agricultural darling that is the most studied and researched, today considered livestock in many countries. *Apis mellifera* is the save-the-bees poster child, the fuzzy yellow-and-black striped star of every movie, illustrated children's book, and honey jar on the supermarket shelf. The western honey bee is beloved because she is an efficient pollinator, produces an overabundance of honey and can regenerate quickly.

Because of this, entomologists have been selectively breeding western honey bees over the last several thousand years. Today's beekeepers can now choose among more than 30 different subspecies and hybrids that have been bred to possess certain characteristics – such as gentleness, strong honey production and hygienic grooming behaviour.

Some popular western honey bee breeds favoured by beekeepers are:

Italian

The most common and widely distributed of all the western honey bee varieties, known for its gentleness and for producing a lot of honey and beeswax. The go-to bee for beekeeping, the Italian honey bee is often golden coloured and adaptable to various climates, and has been cross-bred all over the world. Italian queens are considered prolific egg layers, ensuring large colonies that can fight off pests and predators. This comes with some disadvantages: because of their colony size, they go into winter with a lot of bees that will need a lot of supplemental feeding, especially in places where winters are long. They are prone to starvation, gorging on their own honey – if ample forage or beekeeper-supplied pollen patties and sugar water aren't available. In desperation, they will rob neighbouring hives of honey, or abandon their own and join another colony that has plenty of food.

Carniolan

This bee comes from Eastern Europe, mainly Austria, Bulgaria, Bosnia and Serbia, and is a favourite of backyard beekeepers because their gentle nature makes them especially easy to work with. Carniolans are well adapted to cold regions and more likely to forage on cool, wet days. They are on the smaller side, and their bodies are covered in many hairs that make them appear gray. The colony shrinks down considerably in winter, so they require less feeding during the cold season, but they build back up quickly in spring, making them more apt to swarm during the nectar flow if the beekeeper doesn't give them room to expand. They are considered excellent wax makers, so they are a favourite of beekeepers whose focus is candles, soap and salves.

Caucasian

Originally from the transcontinental Caucasus region sandwiched between the Black and Caspian seas, these bees are greyish-brown and have a longer tongue than other breeds, so they can extract nectar from deeper, trumpet-shaped blossoms. They are considered by many to be the calmest of all the honey bees, making them a good choice for novice beekeepers. They bide their time in spring, then build up their colonies later in summer. However, they are not as productive as Italian bees, and they are great manufacturers of propolis – the sticky 'bee glue' honey bees make from tree sap and use to seal unwanted cracks in the hive, making it difficult to unstick the frames and boxes during hive inspections. Propolis is also known to contain natural plant antibiotics that are beneficial to bees and can be harvested for tinctures believed to boost immunity.

German
Also known as the 'dark European honey bee', these bees have large, stocky bodies that range from dark brown to jet black, without any yellow markings at all. This was the first honey bee brought by settlers to North America in the seventeenth century and the one Linnaeus first classified. German honey bees are well adapted to cold and damp climates, as their original range includes Switzerland, Scandinavia and Austria. They are good for beekeepers in snowy locations, because they are hardy and can last through long periods of freezing temperatures. On the downside, they are considered more easily agitated by hive inspections, and a little defensive. Some say they are not the best house cleaners, leaving wax debris and dead bees in their hives. Furthermore, their honey production is decent, but not as abundant as that of some of the other honey bee lines.

African
Because so much has been written about honey bees from Africa, it's worth mentioning here what the African honey bee is and isn't. There are at least ten western honey bee subspecies in Africa. Depending on where you are on the continent, honey bees are given different names. From Senegal to the Congo, they are known as Western African bees, another strain in South Africa goes by the name Cape honey bee, and elsewhere, beekeepers refer to their bees by a shortened version of their Latin name – *Adansonii*. African bees in general are mostly feral and considered too defensive for most beekeepers, but skilled locals know how to trap and manage wild swarms. African honey bees are not to be confused with the 'Africanized Killer Bee' – a hybridized African western honey bee that's made headlines for terrorizing people (see page 30).

African honey bees thrive in tropical areas, have strong resistance to mites and other diseases, and proliferate quickly, which makes them prone to swarming and abandoning their hive. They are much more interested in gathering pollen than honey. They respond swiftly and aggressively to hive disturbances, sending out three to four times more bees to answer threats, and pursuing intruders for up to 30 m (100 feet) from their home. They will also take over other honey bee colonies by forcing their way in, then executing and replacing the queen. Researchers believe African bees evolved to be more aggressive because of their arid surroundings, as natural selection favoured the bee colonies that did a better job protecting their hives from predators and robber bees.

African honey bees are interesting to bee scientists because they have very few problems with the most serious pest that plagues almost all other honey bee species – the *Varroa destructor* mite. Part of the reason African bees are so mite-resistant is because they keep their colonies small so there's minimal brood for mites to parasitize. Their frequent swarming provides several breaks in the brood cycle, depriving mites of the larvae they thrive on. Also, feral African honey bees are often isolated from nearby colonies, so they are less prone to mite and disease infestations from neighbouring bee colonies.

The western honey bee has also been widely hybridized, either deliberately or accidentally. Some common hybrids are:

Buckfast
Buckfast bees were developed by Karl Kehrle, known as Brother Adam, a Benedict monk at Buckfast Abbey in Devon, England, in response to a tracheal mite that nearly wiped out honey bees on the British Isles in the 1920s. The deadly 'Isle of Wight Disease' prompted the United States Congress to pass the Honey Bee Act in 1922, prohibiting further bee imports from southern England to protect honey bees in the United States. Brother Adam was tasked with creating a bee stock that could withstand the disease. He travelled the world, racking up more than 160,900 km (100,000 miles), interviewing beekeepers and learning about bee characteristics, becoming convinced genetic diversity would produce a superior bee. He crossed British bees with numerous other western honey bees, including Italian, French, Turkish, Greek, and two rare strains of docile African bees.

The resulting Buckfast bees are resistant to tracheal mites and very hygienic, grooming one another of mites and removing diseased larvae from the hive. They are gentle and prolific honey producers. Many commercial bee farms and beekeepers choose Buckfast bees because they have a strong survival rate, as they produce less brood in the autumn and thus do not draw down as much from their winter food stores. They also like to rob honey from nearby hives, much like Italian bees do.

Russian

Russian bees are a cross between Italian, Caucasian and Carniolan honey bees that produce a black or dark-brown hybrid. They are from the Russian Far East, in Primorsky Krai near the Sea of Japan, and were imported to the United States in 1997 by researchers who hoped to use them to breed more mite-resistant bees. Bee breeders worked for several years, and while they didn't get the level of success they hoped for, this strain of bees is considered to be one of the hardier bees; it is, for example, highly resistant to tracheal mites.

Russian bees pay attention to the weather. They are slow to produce brood early in the spring, waiting patiently for the flowers. Once the bloom starts, their population explodes, and they can fill up their hive so rapidly that the colony swarms, looking for more room, making them one of the 'swarmiest' bee types. Although they build fast once they start, they also pull back if there is a dearth. They build many queen cells at all times of the year, always at the ready to replace their queen. Because they overwinter in very small clusters, they require less feeding in winter. Some beekeepers report that Russian bees are a bit testy – they have an erratic temperament that's not aggressive, yet not mild-mannered either. They have dramatic mood swings, which makes it interesting each time the beekeeper opens the hive cover.

Cordovan

Cordovan bees are a subset of Italian bees and remain a bit of a mystery – because it's unclear how and when they became their own separate strain. They are sometimes called blonde bees, distinguishable by their bright-yellow bodies and very faint stripes – a colouring controlled by a single recessive gene. Their legs and head, instead of the traditional black, are a more purplish-brown shade. They are a rare bee that's difficult to purchase, and most often acquired by catching a wild swarm. They are extremely docile, less prone to swarm, superb honeycomb builders, and prefer warm over cold weather. Like their Italian cousins, they consume copious amounts of food and will rob nearby hives to satisfy their hunger.

Africanized honey bee

This bee closely resembles the common western honey bee, yet it is a cross between any of the 30-plus varieties of western honey bee and one species of African bee (*Apis mellifera scutellata*) found in the East African lowlands. These bee hybrids have made headlines as the infamous 'Africanized Killer Bees', but whether they deserve that title depends on who you are and where you sit. While those who have been chased by these ultra-defensive bees see environmental hazard, entomologists looking to build a better bee see possibility, because Africanized bees appear to be the most resistant to the honey bee's worst enemy, the parasitic *Varroa* mite.

The Africanized honey bee began as a lab experiment gone awry and has caused concern ever since. In 1956, renowned Brazilian geneticist Warwick Kerr imported East African lowland honey bee queens to breed them with western honey bee drones in his home country, hoping to produce a hybrid bee that was even-tempered, disease resistant and better suited to the tropical climate. He had just created a first generation of hybrid bees when 26 of the African queens and their small colonies escaped, in 1957, quickly taking over South America and interbreeding with feral and managed bee colonies. Kerr hoped that the more aggressive traits of the escapees would dilute naturally by mixing with 'local' western honey bees, but that wasn't the case. Nearby farmers began reporting wild bees relentlessly attacking their livestock.

Africanized honey bees have unusual guarding behaviour and will chase a perceived threat up to 400 m (a quarter of a mile), and have seriously injured – and even killed – humans, farm animals and pets with their group stings. Africanized bees made their way north to the United States by 1985, where they have since spread through many of the southwestern states.

There have been several recent breeding programmes to course-correct and produce a gentler form of the Africanized honey bee, and now these new lines are some of the most sought-after in Brazil, for their disease resistance and honey production. Brazil is now one of the top ten honey-producing countries, and its beekeepers have learnt to handle Africanized bees with slow, careful movements, wearing full-body suits and using oversized smokers to calm the bees.

Beekeepers everywhere should make sure they are receiving the gentler form of Africanized bees for their hives, and if they suspect they are not, they are advised to remove the queen and replace her with the mellower variety.

Asian honey bee

Besides the western honey bee and all its genetic variations, the only other domesticated species of honey bee is the Asian honey bee (*Apis cerana*). It's found mostly in Southeast and East Asia, including parts of northern Russia, Indonesia, India and Japan, and as far west as the Afghan Highlands. The Asian honey bee was brought to New Guinea in the 1970s and has since spread into Australia and the Solomon Islands.

Asian honey bees are slightly smaller than western honey bees, form smaller colonies and produce less honey. While these bees can adapt to life in an apiary, they are natural migrators and prone to abandoning their manufactured hives in search of better forage.

Because Asian honey bees have lived with the parasitic *Varroa* mite the longest of any bee species, they have adapted strong resistance, using hygienic behaviours such as removing mite-infested larvae from the honeycomb, and cleaning and renewing the brood cells. They are also known to withstand freezing temperatures better than western honey bees.

The Asian honey bees of Japan have evolved an ingenious strategy to deal with the large Asian hornets that try to ransack their hives. They cluster in a ball on the intruder and vibrate their wing muscles, raising their collective body heat to over 38 °C (100 °F) to literally cook the hornet to death.

There are several species of tropical honey bee that are elusive and rare and thought to be offshoots of the Asian honey bee. The Philippine honey bee nests in caves on the Philippine island of Mindanao and the Sulawesi and Sangihe islands in Indonesia. Koschevnikov's honey bee, named in honour of Russian entomologist Grigorii Aleksandrovich Kozhevnikov (1866–1933), and a second honey bee – identified only by its Latin name, *Apis nuluensis* – nest in the rainforest trees of Borneo and parts of Malaysia, Indonesia and Brunei.

It was once believed that the Asian honey bee (right) and the western honey bee were just different races of the same species, but they are now considered separate species.

Undomesticated honey bees

The remaining two honey bee groups are the feral *Megapis* and *Micropis* – the giant and dwarf honey bees. But just because these two types of wild honey bees refuse to be contained by beekeepers, that doesn't stop humans from harvesting their honey. The dwarf and the giant honey bees are precious to modern-day honey hunters, whose ancestors have passed down sacred ceremonies and methods for finding and harvesting their honey.

GIANT BEES

The largest honey bee in the world is the Himalayan giant honey bee, which grows to 2 cm (three-quarters of an inch) long and nests high on remote cliffsides in the Himalayas of Nepal, on half-moon-shaped dangling combs stretching up to 1.8 m (6 feet) across. The only people who dare harvest their honey are the Hindu Kush honey hunters, who carry long poles and buckets up precarious rope ladders to scale the cliffs at night following ancient traditions.

The second of the giant honey bees is called the rock bee, or simply the giant honey bee, and can be found in tropical rainforests of Malaysia, Thailand, Vietnam and Borneo, where they form what look like blankets of honeycomb draped over high tree branches, measuring nearly a metre (or several feet) across. Giant honey bees are known for stockpiling honey quickly and are reliable pollinators of cotton, mango and coconut. One curious behaviour of giant honey bees is that they migrate, leaving their massive nests to follow the nectar blooms, returning later to fill their comb blankets with food.

DWARF BEES

Red dwarf honey bees, named for the red tint to their fuzz, and black dwarf honey bees are both about the size of a standard housefly. They build just a single sheet of wax comb from the underside of a plant branch and hang from it, exposed to the elements. Due to the fact that they are vulnerable, dwarf honey bees choose their locations wisely, deep within the forests of Southeast Asia, hidden away in dense foliage. As a consequence, they are rarely seen.

Beyond the honey bee

While honey bees absorb the limelight, the 'non-honey bees' are right there in the stage wings, diligently pollinating plants without a cheering audience. They show a remarkable range of body types and social styles, some living in communal groups, others in small families, and some by themselves. Here is where we find the humble bumble bees, the stingless bees, and the multitude of diverse solitary bees.

By far the largest group of bees worldwide is the native, or solitary, bees. Solitary bees make up 90 per cent of the 4,000 bee species found in the United States and the 2,000 in Europe. These bees prefer a quieter life, tending to themselves and a handful of offspring inside burrows they build or commandeer, living hidden underground, in rock crevices or the trunks of trees. Solitary bees typically create a small ball of pollen and nectar and lay a single egg on top of it, and there is no overlap of generations, as the female dies before her offspring become adults. Some species build their individual homes close to one another, so while they are technically solitary, they concentrate themselves into dense 'neighbourhoods'.

The diversity and regional adaptations of solitary bees are remarkable. There are solitary bees that nest exclusively in empty snail shells, some that sleep in closed squash blossoms, and others that look like they are made of blue chrome.

Yet they are often overlooked in terms of research, funding and conservation, despite being thousands of times more plentiful, and just as important to the ecosystem. In fact, some say they are better pollinators than honey bees because they like to fly from plant to plant when feeding, rather than concentrating on all the flowers on a particular plant before moving on as honey bees do. According to University of California ecologists, who studied the feeding patterns of honey bees versus native bees, when honey bees co-mingled so much pollen between flowers of the same plant, the resulting inbreeding resulted in 50 per cent less seed production than plants pollinated by solitary bees. Solitary bees flit around more between plants of the same species, so are considered better pollen mixers than honey bees. Honey bees have a habit of staying on one plant until it's depleted of nectar and pollen before moving on. The scientists studying the effect on plants – when comparing the behaviour of solitary bees and honey bees – thereby found that the solitary bees did a better job of co-mingling diverse pollens, and that the plants produced more seeds when they were pollinated by solitary bees versus honey bees.

In many ways, life is more precarious for solitary bees, as they don't live in massive social groups with the luxury of shared resources and better odds of successful defence and survival. Moreover, there is growing concern among conservationists that the growing popularity of beekeeping is putting additional strain on native bees. They say the rise of beekeeping in dense cities such as Manhattan, London and Paris is creating too much competition for limited forage. They warn that high concentrations of domesticated honey bees outcompete solitary bees, wild honey bees, as well as other native pollinators such as moths, butterflies, and ladybirds, pushing them out of their native habitats. The Royal Botanic Garden at Kew – which has a towering, hive-shaped art installation illuminated by LED lights that glow according to the vibrations of the honey bees kept in its nearby apiary – issued a report, in 2020, urging bee lovers to plant native wildflowers to help bees, rather than put another honey bee hive in London.

As entomologists continue to issue reports of a worldwide insect decline, attention is finally turning towards the welfare of the lesser-known bees, leading to a reconsideration of the important role that the 'bumbles', the 'stingless' and the 'solitary natives' play in our delicate ecosystems. While 19,000-plus 'non-honey bee' species are too many to list here, some of the most familiar, and fascinating, are well worth a look:

Bumble bees

These are the large and furry bees with the roly-poly bellies and the lower-octave buzz, belonging to the genus *Bombus*. There are more than 250 varieties, living in colonies of anywhere from tens to several hundred workers for part of the year. The queens overwinter usually in a hole in the ground, emerging in spring to search for a suitable nest site, which, depending on the species, could be under tree roots, in an abandoned bird box or within vacated rodent holes. At first, the queen is very busy – building honeycomb in her nest and laying eggs in it, foraging for nectar and pollen, and feeding her young. When her first generations hatch, they take over house maintenance and food gathering, and she concentrates on egg laying. Her family swells until late summer, when her body flips an internal switch, and she stops laying workers and produces only queens and drones. The colony of workers dwindles, leaving just the new virgin queens, who will overwinter to start the cycle anew.

If you like tomatoes, then you also like bumble bees, because their bulky bodies make them one of the few bees heavy enough to shake the sticky pollen loose from tomato flower anthers. In a process called 'buzz pollination', or 'sonication', they grasp the flower and vibrate their flight muscles, buzzing in the note of middle C, to get the pollen granules to fly off and adhere to their bodies. Because of this, some species – such as the common eastern bumble bee in the United States and the buff-tailed bumble bee in Europe – have been reared in captivity and used commercially inside greenhouses to pollinate tomatoes, as well as squashes, peppers, watermelons and aubergines.

Stingless bees

Contrary to what the name implies, these bees do have stingers, but they are shrunken and useless. Stingless bees are closely related to honey bees and bumble bees but are believed to have evolved more than 100 million years ago, long before honey bees appeared.

There are more than 500 species of stingless bees, most of them in the tropical and subtropical regions of Central and South America, and some species found in Australia, Asia and Africa. They have several distinct behaviours that make them unique. They nest in pre-existing cavities in trees, rocks or underground, and build tubular turrets at the entrance – from a mixture of wax, plant resins, mud and dung – that look like miniature guard towers. These protruding funnels keep wind from blowing debris into and blocking their home. These tiny spouts connect to long tunnels leading to chambers, where they store honey in egg-shaped pots made of the same waxy mixture. Beekeepers have found creative ways to manage stingless bees and harvest their honeypots, by sawing off the section of tree where they live and keeping the log, or by transferring the colony to another container such as a flower pot, water jug or even an empty guitar body. Lacking viable stingers, the only defence the stingless bees have is to bite.

Leafcutter bees

These fuzzy black bees use their jaws as scissors, to cut neat crescents out of leaves and flower petals, then fly with the pieces back to a cavity to line it with their 'wallpaper'. They chew on the edges of their cutouts to make them sticky, then paste them to the inside of bamboo stalks or deadwood. In summer, the female builds a nursery, using multiple cells and provisions, each with a ball made from pollen and honey. Leafcutter bees are widespread, found at all elevations where flowers grow, and show a preference for legume flowers, making them an important pollinator for alfalfa.

Leafcutter bees do not damage plants when they gather nest material, and they carry pollen on a pollen brush located underneath their abdomens, as opposed to their back legs like most bees do. Once a leafcutter finishes her nest, she seals it with more leaves, to protect the next generation until it emerges the following spring. She lives for about two months and can lay up to 60 eggs, but dies before her children enter the world.

Carpenter bees

The largest native species in North America, these bees have a loud, droning buzz and come in all colours and textures, from reflective, shiny black to gold and fuzzy. Their trademark move is to tunnel into deadwood with their powerful jaws, and they reuse their channels year after year, digging a little further each time. The entrance holes to their nests are about the circumference of a dime, and they leave tell-tale piles of sawdust at their front doors. They are also fond of moving into fenceposts, wood sidings and rafters, especially if the building material is soft redwood or pine, making carpenter bees a nuisance to homeowners. They bore long passageways and divide them into a train of pill-shaped chambers, building partitions between each one out of a mixture of saliva and sawdust. The female provisions each chamber with a small loaf of pollen and nectar, then lays one egg atop the food. She lays the females first, and then male bees towards the entrance, before sealing it; that way, the males emerge first in spring and will be ready to mate when the females exit later. While carpenter bees will defend their nests and buzz at intruders, they are not aggressive to humans and rarely sting.

Carpenter bees are large enough to buzz pollinate (sonicate) tomato flowers like bumble bees do. They have also developed an innovative way to suck nectar from tubular flowers, such as salvias, that are longer than their tongue. They will land on the flower and cut a little slit at its base, thus robbing the flower without pollinating it. Honey bees have been seen taking advantage of this shortcut, sipping nectar from the hole after the carpenter bee has vacated.

A striking yellow-striped carpenter bee sipping nectar and collecting pollen.

The males of the valley carpenter bee species, common to the western United States, attract female bees using scent. Groups of these green-eyed, golden-bodied males gather on a non-flowering plant and release a rose-scented pheromone. The females are drawn to the plant, where they choose their mate.

Placing logs or pieces of old lumber near buildings where the carpenter bees like to nest can sometimes redirect them. Homeowners who want to remove carpenter bees from their walls should plug the burrows in spring, right after the new bees emerge and before a female repurposes the tunnel.

Mason bees

Mason bees are the remodellers of the bee world and found on every continent. Often, they do not dig their own burrows, instead preferring to take over an abandoned insect nest and give it a makeover. They use their mandibles to collect small pebbles, resins, and mud, then mix them with chewed leaves and saliva to make a moulding material that they use to sculpt dwellings, to seal their entrances, and to fill any holes in their nests.

One species with a dark-blue body, the blue orchard bee, is an excellent fruit tree pollinator. It has been introduced to almond orchards in California, to aid pollination, and is one of the few solitary bees to be used commercially.

Another species found in the Middle East and known only by its Latin name, *Osmia avosetta*, makes its nest from flower petals, pasting an inner and an outer layer together with a thin lining of mud. These gorgeous floral cocoons have been photographed for art, design and science magazines around the world.

Metallic sweat bees

One of the several thousand species of small, slender sweat bees, the ground-nesting metallic sweat bee stands out for its colouring that looks like green, purple or blue chrome. It also has one of the best rock-star names for a bee, named for the fact it needs salt in its diet along with pollen and nectar. That's why they are attracted to human perspiration. They are found worldwide but predominantly in North America, and they are important pollinators of stone fruit trees and sunflowers. One of the odd things they do while provisioning their nurseries is shape their loaves of pollen and nectar into cubes.

Plasterer bees

There are more than 2,000 species of plasterer bee, most of them found in Australia, with some species in South America and a few in North America and Europe. Their distinguishing feature is their two-part tongue, which they use to excrete unique chemical compounds to create smooth material to line their nests. One species makes a clear, durable material much like cellophane, perfect for keeping the humidity just right for the developing bees in the nursery. Another species, called a polyester bee, lines its nest by producing a compound called *macrocyclic lactone* – also known as *polyester*.

Wool carder bees

This bee's name comes from the textile term for combing wool, 'carding', and it can be found in Europe, North America and parts of East Asia. The females pad their nests with soft hair fibres they pull from plants such as lamb's ear and yarrow, painstakingly rolling the fibres into a ball larger than their heads and flying with the material to their chosen nest site. Wool carder bees are also quite dashing: their black bodies are covered in yellow spots. The males are highly territorial and will stake their claim to a food-rich flower patch, spending the rest of their lives warding off other males, even buzzing a warning when other small animals and humans come too close. Their strategy is to keep the area clear, so they have first dibs to mate with any female that comes by for a meal. Scientists have observed hungry females trying to avoid these dominant males, but eventually mating with them in exchange for food, a practice officially referred to as 'convenience polyandry'.

Mining bees

With a stout, furry body, these bees are found all over the world and are often mistaken for bumble bees. They are plentiful, with more than 1,000 different species. These bees excavate elaborate subterranean tunnels for their nests, often with many side branches and antechambers, and they construct a tiny turret protruding above ground at the main entrance to keep debris from blowing into their labyrinth. Depending on the species, they will mine in sand, hard clay soils, or in the cracks between log cabin or castle walls – and they tend to aggregate in dense miner communities. Some female mining bees lay a single egg on a ball made of pollen and nectar; others lay multiple eggs. The female seals the entrance to her burrow, and when the larvae hatch, they eat the food and spend the winter season transforming into adult bees that emerge in spring. Some male mining bees forage for their own nectar.

Cuckoo bees

Borrowing their name from the bird that sneaks its eggs into another nest for another mother to raise as her own, cuckoo bees are also opportunists, but a tad more vicious, colourful and sleek. They include some black ones with white polka dots, the cuckoo bees lack the receptacles on their legs to gather pollen, and they don't collect honey, either. They don't worry about storing food because they don't have the burden of caring for their offspring. They sneak their eggs into another bee's nest, and when the cuckoo eggs hatch first, the young cuckoo larvae kill and eat the host bee's eggs. Still not satisfied, the cuckoo larvae then eat all the honey and pollen the nest owner had collected for her own family. When the raiding cuckoo bees finish pupating and emerge as fully formed bees, they go on to mate and start the sneaky plundering cycle all over again.

Solitary bees are everywhere, yet rarely seen, as they go about their remarkable lives in their own private microcosmos. But their fanbase is growing, especially among farmers and backyard gardeners who have seen their fruit trees and cover crops flourish as a result of their discreet handiwork. Commercial alfalfa growers are so pleased with native bees that they now use large bee boards drilled with thousands of artificial nest cavities to lure leafcutter bees to their crops. Fruit farmers do the same to attract the blue orchard bee.

Smaller versions of these 'bee hotels' can be purchased or easily made by the home gardener, by creating a nesting container out of an aluminium can, a cinder block, a bucket turned on its side, or PVC pipes, or by constructing a wooden frame and then packing the vessel with hollow tubes. The tubes can be straws, plant stems, bamboo or cardboard tubes – anywhere up to 13 mm (or half an inch) in diameter – with one end plugged and the open ends facing out of the container. The tubes should be anywhere from 13 to 20 cm (5 to 8 inches) long. Plants with hollow stems that work well in bee hotels include asters, sunflowers, honeysuckle, bee balm, sumac and wild rose.

Bee hotels often have other types of rooms and suites to attract a variety of native bees, such as pine cones, small logs with drilled holes, stacks of sticks or wads of dry grass. They should face the morning sun and be placed waist-high above ground, attached securely to a fencepost, building or tree – so they don't shake about in the wind. The chances of native bees moving in will go up if the hotel is placed within 30 m (100 feet) of flowering plants. If the native bees like the hotel, they should move in by spring and should be sealing their nests by the end of summer. Once they emerge the following spring, it's a good idea to put fresh tubes in the bee hotel and clean the old ones, using a solution of around 100 ml to 4 litres (roughly half a cup to a gallon) of water, to prevent diseases from building up in the tubes.

'Bee hotels' are easily made at home using recycled (such as the food tins and olive oil canister here) and natural materials (such as hollow stems, dried grass, and pine cones). A good variety of natural materials should attract a good variety of bee species.

Life cycle of the honey bee

At the height of summer, a vibrant hive may contain anywhere from 20,000 to more than 50,000 honey bees. Bee colonies are matriarchies, made up of tens of thousands of female worker bees, several hundred male drones and just one queen mother. The queen is the lifeblood of the colony because, as the only fertile female, she's the only bee in the colony that lays eggs. Yet she's not the ruler, because a hive is a collective body that makes group decisions, including whether to overthrow their queen if her egg production starts to lag.

Beekeepers must be able to distinguish between the three types of bees inside a hive, because they all have different functions and collaborate to keep the colony healthy. Populations of drones and workers fluctuate during the year in response to the colony's needs and the weather, so it's important to be able to look inside a hive and quickly establish whether the colony is 'in sync' or 'in trouble'.

Workers

The worker bee has always been a she. Everything that needs getting done inside a hive – from cleaning to nursing to wax building – is done by the females that comprise over 90 per cent of a bee colony. Worker bees are also the foragers, gathering all the pollen, nectar and water for the colony. Every bee pollinating a flower is a female.

Adult worker bees are infertile females, whose ovaries have shrunk in response to the presence of the queen's pheromone. If a colony loses its queen, a worker's ovaries can develop and allow her to lay eggs, but because she is infertile, she will produce only male drones.

Worker bees are 12 to 15 mm (up to three-quarters of an inch) in length, with four wings that can hook together, five eyes that can see polarized light, and two antennae that serve as their sense of touch, smell, taste and hearing. They have brushes and baskets on their legs for collecting pollen. Their stingers are barbed and remain behind when they sting, eviscerating the honey bee as the stinger tears away from its abdomen. Because of this, honey bees will avoid stinging unless they believe their nest is under attack and self-sacrifice is absolutely necessary. Before they sting, they give several warnings – buzz flights or headbutts – to get the perceived intruder to move back.

A worker bee lives for up to six weeks during the busy seasons of spring and summer yet can live for several months overwintering in the warm cluster inside the hive. She begins life as an egg deposited at the base of one honeycomb cell: a small white pin about the size of a grain of rice. Within three or four days, she hatches. For her first few days of life as a larva, she's fed a diet of royal jelly, a protein-rich milky-white secretion from worker bees. Unlike developing queens, which are fed a constant diet of this jelly, worker bees switch to feeding their developing sisters a combination of honey, pollen and enzymes they mix into 'bee bread'. Around the eighth or ninth day, workers seal the larva's cell with a layer of wax. Inside, the larva transforms into a pupa and metamorphizes into an adult. At the three-week mark, the new worker bee chews her way out of her cell, ready to go to work.

From the moment the worker bee emerges, she's on the clock. A worker bee spends most of her life in complete darkness inside the hive as a 'house bee', promoted through a hierarchy of increasingly complex jobs. These promotions are pre-programmed, in that her body gains more capabilities as she matures, until after about a month indoors she's ready for her final assignment – foraging outside the hive as a field bee.

Worker bees begin their careers as janitors. Newbies clean the honeycomb, removing bits of wax and dirt from the cells, and polishing them so they can be reused for another egg or to store more honey or pollen. Once their cleaning duties are complete, these bees transfer to nursing care. Nurse bees roam the nursery, feeding larvae the royal jelly they secrete from their hypopharyngeal glands located between their eyes and their brain and mandibular (lower-jaw) glands near their lower jaws – the 'brood food' glands located in their heads. They also take nectar and pollen stored in the honeycomb, mix it together to make bee bread, and feed it to the developing bees. A single larva will be checked by nurse bees over a thousand times a day.

Some nurses are private carers – they bring food and water to only the queen. Because the queen can't feed herself or keep warm at night, she relies on her daughters to bring her honey and cluster around her when the temperature drops, shivering their wing muscles to keep her warm. They do this by unlinking their flight muscles from their wings and gunning their muscular thoracic engines.

Construction is the next stage of life. At a week old, a worker bee's body starts excreting little wax flakes from under its abdomen. Other bees grab those wax flakes with their mandibles and chew them, mixing them with their enzymes until the consistency is pliable. Builder bees cluster together like dangling bunches of grapes and pass these blobs of wax up the line, and then sculptor bees take those blobs and shape them into stacked

Another example of cooperation in the hive. Here, honey bee workers exchange food – in the animal behavioural process known as *trophallaxis*. The exchange of food also serves as a means of communicating information via pheromones.

hexagons to make honeycomb. This assembly line process is called festooning.

After wax building, bees can choose from several career paths. There's warehousing, where they off-load nectar and pollen from the incoming foragers and store it in the pantry. Air conditioning is another possible job. On hot days, bees stand at the hive entrance and fan their wings to circulate cool air and keep a steady indoor temperature of around 35 °C (95 °F). Undertaker bees detect the scent of death and decay – oleic acid – to locate a dead bee inside the hive. They drag the corpse to the entrance and push it out or carry it out of the hive, flying with the deceased in its clutches and dropping it at a safe and hygienic distance from the hive.

Some bees join the security detail. Guard bees patrol the hive entrances, pushing out anyone who doesn't belong. Common intruders are wasps, ants, mice, lizards, birds, and even robber bees from nearby hives that take advantage of weak, defenceless colonies. There is one exception to the intruder rule: if a wayward honey bee comes to the door, bearing a gift of nectar or pollen, sometimes the guards will wave her through.

Finally, after a worker bee has had enough indoor training, she enrols in flying school. She joins a group of students for short practice flights, each time circling the hive in wider and wider circles memorizing landmarks. Her eyesight is extraordinary for such a small creature, and she's aided by five eyes that can see in a 300-degree range. There are two compound eyes on either side of her face, and three light sensors called *ocelli* – shiny bumps in a triangle formation on the top of her head that are smaller than the head of a pin. She uses her ocelli to sense changes in light intensity, especially the sun's movement that tells her which way is up, helping her orient her body in space when flying. Her fuzzy hair senses wind direction and her own speed. She can fly at up to 32 kilometres per hour (20 mph), by beating her wings 230 times per second. Her speed slows to 19 kilometres per hour (12 mph) when she's carrying provisions back to the hive. She can transport loads that weigh as much as half her body weight.

Bees use their eyesight while navigating, but don't rely on it as much as some of their other senses, as sight isn't one of their strongest. They have a combined 7,000 lenses on all their eyes, each one angled slightly differently than its neighbour, allowing them to see a pixelated image of all those different views patched together. They can make out larger objects, such as their hive, in a range of up to 90 cm (3 feet). They see polarized light, which forms patterns in the sky as it moves and assists in navigation. Bees also see ultraviolet light, turning flowers that look like one colour to us into dazzling marquees with colourful stripes like arrows pointing towards the nectar centre. What we see as blue and purple flowers become mesmerizing white beacons to a bee's eyes, which is why they are attracted to so many plants in that colour range. Interestingly, bees are unable to see the colour red.

Once it selects a flower, the honey bee unfurls a long, curled, hollow, tongue – its *proboscis* – into the depths of a flower to suck up the thin nectar. She stores the nectar in a special area in her body, somewhat like a temporary stomach, called a *honey sac*. The nectar mixes with her enzymes as she returns to the hive, where a house bee begs her to regurgitate it by tapping her antennae on the forager's antennae. This prompts the forager to give the nectar to the receiving bee, who presses the substance on her own proboscis, removing moisture as she ingests it into her body. Then she passes the droplet to another bee, and so on, and so on, in a process of communal digestion called *trophallaxis*. Finally, the bees store it inside a honeycomb cell and fan it with their wings until the right amount of moisture has been removed. Nectar begins as 70 per cent water, and when the bees are done passing it around and fanning it, it's honey with a water content of less than 20 per cent. They then seal up the cell with a thin layer of wax to store the honey away to eat later, after the nectar flow dies back.

Some foragers specialize and collect only honey or only pollen. Some do a little of both. Others fetch water. Honey bees collect pollen on the hairs on their body; they then use brushes on their legs to sweep the pollen into hairy depressions on their hind legs, known as pollen baskets. They fly back to the hive with full baskets that look like lentil-sized saddlebags, where house bees are at the ready to help them off-load the pollen bits into the storage cells inside their pantry.

Drones

Drones, meanwhile, are work averse. Their bodies are not designed for labour – they have very short tongues that can't reach nectar inside flowers; they lack stingers; their blunt-tipped abdomens have no wax-producing glands; and their legs lack receptacles to collect pollen. They take about three days longer to develop from an egg than worker bees do. Drones are heavier and stockier than the females, with heads that are almost completely covered by two enormous, compound eyes. This is because they need excellent vision for the one job they were created to do: track down a virgin queen and mate with her on the wing.

Drones spend their lives lounging about the hive, begging to be fed, depending on the females for protection, and waiting for the possibility that a virgin queen will fly by in springtime. If she does, her scent awakens the drones from their restful state, and they spill out of the hive to congregate – high up in a big cloud. These drone gatherings are referred to as drone congregation

Male honey bees, or drones, swarm together in specific aerial locations to mate with queens. Drones can gather in groups of up to 10,000 individuals.

areas, or DCAs, and they can be seen from the ground. They are neighbourhood hangouts for all the drones in a certain radius, which will keep returning in the hope that one day they will get lucky. A virgin queen knows to follow these all-male gatherings, and when she reaches one, she slows down and flies through them, secreting the pheromone decanoic acid, a scent that lets the drones know she is ready to mate. Only the swiftest and strongest drones reach her, and she will mate with up to 20 drones a day, over several days. Unfortunately for the drone, however, he dies immediately after mating. His genitals extrude and rip away from his body, and the castrated male falls to the ground.

If the drones don't die during the spring mating season, they are certain to meet their demise in the autumn. As the colony heads into winter, it's common to see drone corpses piling up outside the hive entrances, as the workers evict them to conserve food resources for the upcoming, lean winter months. Workers turn on the drones, dragging and pushing them out of the hive, where they will soon die of starvation and exposure. The females gang up on the males, tearing at their wings and legs, tussling at the entrance in a final turf battle. The males are considered expendable because the queen will simply make more drones the following year, when colonies start rearing virgin queens and males are needed again.

The queen

The queen bee has only one job – to make more bees. Luckily, she's very good at it. After her series of mating flights, she returns to the hive with enough eggs and sperm stored in her body to lay eggs for the remainder of her life, which can last from one to three years. She can lay more than double her body weight in eggs – up to 2,000 eggs a day at the height of the season – ramping up when flowers are plentiful and then scaling back in winter.

She can keep up this pace because she has an entourage of worker bees bringing her food, water and warmth around the clock. These attendants also encircle her as she searches the honeycomb for a suitable cell in which to lay an egg, clearing a path so she can get a clear view. One way to find the queen is to look for the 'daisy' – a circle of bees, all with their heads faced inwards towards the queen, forming what looks like petals on a flower. These are her bodyguards, who part the crowds for her.

At about 25 mm (1 inch) long, the queen is narrower and longer than the workers and drones. She is easily identifiable by her extended abdomen, where her eggs are stored, which accounts for most of her length. Without the need to fly outside the hive to forage, her head, eyes and thorax are smaller. She has a smooth

Queen (or supersedure) cells – where larvae develop and mature into new queens – protruding from the honeycomb. Shaped like a peanut shell, the cells are around 2.5 cm (1 inch) long, and have a rough surface texture.

stinger so she can sting repeatedly if she needs to defend herself against a challenge to her throne.

Each queen has her own unique pheromone, a scent marker that gets passed around inside the hive to let the workers know their queen is alive and healthy. The queen pheromone is a cocktail of more than two dozen known chemicals that she secretes from her jaws and feet. This chemical signal is picked up by the queen's attendants, constantly grooming and feeding her, who then touch the other bees with their antennae to spread the message. The queen also leaves scent footprints behind on the honeycomb.

Which bee gets to be the queen is a combination of good timing and survival. When a queen is ageing or injured, or has died, her pheromone thins inside the hive and workers get the signal it's time to replace her. Workers choose several fertilized eggs to turn into queens, and while only one will eventually take the throne, the rest are considered insurance. The worker bees feed the chosen larvae a solid diet of royal jelly and begin constructing queen birthing chambers for each that look like peanut shells protruding vertically from the honeycomb. When the first queen is about to emerge, after 16 days, she makes a series of high-pitched peeps by pressing her thorax against the comb and vibrating it. This 'piping' sound is an audible pulse, sent as a vibration message through the honeycomb, and serves two purposes: it alerts the workers to help her chew her way out of her birthing chamber, and it is a battle cry to the remaining queens who are still in development.

Once the queen bites a circle into the tip of her wax enclosure and pushes it outward like a little trapdoor, she's free. Her first order of business is to kill her competitors. This is where her smooth stinger comes in handy, allowing her to sting repeatedly unlike the one-and-done barbed stingers of the workers. She follows the piping sounds coming from the remaining sealed queen cells and chews a small hole in the side of each so she can sting her rivals to death.

Sometimes, two queens release themselves at the same time. In that case, there will be a duel to the death. The two queens vying for the throne instigate a no-holds-barred wrestling match, seizing one another with their legs, grappling and biting, bending their abdomens to try to get the first sting. Their battle draws an audience that waits eagerly for the victor. As soon as a queen tears off a leg or an antenna, or stings first, the rest of the bees form a ball around the losing candidate and suffocate her.

Victory is not all that sweet, however, because the slim virgin queen is largely ignored by the colony until her pheromones change a few days later, signalling that she is sexually mature. Suddenly, the workers are highly interested. They follow her, vibrating with excitement, tugging on her wings to motivate her to leave the hive for her mating flight.

When the newly mated queen returns to the hive, her abdomen swollen and elongated, she remains fertile for the rest of her life. It takes only a few days after her successful mating flight for her to start laying eggs. She deposits one egg per honeycomb cell, along with a drop of sperm, to create a worker bee. If she deposits only an egg without fertilizing it, the egg becomes a drone.

It's the beekeeper's job to ensure that the factory inside the hive is humming along, that everyone is present and accounted for, and satisfied with their work environment. Which can be boiled down to one very important question: Is the queen happy?

The answer is yes if she's being followed by an entourage of adoring attendants, and if her laying pattern is on point, meaning she is distributing her eggs in wide, solid swathes in the warmest centre of the nest. If her laying pattern is haphazard, or dwindling with each inspection, it could mean the queen is failing. Another way to tell if things may be off with the queen is by the bees' response upon opening the hive. Do they make a hum or a roar?

Relaxed bees ignore the beekeeper during hive inspections, too busy going about their chores to pay much attention to anything else. Unsettled bees with a troubled queen are jittery – they run instead of walk on the honeycomb, they tremble, or show defensive behaviours such as crouching together and peering up from between the frames – or headbutting the beekeeper's veil.

If there are excessive drone cells in the nursery, or eggs laid haphazardly – with multiple eggs in one cell, or sticking sideways from the cell walls instead of standing neatly upright at the bottom – that means a worker's ovaries have developed in response to a missing queen. The worker is trying to lay eggs to save her family but, because she's infertile, all she's doing is producing non-worker drones, which will inevitably lead to the colony's downfall.

Regular hive inspections help beekeepers to notice a failing queen while there's still time to turn things around by replacing her. While hobbyists can see good queens last several years, many commercial beekeepers replace their queens annually rather than spending labour-intensive hours monitoring thousands of hives for queen health.

Beekeepers can buy mated queens from suppliers or raise their own. The benefit of buying is that it saves time and effort, especially in an emergency, when a colony has entirely run out of eggs, but the downside is that it's not a sure bet that the new queen will do well in your microclimate. The advantage of the DIY method – taking developing queens from your strongest hive and placing them into your weak ones – is that it is a more reliable way to produce bees already adapted to your location.

Selectively breeding queens with strong genetics is the hallmark of a self-sufficient beekeeper. By keeping an eye on which colonies are mite-free, produce lots of eggs, and have bees that are gentle and make a honey surplus, the beekeeper can intentionally reproduce queens from their best stock and strengthen the entire apiary.

To do this, beekeepers use a grafting tool to carefully remove eggs from a strong hive and transfer them individually into specially designed cups on the underside of the top bar of a wooden 'queen frame'. The circumference of the cups spurs the bees to start building queen cells and to rear the larvae as queens. Workers start feeding the transferred larvae royal jelly and enclose them in queen cells dangling from the cups. When the developing queens are finally sealed inside wax birthing chambers, the beekeeper can carefully remove one of these queen cells and put it into a hive that has been without a queen for at least one day.

The bees will start caring for the developing queen as one of their own, and if all goes to plan, a locally adapted queen will emerge after 16 days and right the troubled colony. Provided she mates successfully and starts laying eggs, the hive can restore its workforce and bounce back.

A beekeeper holding a queen frame, where worker bees develop queen cells below the plastic cups. Inside these birthing chambers, larvae are developing and maturing into new queen bees.

Breeding queens at home only works to strengthen hives if the beekeeper can keep good records and remember which colonies produced solid queens. One way to keep track is to mark queens on their thorax with a dab of coloured paint or an adhesive number to record the year a new queen was introduced to a hive. Queen marking helps beekeepers to keep tabs on which queen is producing which results. Also, if an unmarked queen suddenly appears on the scene, beekeepers will know immediately that the colony has replaced its original queen.

Life in the hive: communication and survival

Life inside the hive is pitch dark, and what we would consider sweltering. The temperature is kept at an average 32–35 °C (90–95 °F), with 60 per cent humidity. It's also quite noisy. A hive emits all types of sounds, depending on the group conversation inside. Standing next to a hive, you can hear a contented purring; a staticky crackling; sometimes a hive sighs; other times a worker inside lets out a high-pitched screech. If you rest your ear on the hive wall, you can hear a sound like chewing, and the ping of bees dropping to the floor, and feel the vibrations contained within.

Over millions of years, honey bees have developed ingenious ways of communicating in their dark sauna. Without the ability to hear audibly, they rely on scent, touch and sound vibrations that are passed through the surface of the comb as an in-house PA system. For a species that must defend a hidden sugar cache from sweet-toothed invaders, its survival has depended on its ability to pass messages broadly and quickly to alert the colony to danger, food sources, and to the health of their queen.

The main way honey bees sense the world around them is through their antennae. These two swivelling, bent appendages behave as their ears, nose, tongue and fingertips, allowing them to recognize fellow hive members and talk to one another. Their antennae have taste receptors, as do their mouthparts and their feet. They use their antennae to feel the texture of flowers and decipher where different blooms are hiding nectar.

Their antennae are covered in thousands of sensory hairs that can detect air movement inside the hive from beating wings, and scent receptors on the tips allow honey bees to parse out the hundreds of unique odours their bodies release as messages, lures and repellents. Each antenna contains approximately 65,000 olfactory receptor cells, and – because their antennae can move independently of one another – honey bees also gain directional information about an odour. They experience a smell, but also the three-dimensional cloud-shape of it. They can literally 'see' the scent hovering over a patch of flowers.

Honey bees have one of the most complex forms of scent-communication in nature, with at least 15 known glands that produce a menu of odours. One of the most important is the queen's pheromone, which is kept at a steady level inside the hive when her attendants touch her with their antennae and then touch their hive mates, who then distribute it bee-to-bee throughout the hive. This assures the whole colony that everything is all right with

This extreme close-up, head-on shot of a honey bee shows the antennae, huge compound eyes, and, at the bottom of the picture, the mandibles – the last used for a variety of tasks such as cutting, carrying, fighting and grooming.

the queen. A weakening queen 'pheromone signals' the workers to start building queen cells to replace her.

When confronting enemies, honey bees release an alarm pheromone when they sting that smells like ripe bananas. It's a rallying cry that attracts hive mates to assist in the attack. This is the primary reason beekeepers use smokers, to overpower the chemical alarm so the bees won't receive the call for back-up. Honey bees have a second alarm pheromone that releases 2-heptanone from their mandibular glands, a chemical that temporarily paralyzes robber bees and other invaders, giving the honey bees time to drag the criminals out.

A lemony scent is used to summon workers to important areas, such as a food source or a nest site. Honey bees release the odour from the Nasonov's gland located in the tip of their abdomen and then fan their wings to disperse it. Honey bees use this aggregation pheromone to call foragers home after a rainstorm, or to gather the colony back together after a disruption, such as being relocated to a new hive by the beekeeper. Scout bees will direct a swarm to a new nest by zipping through the travelling cloud of bees and releasing the scent. The chemicals smell like lemongrass oil, which is why some beekeepers douse cotton balls or paper towels with this oil to try to lure swarms to empty hives.

Talking via odour is not unique to adult bees. Developing brood release a pheromone that helps nurse bees to distinguish between the hungry young larvae that need their attention and the cells that are already sealed with developing pupae. Drones release a scent that recruits other male drones to congregate in areas where there are virgin queens.

Although honey bees don't have auditory hearing, they can sense vibrations across the surface of the honeycomb and pick up sounds through 'vibroacoustics'. They can feel the piping and quacking sounds a developing queen makes before she releases herself from her cell, alerting them that an overthrow is coming. They can feel the buzz-running of their nestmates as the colony prepares to swarm. They pick up vibrations with their antennae and with thin membranes inside their legs that ripple in response to soundwaves. Bees also feel the 200- to 300-hertz frequencies produced by the vibrating flight muscles of their dancing sisters.

Dancing is one of the most remarkable ways that honey bees communicate. Animal scientists have discovered that the duration and intensity of their dance, plus the direction of their dance in relation to the sun, all serve as GPS co-ordinates to tell the other bees where to find flowers or a new nest site.

Austrian zoologist Karl von Frisch (1886–1882) was the first to discover and explain honey bee dancing in 1927, for which he later won a Nobel prize. He got there by wondering why so many bees from a single hive gathered on the same plant to forage. He watched their comings and goings very closely and observed foragers returning to the hive and repeatedly walking in circles on the honeycomb, and then switching directions and doing it again. The movements seemed deliberate and urgent to von Frisch. By following the circling bees back to their food source, he was able to determine that this round dance was a type of message, a signal that food was relatively close to the hive, within a distance of approximately 50 m (165 feet).

However, when the bees did a more elaborate waggle dance, crawling in a figure of eight and shaking side to side each time they crossed the middle of the eight, that meant the food source was beyond 50 m (165 feet). Von Frisch determined that the angle of a bee's dancing body represented the direction of the nectar or pollen source in relation to the sun, so if she turned right after crossing the middle of the eight, the flowers were to the right. A left turn indicated the opposite direction. If the bee flew up, it was an indication to fly in the direction of the sun. If she dipped down, the flowers were in the opposite direction to the sun. The longer the dance went on, the further the distance to the flowers. A honey bee dances with more enthusiasm if her find is particularly sweet, and with less gusto if there are threats or obstacles to negotiate en route to the blooms.

Sometimes, the audience disagrees with the dancer's message. If there's a danger that's been discovered near the flower source, workers will headbutt the dancer to get her to stop. Nestmates will do the same thing to dancing scout bees, urging a move to a new location, if they prefer a different home to the one that's being advertised.

Without the ability to see in the dark, the audience picks up the dancer's information from vibrations on the dance floor and by touching her with their antennae as she shimmies. They also gather information by tasting the nectar and pollen samples the dancers pass out to recruit others to bring back more. Subsequent studies of honey bees reared in isolation have shown that bee dancing is innate, not learnt from observation. Honey bees, in other words, are born to dance.

Keeping the hive happy

Successful beekeepers understand how their honey bees interact with their unique environment and keep their hives happy by giving them the right supports at the right time. The key is knowing how to read a colony and interpret what the bees are planning to do, then supporting their natural instincts, rather than trying to force the bees to conform to human will.

A colony's size and shape changes dramatically with the seasons, going from a small overwinter cluster to quadrupling in size once the nectar starts flowing. If a colony can be spared the work of having to warm a draughty hive or cool a crowded one, the bees will have more energy for honey and brood production.

For honey bees to thrive, they must be kept healthy in a place that's as pristine as possible, free of chemical exposure, and with access to abundant, year-round food and a reliable water source. They will need to be kept warm and well fed to ease the stress of getting through winter and monitored regularly for mites. Furthermore, they need an attentive beekeeper who has the will, and the time, to keep careful notes on the health of each hive.

Beekeepers typically don't take vacations in spring and summer at the height of bee season, when they are monitoring their hives multiple times a month, moving their hives to croplands, or harvesting honey. To share a life with bees means a measure of personal sacrifice, adjusting and adapting to the bees' schedule. One of the biggest mistakes new beekeepers make is thinking honey bees are 'plug 'n' play': that all they need to do is put the hive in the garden and watch the bees go to work pollinating the landscape. Excited about the honey, the new beekeeper harvests too much, before the colony has built up enough for its own needs, leaving the bees to starve over winter. Newbie mistakes are just one of the myriad reasons a hive can dwindle; besides beekeeper neglect, a hive could perish from poor nutrition, a weak queen,

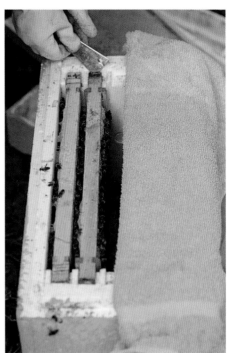

Top left: The beekeeper has added a mouse guard to protect the hive entrance from invasion.

Top right: A polystyrene hive box helps keep the colony temperature at an even, warm temperature during the winter months.

parasites, pests, pesticides, or some combination of any of these.

The beekeeper who stays ahead of a hive's needs can eliminate potential pitfalls, strengthen weak hives, multiply strong ones and help the bees to produce excess honey, so that the keeper can harvest a portion. It's the beekeeper's responsibility to make sure the bees always have a clean, comfortable home with a strong queen and enough food, so they have the best possible platform for combatting predators and diseases.

To achieve this, it is important to monitor the ever-changing size of the colony, to make sure the bees always have the right amount of space. This means adding more brood boxes and honey supers in spring and summer, when the population is expanding, removing entrance reducers to permit more traffic, and replacing solid bottom boards with screened ones to increase airflow.

Hive equipment can't be used for ever. An attentive beekeeper knows to throw out old honeycomb frames and hive boxes that have holes and cracks. Fresh wax is brilliant white and translucent, but it starts yellowing with age. As it thickens over months and years – infused with propolis, pollen, silken cocoons and larval faeces – it will turn black and harbour mould and disease. It looks nasty, and the bees tend to agree. They will get sick and/or leave.

Depending on location, an apiary may need a good windbreak, so if the hives are not positioned near large trees, fences or walls, beekeepers can use tie-downs or heavy rocks to secure the hive covers. In places with lots of snow, the hives may need to be wrapped and insulated. In cold weather, honey bees hang together and shiver their wing muscles to keep warm, with those on the outer edge of the cluster constantly cycling back to the centre, so the heat disperses evenly between all the bees. If the temperature inside the hive drops below 10 °C (50 °F), the bees can't travel far beyond the protective warmth of the cluster, and if stored food is too far away, they'll starve. Beekeepers can help them to keep warm by placing large boxes over hives with insulating material, wrapping hives in blankets, or covering hives in black roofing paper to absorb heat. Some beekeepers put an empty super hive box on top of the inner cover, with the escape hole screened, and fill it with leaves, newspaper or cloth. Warm air rises from the colony through the screened inner cover hole and is captured in the absorbent material above.

Infrared cameras can reveal the relative size and warmth of the colony inside the hive. There are infrared camera attachments for mobile phones, making it relatively easy to get a picture of what's going on inside without having to open the hives and sacrifice precious heat.

Honey bees also need enough food to get through the winter. A colony should have at least one hive super filled with honey-laden frames, placed directly over the brood, with more frames

Here, the beekeeper is feeding their bees with a jar of homemade sugar syrup to help them through the cold, nutrient-poor winter.

of honey and pollen on each side of the nursery. This is the time to thicken their supplemental sugar water, in a ratio of two parts sugar to one part water, and replenish it as soon as they consume it. If they are low on pollen, they can benefit from manufactured or homemade pollen patties.

As one of the oldest creatures on the planet, arguably honey bees have developed exquisite survival techniques. But there are ways to help them fight pests and predators, so they don't have to deploy them. If you see scratch marks near the hive entrance, that means the hive is too low to the ground and accessible to skunks, squirrels and racoons, which scratch at the hive at night to get the bees to come out so they can eat them. Make sure your hive is on a stand, or cinder blocks, placing it out of reach. Metal mouse guards that cover the hive entrance – allowing just a row of small holes large enough for the bees to pass through – can help keep out not only mice, but also snakes and lizards.

Depending on where you live, creating a fenced-off apiary might be a wise decision in order to deter foxes, or even human vandals! Motion lights pointed away from the hives can also keep unwanted intruders away.

When it comes to battling pests and parasites inside the hive, there are many different types of natural and chemical treatments, which will be further explored in the forthcoming chapters. That said, there are a few things beekeepers can do to prevent these problems from occurring in the first place. The main action is to check colonies regularly for mite infestations, but especially in the autumn – when *Varroa destructor* mites are at their seasonal high. Beekeepers can use icing sugar, or alcohol washes, on a sampling of bees to extract the mites, count them, and extrapolate the size of the infestation.

Other methods of keeping mite counts low include using a screened bottom board – so that the mites that fall through can't return. Because mites feast on larvae, some beekeepers encourage the bees to build excess drone larvae, by placing a shorter honey frame in a deeper brood box. The bees will build a hanging sheet of drone cells from the small frame and – once the cells are capped with developing drones – the beekeeper can slice it off. This will remove the drones, as well as all the breeding mites feasting on drone larvae behind the closed cells, reducing the overall mite load. Instead of throwing away the drone bait, consider this: if there are chickens nearby, they will gladly tear open the drone brood and have a feast, with no dangers posed to them by the mites.

Individual intelligence versus hive mentality

The bee's brain is roughly the size of a sesame seed. But there is a lot of intelligence packed in there, from the way they build mathematically uniform hexagon honeycomb, to how they make democratic decisions about when to swarm, to – as more recent studies have indicated – the capacity to count, to recognize human faces, and even to reverse their age.

In 2022, German zoologist Lars Chittka (born 1963), of Queen Mary University in London, published *The Mind of a Bee*, which argues that the most plausible explanation for bees' ability to perform so many different tasks, and to learn so well, is that they possess a form of general intelligence – a bee consciousness that puts them on a par with dogs and cats as sentient creatures.

Chittka and his colleagues trained bumble bees to roll a small ball into a hole for a sugary reward, leading to a viral video of 'bees playing football'. His team discovered the bumble bees could train one another to push the ball into the hole, yet – even more surprisingly – the student bees could also find better solutions than their teachers; they didn't blindly follow instructions, but used their own individual intelligence to score a goal faster.

This, Chittka argues, is exactly the kind of cleverness a bee uses when foraging alone. It takes some amount of learning and memory to be able to fly miles from home, visit thousands of flowers, disregarding the poor ones in favour of the nectar-laden blooms, only to navigate back to the correct hive to off-load, then go back out again, remembering the previous route. Not only are bees memorizing their flight paths, but they are also constantly updating and re-learning them, when one food source withers and another comes into bloom.

Behavioural ecologists study the ways in which honey bees interact with each other and solve practical or complex problems. Here, a bee returns to the hive and 'dances' to communicate the location of a nectar source to other workers.

Perhaps bees memorize their routes by counting landmarks. In one of Chittka's bee experiments, forager bees were trained to fly past three identical landmarks – in this case, 3.5-m-high (11-foot-tall) yellow triangular tents – to a food source. Then he added more identical tents over the same distance. The bees tended to land closer to tent three, before reaching the food source, leading Chittka to conclude that the bees were going off memory, counting to three and stopping. When he reduced the tents to just two, the bees flew past the food source, presumably searching for an expected third tent.

There is an old beekeeper myth that honey bees can recognize their beekeeper's face. In 2004, visual scientist Adrian Dyer, then at the University of Cambridge, tested it out. He and his colleagues pinned black-and-white photographs of four different human faces onto a board. By rewarding the bees with sugar water, the team repeatedly coaxed them to fly towards a target face, even after moving it to different locations. When the sugar reward was removed, the bees continued to approach the target face up to 90 per cent of the time. Amazingly, the memories stuck; the bees could pick out the target face up to two days after being trained. It's also likely the bees were simply being trained to think the faces were 'bizarre flowers', but the experiments caused a stir in both science labs and popular culture, because they illustrated the flexibility of bee learning.

Later, in 2012, researchers took the plasticity of bee intellect even further, with a study saying that older honey bees may be able to reverse brain ageing. When older foragers with typical age-related cognitive decline changed social roles and reverted to nursing care inside the hive, their brains started producing proteins associated with more youthful nurse bees, according to a study by scientists at Arizona State University and the Norwegian University of Life Sciences. Researchers found that when foragers returned to a social role designed for younger bees, their learning ability increased. Looking at the brains of these role-reversal bees, researchers found increased levels of antioxidant proteins that maintain and repair brain cells, including one similar to the human protein peroxiredoxin-6 that defends against inflammation associated with Alzheimer's disease and Huntington's disease. Scientists are now looking to the honey bee as a potential source of dementia research innovation.

Either together or apart, bees are clever. As for the collective consciousness of bees, one of the most astonishing examples of 'hive mind' is what's known as swarm intelligence – how honey bees make a democratic decision to relocate to a new home.

When a hive is full, with no more space to store honey or eggs, it will divide itself in two. This is how bee colonies naturally reproduce in the wild. Managed beehives swarm, too, especially if the beekeeper hasn't provided enough room for the expanding colony in spring and summer. While this poses less of a problem in rural areas, where such swarms can return to the wild and rehome themselves in a crook of a tree or rock crevice, it creates more of a problem for the urban beekeeper whose swarms can settle inside house walls, under bonnets of cars, on fences, in trees in public parks, and in all sorts of inconvenient places that often make the local news.

Inside an overcrowded hive, the queen's pheromone spreads too thin, diluting as it gets dispersed among so many bees. When a colony starts swelling to above 60,000 or 70,000 inhabitants, the bees are pushed so far away from the queen that they start to lose her scent. This triggers them to start rearing new queens from a handful of the eggs in the nursery. Once the new virgin queen emerges, half the colony will swarm away with the old queen to re-establish themselves in a new location.

When a colony is getting ready to swarm, the first thing it must do is put its queen on a diet, so she loses enough body weight to fly. Her attendants, who had been grooming and feeding her daily, start rationing the queen's portions. They start forcing her to move more, grabbing her with their forelegs and nipping at her to keep her going. Like personal trainers, they prod her to run all over the honeycomb, so she slims down.

Meanwhile, the queen's daughters have a feast. They gorge themselves on honey inside the hive, so that they'll have enough calories stored to carry them through the move. The wax glands of young bees start activating, sensing they will soon be put to work building fresh honeycomb somewhere else. Tiny, transparent wax scales start protruding from the undersides of their abdomens, which they will chew and mould into a building material.

Life inside the hive during a lead-up to a swarm is as loud as rush hour, all the bees urgently running in a roiling cacophony of sound. If you put a microphone in a beehive as it's preparing to swarm, you will record what sounds like driving rain, with occasional motorcycles revving, flocks of angry seagulls squawking, and whining dentist drills. These are the sounds of scout bees, buzz-running over the comb, emitting high-frequency squeals to rouse their sisters into swarm mode. They shake their abdomens against the comb to create a vibration that other bees feel as pulses in their feet, rising to their knees, which are sent as nerve impulses to the brain. The scouts nudge, push and alert their nestmates that it's time to go.

A honey bee working in the hive collects fallen wax scales, produced by other workers, to build comb.

Then, just before the swarm takes off, everything goes quiet. The bees stop moving and hang on the combs, as if exhausted and catching their breath. If you happen to be standing outside a beehive at this very moment, you will suddenly see tens of thousands of bees pouring out of the hive and rising into the air, a moving inkblot in the sky, with their hungry queen safely hidden in the middle of the swarm.

The colony will land in a clump not far from the hive, typically on a fence or a tree branch, and hang there for several days while deciding where to go next. Scout bees leave the cluster to go house-hunting for a permanent home, and when they find a spot they like, they return to the swarm and dance to advertise the address of the tree cavity or rock crevice they found. Dr Thomas D. Seeley (born 1952), professor at the Department of Neurobiology and Behavior at Cornell University, followed individual bees as part of his research for a book on swarm intelligence, titled *Honeybee Democracy* (2010). He discovered that many scouts go house-hunting at once, and they fall in love with different properties. They dance on top of the bee cluster, each scout campaigning for the home they like the best. The audience takes the information, goes out to inspect the homes, and then picks their favourite. They return and dance with the scout whose home they prefer. Over time, whichever scout assembles the largest dance crew, and thus the largest number of votes, wins. And the colony flies off once again, typically within a week of leaving its hive, to the chosen spot.

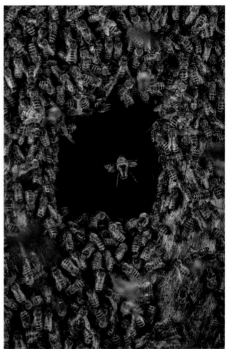

Top left: A honey bee swarm can be a disconcerting sight, as on this fencepost, but is a perfectly natural part of a colony life cycle.

Top right: Here, a honey bee swarm has created a colony in an abandoned black woodpecker nest in a tree.

Bottom: A bee swarm hanging from a tree.

If the colony's new home is away from human eyes, then people are none the wiser. But if it moves into the walls of a building or a public place that interferes with people, that's when it's time to call a beekeeper, not an exterminator. Local beekeeping clubs keep lists of 'swarm catchers' – area beekeepers who will remove outdoor swarms or cut them out of walls and collect the bees. Typically, the service is free in exchange for the bees. An exterminator, on the other hand, will kill the bees using a chemical spray and charge a fee for the service.

One way to prevent a hive from swarming is to split a crowded colony in two before the bees take matters into their own hands. There are signs to look for in a hive that wants to swarm. Look for small, open cups near the bottom of the frame, with the cup openings pointed downwards. These are signs that the bees have begun building peanut-shaped queen cells that protrude from the comb. Now is the time to divide the hive by removing the original queen and half of the colony into an empty hive, along with some frames of honey and pollen. This way, the beekeeper has preempted the future swarm by moving it before it is left on its own, eliminating the need for the swarming bees to search for a new home. The bees left behind in the source hive will quickly realize their queen is gone, select some eggs and start feeding them a constant diet of royal jelly to develop them into queens. The strongest of the royal candidates will take over as the new virgin queen, and – after she goes on her mating flight – she will return to the hive to begin laying eggs.

Splitting does have its risks – the new queen might not be strong, she might not mate properly because the available drones are genetically weak or too few, or she might get injured or eaten by a bird during her mating flight. Some beekeepers like more control over the outcome of splitting, so, instead of waiting for the bees to make a replacement queen, they may instal a mated queen instead. If the colony accepts her, she can begin laying right away, and the colony doesn't have to wait for a virgin queen to be born, her ovaries to develop, and for her to embark on her mating flight.

Whichever way a beekeeper manages the issue of swarming, it's important to provide plenty of sugar water to the newly divided colonies – because splitting is stressful to the bees, even at the height of the honey flow. They need easy access to food as they adjust to a new home, a smaller family and a new queen. Learning to read hive dynamics can bring beekeeping to the next level, pulling the beekeeper and the bees into a closer relationship, one that is not only mutually beneficial, but full of wonder and boundless discovery, too.

BEEKEEPING TASKS
AND EQUIPMENT

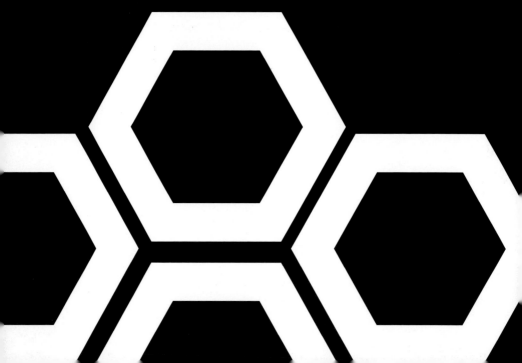

Beekeeping Tasks and Equipment

A beekeeper's year

Beekeepers typically spend a minimum of 15–30 hours each year managing a single-colony apiary, to ensure they are meeting bees' needs and keeping them healthy. Count on another 12 hours for each additional colony. More experienced beekeepers, with at least five to ten years of beekeeping know-how, typically spend less time on their tasks than a newbie beekeeper who is still learning to master the basics.

Beekeeping is strongly tied to the seasons and temperature, so it is helpful to follow a calendar of tasks to guide you as you seek to raise strong and healthy colonies. Even experienced beekeepers benefit from a checklist. Shifting the dates according to your local area and variable weather patterns, your beekeeping year will vary widely depending on your location. The warmer your weather, the earlier in the calendar year you will start actively managing your colonies. In parts of the southern United States, bees can be active 12 months of the year because of the moderate temperatures. The calendar shown over the page, however, assumes that you and your bees experience four distinct seasons every year. It also assumes that you and your hives are in the northern hemisphere – in the southern hemisphere, simply swap January for July, and so on.

The aim for this calendar is to provide a checklist of chores month to month, including feeding, hygiene, requeening, ventilation, protection, swarm reduction and extraction. The beginning of the year sees the buildup of the bee population, and the later part the contraction of the population.

Previous page:
An apiary in a
city allotment.

Opposite:
A beekeeper
inspects the
honeycomb
in their hives.

JANUARY
Early inspections
(only in good weather – at least 4 °C / 40 °F)
1. Close and remove dead colonies.
2. Clean colony entrances, removing any drifted snow or ice.
3. Lift covers *briefly* to check three things:
   - amount of food stores;
   - cluster location;
   - presence of brood.
4. Feed weak colonies with fondant, loose sugar and/or winter patties.
5. Clean/sterilize and refurbish old equipment.

FEBRUARY
Preparation for the coming season
1. Order new equipment and bee nucs or packages.
2. Undertake a *Varroa* count and plan treatment.
3. Cull frames, disposing of old, damaged ones (over three years old) and ordering new ones.
4. Make swarm boxes.
5. Feed weak colonies with fondant, loose sugar and/or winter patties.
6. Make any hive checks brief, picking a sunny day.
7. Paint beeswax on frame foundations.

MARCH
Often known as the 'starvation month' – due to stress of brood rearing
1. Clean and scrape bottom boards, removing dead bees.
2. Remove mouse guards and entrance reducers.
3. Stimulate colonies by feeding with pollen patties and 1:1 sugar syrup.
4. Equalize colony strength by moving brood from strong to weak colonies.
5. Install packages mid-month.

APRIL
Build-up
1. Maintain active brood-rearing colonies by inspecting hives every seven to nine days:
   - Check on queen's status and brood pattern.
   - Check for presence of disease.
   - Practise good hive hygiene, cleaning tools after inspections.
   - Reverse brood boxes if necessary.
2. Practise swarm prevention by looking for queen cells.
3. Continue feeding as needed.
4. Start nucs or split strong colonies to increase colonies.
5. Set out baited swarm traps or boxes.
6. Begin testing and treating for *Varroa* mites.
7. Unite weak colonies.
8. Have extra hive bodies on hand for growing colonies.

MAY
Swarm season
1. Inspect colonies (*see* April).
2. Capture swarms, checking swarm boxes regularly.
3. Feed as necessary with 1:1 sugar syrup.
4. Add queen excluder, if using, and supers for honey flow.
5. Plant bee forage flowers.

JUNE
Queen rearing
1. Inspect colonies (*see* April).
2. Provide extra ventilation as weather warms.
3. Add more supers, as needed.
4. Trap pollen for storage (if desired).
5. Rear queens, create nucs and requeen.
6. Order honey containers and labels.

JULY

Honey harvest

1. Inspect colonies (*see* April).
2. Remove supers, extract honey from supers if full; adding 'wet' supers on top for bees to clean.
3. Remove cut comb from supers.
4. Clean supers before storing with a wax moth prevention chemical.
5. Add entrance reducers to limit honey robbing.
6. Check for *Varroa*/tracheal mites.

AUGUST

Wind-down

1. Inspect colonies (*see* April), reducing frequency of inspections to every two to three weeks.
2. Extract honey, if not extracted earlier.
3. Unite weak and queen-less colonies.
4. Treat for tracheal mites.
5. Add entrance reducer to prevent robbing.

SEPTEMBER

Feeding and requeening

1. Inspect colonies (*see* April); look for weak colonies that should be united with stronger colonies.
2. Requeen hives.
3. Check on food stores going into winter; feed colonies, as needed, with 2:1 sugar syrup.
4. Add mouse guard at hive entrance.
5. Clean all boxes containing wax before storage, using a wax moth prevention chemical.

OCTOBER

Hive reduction

1. Finish feeding sugar syrup for winter.
2. Remove queen excluder, if using.
3. Reconfigure hive bodies for winter, adding ventilation to avoid moisture build-up.
4. Add mouse guard now, if not added earlier.

NOVEMBER

Winter preparation

1. Add windbreak and tie down hives, making sure hives are secure against bad weather.
2. Add insulating covers around hive (single).
3. Group and wrap hives if preferred to better insulate for winter.
4. Do *Varroa* mite counts and treat if necessary.

DECEMBER

Equipment checkup

1. Check entrance to see whether clear and not blocked with dead bees; the bees should be in a cluster during cold weather.
2. Do *Varroa* mite counts and treat if necessary.
3. Repair and refurbish equipment; assemble new equipment.
4. Feed fondant, loose sugar and/or winter patties as necessary to colonies with low stores.
5. Check your equipment for signs of wax moth or other infestation.

Personal safety and hygiene

Caring for and managing your bees involves some degree of risk. Bee stings are the obvious hazard, though there are many ways to reduce this. There are various other risks that might surprise you when you begin beekeeping. But once you understand the physicality of this hobby and know your legal responsibilities as a beekeeper, you will be able to prevent and prepare for adverse outcomes.

There are a few general precautions:

- Have an emergency plan written out and stored in a convenient, accessible location for when you have a sting emergency; know the location of the nearest medical facility and have your route planned and ready.
- Always carry your mobile phone with you in case there is an emergency, and – if you are working alone – let someone know where you are going and when you expect to be back.
- Keep a first aid kit handy, either in your home or your vehicle if you are travelling to your hives, stocked with antihistamines, pain relief, bandages, and so on.
- Keep hydrated. The importance of hydration while working in a confining bee suit on a hot day can't be overstated. Keep drinking water handy at all times. It can get very hot in a bee suit on a 35 °C (95 °F) day, so hydrate prior to working with bees as well as afterwards, as it is difficult to drink while wearing a bee veil.

Allergies

It's a good idea to ask your GP to refer you to a specialist allergy clinic before keeping bees – to make sure you have no severe reactions to honey bee stings. Even though you might have had itching, swelling and some pain at the site of a past sting, that is a *localized* and normal reaction. If, however, you have ever reacted negatively in a *systemic* way to a bee sting – difficulty breathing, swelling of your tongue and throat, dizziness, nausea or a racing pulse (symptoms that can lead to anaphylaxis, a severe and life-threatening allergic reaction) – you should think twice before jumping into beekeeping. You can still become a beekeeper, but you will need an auto-injectable device of adrenalin (an Epipen) in your toolkit as a safeguard. Many people have more severe reactions to wasps, hornets and yellow jackets, which are much more likely to sting than honey bees. If you are stung, it is important to scrape the stinger out as soon as possible (see page 203).

Soon after a bee stings, a red, itchy swelling will normally appear on the skin. This can be easily treated with home remedies or antihistamines.

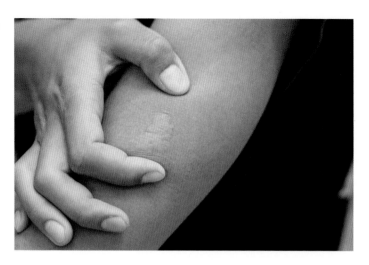

Normal reaction – easily treated with home remedies or antihistamines:
- sharp pain at the sting site that subsides within an hour or two;
- swelling;
- redness and itchiness.

Severe reaction – call an ambulance immediately:
- hives or extreme itching;
- swelling of the throat or tongue;
- difficulty breathing;
- nausea or stomach cramps;
- Racing pulse.

Ergonomic safety

Lifting heavy hive boxes can lead to 'beekeeper's back', if sensible daily practices are not put in place. Hive boxes full of honey can weigh from 18 to 41 kilograms (40–90 lbs), depending on the size of your hive bodies. When you stack heavy hive bodies on top of each other, the additional added height makes each one increasingly more difficult to lift. Bending your knees while lifting is important to avoid injury. Make sure your hive stand is at the proper height (45–60 cm / 1½–2 ft) so that the hive is at a good working level, and that there is a raised platform adjacent to the hive for setting your tools and equipment at a convenient level. Also, using some kind of wheeled vehicle will help in transporting heavy boxes and equipment. Think about using a Langstroth or top-bar hive instead

Bending your knees while lifting heavy hives is essential, to avoid developing the condition known as 'beekeeper's back'.

of a Warré hive, as the Warré requires heavier lifting. In addition, using smaller hive boxes, to lighten the load, or getting help lifting the boxes is a way to minimize this all-too-common hazard of beekeeping. Consider using a back brace or knee support when inspecting your hives. Get into the practice of performing some simple warmup exercises prior to beekeeping activities.

Picking the right breed and temperament – colony temper

Research the bee breeds available in your area. This should be one of your first decisions before you even set up your equipment. Several breeds or races – such as the Carniolan (*Apis mellifera carnica*), Caucasian (*Apis mellifera caucasia*) and Italian (*Apis mellifera ligustica*) – are known for their gentle disposition, great honey production and range of availability (see page 26). In addition, there are hybrids of these three (above) and many other breeds out there that might be better suited to your area. There are advantages and disadvantages to each bee variety, and it is a very good idea to talk to local beekeepers to see which breeds they have had the most success with and are the easiest to work with.

But even with all your research into honey bees' genetic predisposition, your success with a productive hive ultimately depends on your proactive management style. With keen observation you will be able to see how each hive has a character and personality all of its own, and that bees, like all living things, vary in their traits across the species.

Infiltration by Africanized bees

Africanized honey bees, which are much more aggressive, are mating with the Western honey bee in parts of the southern United States. The Africanized honey bee looks just like the Western honey bee, and its sting is no different from a single sting of a European honey bee. While a single sting might not be dangerous, Africanized honey bees aggressively attack in large numbers, which can be very dangerous for their target. Stay away from all honey bee colonies in areas known to have Africanized honey bees. If there are Africanized bees in your region, mark all your queens – using a dot of bright paint, nail varnish or a non-toxic, water-based paint pen – so you know an African queen hasn't taken over. Be wary of swarms moving into empty hives or swarm boxes, as these could be Africanized ones. In addition, watch out for parasitic swarms – Africanized bees can invade a colony of Western honey bees and take over the nest.

Preventing the spread of disease and pests

Apiary hygiene is key to preventing the spread of disease and pests, primarily as a result of dirty bee suits, tools and the transfer of combs between colonies. Using dirty equipment risks the spread of infection between each colony, including a range of insects, mites, viruses, bacteria and fungi that can lead to American foulbrood (AFB) and European foulbrood (EFB). An annual cleaning and disinfecting of brood boxes and frames is necessary, using one of three methods: placing them in a freezer for 48 hours; scouring them with a blowtorch; or sterilizing them chemically with disinfectant. Old brood combs can carry disease, and it is recommended that no brood comb should be used for more than three years.

Wax moths (*Galleria mellonella* or *Achroia grisella*) are an ever-present hazard which will attack your stored frames that contain wax. There are chemicals available as a preventative treatment that controls wax moths and is safe to use and harmless to honey bees, as well as an environmentally friendly treatment that contains a concentrated solution of *Bacillus thuringiensis*, a microorganism. Applied as a solution after your honey harvest, this will kill young wax larvae. One application is effective against wax moths through the following season. The best way to protect stored frames from wax moth damage is to apply the solution to your frames using a spray bottle, and then allow it to dry. The frames should then be stored in sealed containers to prevent reinfestation.

Location, location, location

Hive placement is incredibly important: a good position will have an enormous positive effect on your hive health and keep you and any other people in the vicinity safe. On a sunny day during active season (spring into autumn), the area in front of the hive entrance can be quite congested with bees launching out from the front entrance and returning laden with stores of water, nectar and pollen. Because of this, the immediate area in front of the hive – about 3–4.5 metres (10–15 ft) – will be crowded with lots of bees, especially during honey flow (when one or more nectar sources are in bloom and the weather is favourable for bees to fly and collect nectar in abundance). With this in mind, be sure to place your hives away from walkways and where people and pets congregate. If your space is limited, you can place a privacy fence or living hedge to screen the hive from view, which also adds a barrier to keep people out. Electric fences are another option to keep people out of the area and bees out of danger from predators and pests – but these should be adorned with warning signs.

As a beekeeper, you ought to be able to see, access and observe your hives easily from your house or garden. The earlier you spot problems occurring in a hive, the more success you will have in solving any resulting issues.

In urban areas, there should be a good 3 metres (10 ft) of space around the hive where there is no daily activity. Situate the hive

This blossom- and bloom-filled garden in Borjomi, in Georgia (the country), provides bees with plenty of pollen and nectar.

entrance so it doesn't point at your neighbour's garden or pool. Consider elevating your hives if you are in a congested area so the bees' path passes over any activity on the ground. Rooftop hives will solve a lot of urban congestion problems, avoiding any interactions with wary neighbours. Check the rules with your local authorities and homeowners' associations, and apply for any necessary government of council permits before bringing your first colonies home. It is an extremely good idea to inform your neighbours that you are keeping bees – and don't forget to offer them some honey from your hives, if you have some available.

All these measures ensure a healthy hive and increase your chances of establishing a peaceful coexistence between your bees and humans – and any other neighbouring animals.

Protective clothing

Bee behaviour can be unpredictable. To ensure you have the best sting prevention, it is important to wear protective clothing, including a beekeeping veil, gloves and suit. In fact, these aren't completely sting-proof, but they greatly lessen the occurrence and severity of stings. Bee clothing made of ventilated, heavy-duty woven cotton or polyblend is comfortable and gives excellent protection. If you don't want to buy a bee suit, be sure to wear light-coloured clothing, preferably white, as bees show no interest in the colour. Use masking tape to close the wrist and ankle areas so that bees can't get in. Bees are attracted to bright colours, so avoid wearing these. Avoid wearing any scents, as bees are naturally very sensitive to odours.

Your bee suit should close with a front zip, and all sleeves and trouser legs should be tucked tightly into your gloves or footwear. Inspect your suit regularly for tears that bees can get into. The mesh in the bee veil shouldn't rest on your skin; otherwise the bees will be able to sting through it. The gloves should be of soft leather or goatskin and extend up to your elbow with an elasticized gather to ensure no bees can enter. Unprotected hands are always the first thing to get stung when opening up a hive.

All-encompassing bee suits worn on a hot day in August can become extremely stifling and also cause heat exhaustion if worn for too long without a break for water and rest. Hydration before donning your bee suit and after removing your bee suit is important; you should also take regular breaks. Be aware of heat exhaustion symptoms and carry your mobile phone will you at all times. Many bee suits have pockets sewn in the front for housing a phone. Boots or work shoes – the type that allow you to tuck the bee suit into them – are highly recommended.

If applying chemicals in the hive, check the product labelling to make sure you have adequate protective clothing, such as rubber gloves, eye protection and a face mask.

Ticks are becoming a problem because they are vectors for Lyme disease. Be sure to inspect your body for ticks after making a visit to the apiary, which may have tall grass present.

Equipment safety and hygiene

Sting pheromones and diseases will cling to your equipment and clothing for a long time, so it is important to keep all of your beekeeping tools and garments as clean as possible in order to avoid being stung. Experienced beekeepers clean their equipment frequently and before use in different apiaries. Hive tools are especially important to keep clean as they are used constantly inside a hive. A good apiary hygiene procedure is to scrub the hive tool clean with soda crystals (sodium carbonate), using 100 grams (half a cup) of washing soda to 500 millilitres (1 pt) of water, between inspecting one hive and the next. A spray bottle loaded with this solution is helpful to keep with your hive inspection equipment. Wear rubber gloves and eye protection when scrubbing with washing soda and dispose of any waste responsibly. Another method is to scorch your hive tool with a portable blowtorch.

Clothing hygiene

Clothing such as veils, hats and gloves should be washed by hand to remove the stickiness of honey, wax and sting pheromones. Scrape off as much wax and propolis as you can first. Soaking and scrubbing with detergent is very effective for leather beekeeping gloves that can become covered with honey and propolis. A suit can be thrown into a washing machine after removing the veil or hat. Avoid using any highly scented detergents. If you don't have the time to wash your beekeeping gear frequently, the next best thing is to air it outside, as this helps in dispersing alarm and sting chemicals.

Timing/poor weather conditions

Inspecting a hive on cool, windy or rainy days can be problematic and unpleasant for a beekeeper. Wait for a warm, sunny day during the middle part of the day. More bees will be out foraging during this time, which reduces the population of the hive. Also, when there is a dearth of nectar – as in early spring or late autumn – bees will be irritable and defensive when you start inspecting the hive. Pick your time carefully, and you will avoid having to deal with stinging, defensive bee behaviour.

Calmness and slow, deliberate movements are key to good beekeeping.

Calmness/gentleness around the hive

Relaxed, calm behaviour around your hives is crucial for your safety. Jerky, sudden movements can turn good-tempered bees into bad-tempered bees. Approach your hive carefully from the rear, never from the front entrance, and avoid sudden movements. Bees will react instantly if you bang your hive lid down or use rapid movements during inspection. When moving the hive bodies around, try not to crush any bees as they can release an alarm pheromone that will put the entire colony on alert. If you do crush some bees during an inspection, use some smoke to block and dampen the defensive pheromone from spreading. A defensive bee is more likely to sting. If you are stung by your bees, move away immediately. When a bee stings, it releases a pheromone that signals to the other bees to go on the defensive and you are more likely to get stung again. Let them calm down for a while before going back to finish your task.

Using a smoker safely

Learn how to use a smoker correctly: every time you fire up your smoker, you are starting a small fire, so you should always practise fire safety precautions. Aim the smoker away from your face and body when you fire up the smoker and snap the nozzle top closed before the flames can cascade out. The flames from a smoker can easily set your suit or veil on fire. You can also burn yourself on the hot sides of a smoker, so handle with care. If you are working in dry grass, be careful to avoid shedding any hot coals as these could start a brush fire very easily. Smokers build up creosote, which can ignite, so remove it regularly with a wire brush.

The smoker will have a hanging hook on the side, so use this hook to hang the smoker from an open hive, so it is readily at hand instead of on the ground, where it could start a brush fire. Smoke masks the hives alarm pheromones that the bees emit when on the defensive. When initially inspecting a hive, it is helpful to shoot a few puffs of smoke at the entrance before opening the hive top cover. When you open the top cover of the hive, puff some smoke into the inner cover hole. Once you pry up the inner cover, waft smoke over the frame tops and you will see the bees retreat down into the hive. Use your smoke in moderation to calm the hive and only as needed if they get agitated.

Smoking doesn't harm bees, so long as it isn't used excessively. New beekeepers tend to overuse smokers because they are more nervous when manipulating a hive. As you gain experience, a beekeeper should use less smoke and a few brief squeezes of the bellows should be sufficient. Most importantly, when you are finished with the smoker, make sure the embers are completely extinguished, even if it is just smouldering, as embers can start a field or forest fire quite easily.

As beekeepers gain experience, they will use their smoker less frequently and more judiciously. Too much smoke can harm bees.

Drifting

Drifting – where bees enter hives that are not their own – carries the risk of spreading disease between colonies, but you can reduce its occurrence. If there is a prevailing wind or the hives are in a location exposed to winds, a living or fence windbreak near the hives will diminish their effect. Other useful tactics are to arrange your hives in an arc, point the hive entrances in different directions, space your hives further apart or mark your hives with distinguishing features such as different, bright colours or patterns – all of which may assist your bees in returning to the right hive.

Creating and setting up your hive

Becoming a beekeeper

Having been in decline for more than half a century, beekeeping has become popular again, especially with women and young people. However, as newer people take on the hobby, it has been estimated that 80 per cent of new beekeepers quit within the first two years – a staggering statistic! So how can you be better prepared to take on this fascinating and rewarding hobby or business and stick with it?

Responsible beekeeping means a lifelong commitment to education, with a good understanding of bee biology and beekeeping methods. Learning beekeeping takes time. Before installing that first hive, read, listen and learn. Even a Master Beekeeper – a position that requires years of study, passing exams and certification – will admit there is always more to learn. Before you order your first bee package, take some time to reflect and consider whether beekeeping is a good fit for you. Ask yourself the following questions:

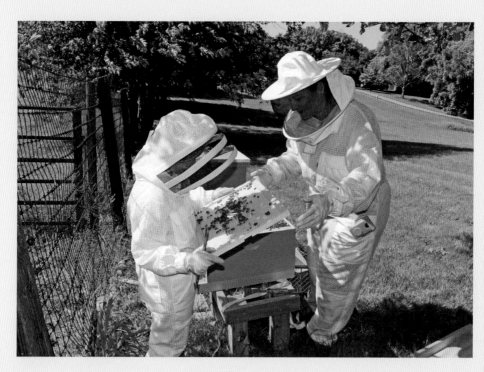

1. **Do you have an interest in the natural world?** Bees are one of the most fascinating animals to work with, and there are enormous benefits in satisfying an urge and curiosity about the biology, behaviour and management of honey bees. Expect to be nervous when first working with bees, but this should diminish over time as you learn to manage your hives.

2. **How much time do you have?** Beekeeping requires both time and attention, particularly when you are beginning. Indeed, the time commitment, dedication and responsibility are more than most new beekeepers expect, especially during the spring build-up and honey harvest time. Don't expect to place some hives outside, ignore them and simply harvest honey at the end of the season.

3. **Can you commit to continuing education?** There are always new methods and new diseases or pests that crop up in beekeeping, so you need to keep abreast of developments and procedures by taking courses, joining clubs or finding a mentor (see below).

4. **Can you afford the on-going costs?** An initial investment in equipment and bees is just the beginning. As you get more into beekeeping, you will usually buy an extractor and additional equipment for harvesting honey, which can add up. Of course, if you sell honey, you can recoup some of your investment – and by catching swarms, and raising your own queens, you can economize on the cost of buying bees.

The following may help you make your decision to become a beekeeper – or during the first year or so after you become one:

Find a mentor. Find someone in your area who will mentor you and guide you through the many questions that will crop up while beekeeping. Several mentors are a plus, as beekeepers use multiple strategies for managing their bees. Contact someone who has been beekeeping for years and ask to observe them working with their bees on a long-term basis. Experienced beekeepers are usually very forthcoming with new beekeepers and ready to share their hard-won knowledge.

Learning about beekeeping is best done at the side of an experienced beekeeper. Here, a mother shows her child how to look for a queen in a Langstroth hive.

Take a beekeeping course. Many beekeeping organizations offer introductory beekeeping courses, as do colleges and online educational websites. Basic and advanced courses are both available. By taking a course, which is usually with a specialist beekeeping organization, you can form a network with new and experienced beekeepers that will aid you in the future.

Join a beekeeping association or club. There are beekeeping associations all over the world that teach beekeeping and hold field days or 'open hive' events, where you can observe a Master Beekeeper opening and inspecting hives. Hands-on experience is invaluable in learning the best practices of beekeeping.

Attendees and tutor at an introductory beekeeping course in the UK.

Starting a safe and productive apiary

CHOOSING A SITE

Choosing a good site to locate your apiary is critical to the colony's health. There are many factors to consider in deciding the best possible area to place your hives. You are looking for certain criteria to be met before setting up your apiary. Not everything will be perfect, though, and bees can thrive in many situations, suburban and urban (including rooftops).

Recommended features:
- Access to clean water;
- Access to good-quality uncontaminated forage;
- About a metre (3–4 ft) of firm level ground in every direction so the hives are easy to access;
- Seclusion from neighbours or the public, with a hedge or fence between your apiary and public/other private land;
- Vehicle access;
- View of your hives from your house – not mandatory, but very helpful;
- Morning light exposure;
- Large enough area to provide enough space for the number of hives you want to keep (it is recommended there should be at least 1.5 metres (5 ft) in every direction per hive).

Not recommended:
- Low-lying, damp locations;
- Area close to high pedestrian traffic;
- Area prone to flooding;
- Shade all day;
- Proximity to industrial agricultural fields;
- Proximity to another apiary.

Other factors to consider:
Sun exposure (south or east facing) is crucial to increasing your honey crop, as the bees will fly earlier in the day – and sun exposure has also been linked to lower *Varroa* mite populations (see page 223). Keep all your entrances free of vegetation to promote good air circulation, and site your hives to reduce drifting between colonies. This might mean situating the hives to face in different directions or close to different landmarks. You can also add different colours or patterns onto the hive bodies to make them more distinctive.

LAWS AND REGULATIONS

To determine if it is possible to keep bees on your property, check the legal requirements with local authorities, homeowners' associations or your individual lease, as well as with animal control ordinances. These vary widely between communities and countries. Many local authorities will regulate the following:

- Minimum size of property or site for keeping bees;
- Water requirements for on-site water sources – to minimize drift onto adjacent properties with ponds and pools;
- Maximum number of hives;
- Installation of warning signs;
- Permissible types of bees (e.g. no Africanized bees);
- Requirement of whether fences or enclosures are necessary;
- Minimum setbacks to property lines and adjacent structures.

In the UK, you are not required to hold a licence to keep bees. However, ensure that you check with your local council or allotment association in case of specific restrictions. Conversely, in the United States, all states have some laws that are pertinent to beekeeping and the registration of hives.

In terms of transportation: in the UK, beekeepers take out insurance in order to move bees and to remove swarms. Contact your local bee inspector in the UK – care of the National Bee Unit. You may also wish to contact the British Beekeeper's Association.

SURROUNDINGS AND BEE DENSITY

Be aware of your adjacent areas – fields, wild areas, busy footpaths and neighbours. Look at the environment and observe if there any are nearby floral sources. Bees can forage up to 4 kilometres (2½ miles) from the colony. Consult nearby beekeepers to see how many colonies they manage in their apiary as there might be a lot of competition for forage if there are too many colonies in the neighbourhood.

In urban and suburban areas, there may be a lot of forage available, with a variety of flowering shrubs, trees and other flowering plants, especially if there are many green spaces, such as parks. In rural areas with crop fields, such as sweetcorn (maize) or wheat, these provide little to no nutrition. The plant diversity diminishes greatly near to industrial agricultural areas that are treated regularly with pesticides. With very few plant species available for foraging, this situation would overtax a hive and impact its health greatly. Forests and public lands are a mixed bag of trees and shrubs, but spaces such as unmown utility lines and

Top left: Rooftop urban beekeeping in Bankside, south London.

Top right: Hives on the roof of the InterContinental New York Barclay Hotel, USA.

Cities, with their numerous parks and gardens, can provide bees with a rich banquet of flowering plants.

right of ways can be highly desirable as forage resources, as long as they aren't controlled by pesticides.

Pay special attention to prevailing winds if you are installing rooftop hives. The amount of wind on rooftops could be a limiting factor for honey bees carrying nectar and pollen, as it would require too much flight energy for the hive to handle. An urban rooftop or balcony will easily support two or three hives but more than that would be difficult. Too many colonies in some cities have become a problem where there is too much pressure on available resources. In urban locations, make sure that there is undeveloped lands and parks to support the number of colonies present in the area.

If there are already beehives in the area, make sure that you aren't placing your hive next to them. The more isolated your apiary is, the less likely it will share the diseases and problems of another apiary.

WATER SOURCE – NATURAL OR ARTIFICIAL

Like any animal, bees need a safe and dependable water source. You want to provide one that won't go dry, won't drown the bees and won't be shared by people, pets and livestock. Bees use water not only for drinking, but also to adjust the temperature of the hive

Bees should have, or be provided with, a source of fresh, clean water, such as this garden fountain.

and use it in honey production. Water that has a smell – such as of wet earth or leaves, aquatic plants or chlorine – will attract bees.

Providing an attractive and close water source before your bees find your neighbour's pool or dog bowl is important because bees are creatures of habit, and it can be extremely hard to change their chosen source. Your neighbours might be upset if your bees start using their swimming pool as a drinking bowl! The solution could be as simple as providing a bowl of water with large stones or sticks added to provide landing areas for bees, so that they don't drown. A small, gravity-fed pet feeder holds about a gallon of water and is a quick and inexpensive solution, as is a bird bath filled with stones. Initially, adding a drop of chlorine or a weak sugar solution will attract the bees and head off any problems with the neighbours. Establish a pattern early, before your bees develop any bad habits and cause problems.

TWO COLONIES CAN SHARE

Many beekeepers start off with one colony and become very disappointed if the colony fails. More than likely this happens towards the end of the season, when it is too late to start a new one. A minimum of two colonies is recommended for both inexperienced and experienced beekeepers, as it is helpful to compare both colonies and trade resources between them. Each colony has its own personality, sometimes vigorous, sometimes less so. If one colony is weak, you could transfer a brood from the strong hive to the weak hive to bolster its strength. Also, if you are using a new technique with one hive, such as pesticide management, you should have a control hive to compare between the two. The whole hive set-up will cost more in the long run, but it will allow you to compare and contrast between the two hives. Plus, if you end up with two strong, honey-producing hives, your honey harvest will double. If you are a new beekeeper, keep your hives to a minimum – below five – until you gain more experience.

PROTECTING APIARIES

Wildlife, livestock and wind can be very damaging to your apiary. Consider planting a windscreen, erecting a barrier or a lockable security fence, and add 'mouse guards' to your hive entrances (see pages 95 and 254). An electric fence should be installed if your area has large animals that are likely to prey on beehives. If you have an electric fence, set up a visible 'caution' sign stating that there is an apiary located nearby.

HIVE STANDS

Provide a sturdy hive stand that keeps your hives at a good height for working (4–5 cm / 1½–2 inches high). Use screened bottom boards to aid air circulation and to allow debris to fall through and out of the hive area. Make sure the hive entrance is high enough off the ground, so that small animals cannot enter. It is also a good idea to tilt your hives slightly forwards, using wedges, so that condensation cannot collect, leading to mould.

Prevailing winds are an important consideration when siting hives. Natural windbreaks such as hedges are best. Here, the hives have been given extra protection in the form of wadding.

Choosing and setting up a hive

DIFFERENT TYPES OF HIVE

There are many options for equipment, types of bees and designs for hives. Your very first decision is what type of hive you would like to use. There are three major types of beehives used today – the Langstroth, the Warré and the 'top bar' – plus a myriad of combinations of these types. The Langstroth is the most commonly used and the one most people are familiar with. There are pros and cons to each type, so find one that suits your needs most closely. Whichever type you choose, preassembled starter equipment is recommended: hive boxes, tops, bottoms and frames. You can even buy your hives pre-painted!

The Langstroth hive

Invented in 1852, by US apiarist and minister L. L. Langstroth (1810–95), the Langstroth is a modular, expandable hive that uses vertically hanging frames on which bees build their comb. Each movable frame hangs with gaps between the frames of between 6 and 10 millimetres (¼–⅜ in), known as the 'bee space' (see below). Langstroth's invention is still being used today with a few modifications and has become a standard. The hive is expandable, with hive bodies that come in various depths – deep, medium and shallow – and which stack on top of each other. The beekeeper can mix and match the different components to configure the hive so that it fits their physical strength and the bees' needs. Available to purchase anywhere, the components are standardized, which allows you to purchase them from different manufacturers. Langstroth is a standard beehive that is used worldwide and is considered the benchmark for most beekeeping today.

BEE SPACE

Hives are designed based on the concept of 'bee space'. Bees build extra unwanted wax comb in any space larger than 10 millimetres (⅜ in), and any area less than 6 millimetres (¼ in) will be filled with resin-like propolis (see page 167). The ideal bee space is somewhere between 4.5 and 9 mllimetres (³⁄₁₆ and ⅜ in). Bee space allows the bees to travel unhampered around the hive. If a beekeeper breaks the bee space rule, by not using enough frames, this will result in a totally glued-together hive that they will be unable to pull apart and inspect.

Langstroth beehives in Chimacum, Washington state, USA. Note the brick weights placed on top of the hives to hold down their top covers.

The Warré hive

Looking like a mini-Langstroth hive, this square-boxed hive is also named after its inventor, French country priest Émile Warré (1867–1951). Warré's aim was to design a hive that mimicked a natural setting such as inside a tree, where wild bees would set up a home. The main difference between the Langstroth and the Warré is that boxes are added beneath the existing boxes of the Warré, rather than on top, as in the Langstroth. For a beekeeper who is concerned about lifting the heavy elements of a hive, this could be a non-starter, as you have to move all the top boxes off before adding new boxes underneath. Rather than supporting vertically hanging frames, the Warré has a series of slats spanning the top of each box, from which the bees build their comb vertically downwards. Some beekeepers use the Warré with frames that have modifications to fit the different-sized boxes. A great feature of the Warré is the peaked roof, which includes material to absorb the condensation that bees can generate in regulating the hive – an important issue during the winter.

The top-bar hive

The most unique design, the top bar is also the latest. A structure supports the hive at a convenient height, so there are no heavy boxes to tote around, just individual combs hanging off of the 'top bar' that runs across the box. Because this simple design is composed of one very long box, there is no way to expand the colony unless you get another top-bar hive. Starter strips hang from the bars from which the bees start building vertically hanging comb. The design attracts many new beekeepers, as the equipment needed to maintain and harvest honey is minimal. Harvesting honey is accomplished by the 'crush and strain' method (see page 160). Often, top-bar hives even have a viewing window located in the body, so that the beekeeper can observe the bees without disturbing them. This can add considerably to the enjoyment of beekeeping.

Inner cover

Polystyrene
hive boxes

CORE COMPONENTS OF A LANGSTROTH HIVE

Hive boxes of the most commonly used hive, the Langstroth, come in various sizes and are known for their versatility and expandability. The topmost boxes are known as 'honey supers', which is the space where bees deposit their nectar that ripens into honey. These, when full, are removed for the honey harvest. The basic components of a Langstroth hive comprise the following:

Outer top or telescoping cover The sides telescope down over the top box to keep out the weather.

Inner cover This creates a dead air space to help insulate the hive. There is a hole cut out that serves as a small observation window, feeding hole and ventilation point.

Hive boxes Available in wood or polystyrene, all the components can be purchased as a unit already assembled from various bee supply vendors. Polystyrene can offer better insulation as there are fewer temperature fluctuations within the hive, which can allow an earlier spring build-up. Since the Langstroth is a universal system, the beekeeper is able to use various numbers of different-sized boxes to come up with a configuration that works for their individual preferences and the bees' requirements. All the Langstroth boxes used in a single hive are the same length and width but can vary in depth. The keeper can use the now popular eight-frame hive bodies or the more commonly used ten-frame bodies. The advantage of using eight-frame bodies is the lighter weight (so they are easier on one's back). The hive box width for an eight-frame is 36 centimetres (14 in), and for a full ten-frame it is 41 centimetres (16 in). Consider this difference when purchasing your hive, as you will be lifting these boxes frequently. You must stick with one size of frame body for the entire hive. Within an apiary, however, you can vary between eight frames and ten frames. Boxes of different depths can be mixed in the same hive with the following sizes available:

1. **Deep: 24 centimetres (9⅝ in)** – used as brood boxes, where the queen will mostly live depositing her eggs;
2. **Medium: 17 centimetres (6⅝ in)** – used as brood boxes or honey supers;
3. **Shallow: 15 centimetres (5⅞ in)** – usually used as honey supers.

Bottom board

Entrance reducer

Queen excluder

Feeder

Mouse guard

Bottom board Providing a base for the hive boxes to stand on, this also provides an entrance to the hive that extends to around 8 or 10 centimetres (or a few inches) further than the hive body.

Hive stand This bottom support raises your hive to a working height, preferably with some area included on which to place equipment. A reused level wooden pallet raised up on concrete blocks makes an excellent hive stand.

ACCESSORIES:

- **Slatted racks** These provide dead air space below the brood boxes to help with ventilation.
- **Screened bottom boards** These act as the hive floor with a screen, protecting bees from pests and animals. They help with controlling ventilation, and especially with controlling *Varroa* mites. Mites inside the hive attached to bees will fall off and pass through the screen onto the ground and die.
- **Entrance reducer** Blocking a portion of the entrance, a reducer limits the area the bees need to defend. A new colony with a small population needs this more than an established one, which will have plenty of available guards.
- **Queen excluder** This is a metal or plastic grid placed on top of the brood boxes to keep the queen from migrating upwards and laying eggs in the honey supers. The openings are just large enough for worker bees to pass through, but not the larger queen or drones. Beekeepers are divided on the efficacy of the queen excluder, with some arguing that it slows down worker bees passing into the supers. You can combat this by placing an upper entrance into the supers.
- **Feeders** You can select either internal feeders ('frame' feeders) or external feeders ('bucket' or 'gravity' feeders). For more on this, see 'Feeding honey bees' later in this chapter (page 134).
- **Mouse guards** There is a high chance of mice getting into your warm beehives for winter protection. Avoid this by placing mouse guards – expandable metal contraptions with holes punched through for bees to pass – at least a month before winter arrives.

Top: Beekeeping equipment should be kept together in a toolbox, ready for use.

Bottom: A wooden honeycomb frame taken from a Langstroth hive.

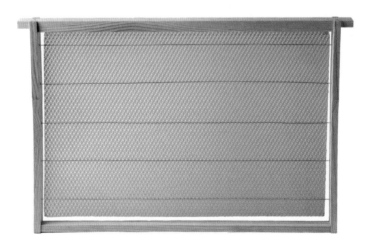

HIVE TOOL AND TOOLBOX

Used for numerous beekeeping tasks, the hive tool is a beekeeper's most important possession when working with bees – perfect for everything from levering up screens from bee packages and prying apart a queen cage, through to lifting frames and loosening and prizing apart the hive boxes. Have an assortment ready to use as they are easy to misplace. Available in a 'J' or a standard type, the tools are made out of stainless steel and have a bevelled edge that's perfect for scraping and prying. The J-type hive tool has a hook on the end that's great for levering up propolis-glued frames out of a box. Keep a dedicated toolbox with all your equipment ready to go.

FRAMES

Wooden or plastic rectangles that support the comb, with an outside supporting structure, frames are the building blocks of the Langstroth hive and sometimes of the Warré, too. The frames are self-spacing so that they fit snugly in the hive with the proper bee space (see page 90). A six-sided imprint is embossed into the foundation, a rectangle that bees build their honeycomb on. There are frames that are made completely out of plastic – the frame and the foundation – and others that have a mix of a wooden frame and plastic foundation.

Some foundations are simply made out of beeswax supported by two supporting wires that run across the frame. This type of frame is called 'foundationless', and some beekeepers swear by this method, as they believe bees prefer to build their honeycomb from scratch. It definitely gives the bees more freedom, and it is a lot less expensive. Using foundationless frames certainly involves a steeper learning curve for the beekeeper – so it's best that you only start replacing your frames with these once you have become more experienced. You can use this type if you want to harvest cut-comb (see page 162), or you decide to have a more 'natural' hive. If you decide to go with a plastic foundation, you should paint beeswax across the foundation, so that bees will readily accept this type.

Pre-assembled frames that go into pre-assembled hive boxes provide the easiest option for the novice beekeeper. Alternatively, there is the top-bar hive (see pages 92–93): instead of frames, a top-bar hive has bars across the top of the hive body. In this type of hive, the bee builds the hanging foundation from scratch, as it would in a wild hive.

THE ART OF THE SMOKER

Perfect your smoker technique even before you purchase bees. The smoker is a must-have tool when starting out in beekeeping, and there is definitely a good way and a bad way to manage a smoker. It is very important to keep your smoker lit the entire time you are inspecting, as you don't want to have to leave your uncovered hive open with lots of bees flying around. Your preferred smoker fuel will burn slowly and have a cool smoke.

Follow these steps:

1. Gather your smoker and fuel with matches or portable propane blowtorch. The fuel could be dry grass, pine needles, newspaper, wood shavings/chips, untreated hessian or a commercially prepared fuel.

2. Lightly ball up some newspaper and push into the bottom of your smoker (firebox) using your hive tool.

3. Using matches or the blowtorch, light the newspaper and squeeze the bellows several times – you will see the newspaper flare up.

4. Add some other fuel, like the hessian or pine needles, then place on top and squeeze the bellows a few more times until the hessian catches fire. Push the hessian down into the smoker, squeezing the bellows a few more times.

5. Continue to add more fuel, squeezing the bellows to keep air circulating, making sure you don't smother the fire with too much fuel. Keep pushing the burning fuel down into the chamber.

6. Once smoke starts to puff out and the fire remains lit, even when you have stopped squeezing the bellows, you can close up the smoker – it should now stay lit for at least a half hour. If the smoke starts to subside, squeeze the bellows a few more times to reignite the embers.

A bee smoker, with hand-operated bellows, fire chamber and nozzle.

Starting or replacing colonies

To start new colonies in the spring, or just to replace colonies that have died over the winter, beekeepers can use one of the following methods:

- **Purchase bees** – in the form of a full-sized working colony from a local beekeeper; a nuc (nucleus) colony; or a package in several sizes.
- **Make new colonies** – by splitting or dividing one of the stronger colonies from their apiary.
- **Capture a swarm** – using swarm traps or by locating ones in the wild.

A queen bee in a plastic cage, as she might arrive as part of a package, separate from the rest of the colony.

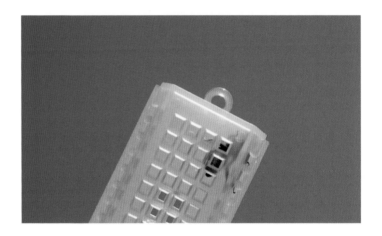

PURCHASING BEES

If you are purchasing bees, select them according to your preferences – for example: docile, hardworking, well-behaved, good at honey production, able to survive severe winters, well adapted to your location and/or resistant to pests and diseases. Not all bee types will have every characteristic that you want, as each line of bees is different and has strengths and weaknesses, but once you start, you can gradually select and develop better bees for your conditions.

Seek out reputable local producers if possible, as their bees are more likely to be adapted to local environmental conditions and pest and disease strains endemic to the area. If this isn't possible, purchase them online and be sure that the bees are certified as disease-free. For full-sized colonies, some beekeepers will sell you an entire working hive, but make sure it is disease-free and that you can move it to your new location safely – usually at night.

INSTALLING PACKAGE BEES

A package is a plastic box or wooden shipping container holding a separately caged queen with a sugar plug and sugar feed source containing between 8,000 and 20,000 bees. Purchased package bees are usually shipped and picked up at the post office, and once retrieved should be installed soon after or, at most, within a day or two. Inspect the package carefully, making sure the queen is healthy and moving and most of the worker bees are alive. (It is normal to have an inch of dead bees on the bottom.) Lightly spray the bees through the screen with 1:1 sugar syrup. Store in a cool, dark and dry area prior to installation. The ambient temperature should be between 10 °C (50 °F) and 15 °C (60 °F). In these conditions, the bees will be calm and cluster around the queen.

There are two methods for introducing a package: the shake method and the package in the hive method. For both methods, you need an empty (and usually deep) super with ten frames, either with old drawn comb (the wax sheet created by the honey bees) or new foundation, a hive tool, a spray bottle filled with sugar syrup and a small nail or tack. Wear all your protective equipment. Choose a calm, warm day towards the end of the afternoon, as the bees are less likely to abscond in the evening.

Shake method

1. Set up an empty (usually deep) hive body on your hive platform along with a bottom board and slatted or screened rack in your apiary.
2. Transport your bee package to the apiary along with your tools. When handling the package, be sure not to put your hands close to the screen as the bees can sting through it.
3. Slot in two frames on either side of the deep (or brood) box – which is the largest hive body – leaving six frames out to make space in the centre for the bees.
4. Add an entrance reducer.
5. Spray the bees in the package with sugar syrup again.
6. Remove the wooden panel from the top of the bee package with your hive tool.
7. Gently remove the can feeder and queen cage from the hole in the top of the package, replacing the wooden panel on top to prevent bees from escaping.
8. Gently shake the queen cage to remove any clinging bees into the deep, keeping the queen inside the cage, and inspect the queen to make sure she is healthy. The queen should be marked for easier spotting in the hive. Place the queen cage to one side, in the shade.

Top left: A beekeeper shakes a purchased box of bees into a new hive.

Top right: A hive being prepared to house a new colony.

9. Remove the wooden panel again and invert the package over the hive and firmly and vigorously shake the bees into the centre of the deep (where frames are missing). If you prefer, you could remove the entire screen on one side of the package and then shake the bees.

10. Prop the package in front of the hive so that any remaining bees can travel into the hive.

11. Gently return the frames into the deep, slotting them in carefully so as not to crush the bees.

To instal the queen:

1. Remove the plastic plug or cork from the queen cage on the side containing the candy (or 'sugar') plug. The other end has another plug – leave this one alone. The bees will eat the sugar and eventually release the queen within one to two days. The bees will gradually become accustomed to the queen's pheromones, minimizing the chances that they will reject the new queen.

2. Place the queen cage, candy side up, between the two centre frames of the hive, making sure the cage is secure between the frames, so it doesn't slip to the bottom of the hive, making it harder for the queen to emerge. If your frame already has drawn comb, embed the cage into the wax to mount it, adding a rubber band for safety. Otherwise, you can tack the cage to the frame with a small nail or use a provided metal tab folded over the top of the frame.
3. Close up the hive and add a feeder with sugar syrup.
4. Inspect the colony after five to six days to ensure the queen is released and alive. Check for evidence of egg laying, which will appear as single small grains of rice in each cell. Continue to feed until there is adequate forage.

Sometimes the workers won't accept the queen and you will see the results if the queen is dead in the cage or missing from the hive. If this is the case:

- *Either:* obtain a replacement queen quickly (within a few days) and instal her – as outlined above.
- *Or:* unite this queen-less colony with an established colony using the following method:

1. Remove any top boxes on an established colony, revealing the brood box(es) underneath, and place a single sheet of newspaper on top.
2. Poke holes in the newspaper with your hive tool.
3. Place the queen-less colony on top of the newspaper, uniting it with the established colony, and close the cover.

The bees will chew through the paper and unite the two colonies. Be sure to supply daily infusions of sugar syrup to help the new colony to thrive.

Package in the hive method

In this hands-off approach, you are relying on the bees finding the queen and coming out of the package on their own. It is a less intrusive way of introducing bees, and one by which many beekeepers swear.

1. Follow steps 1–7 in the 'shake' method above but, using the tip of your hive tool, remove the plug on the end of the queen cage with the sugar plug.
2. Rubber-band your queen cage horizontally on a removed frame, or, if the frame has drawn comb, embed it in the wax.
3. Take the package of bees and rap it on the ground to dislocate bees inside the package – and then immediately dump a *few* bees onto the frame holding the queen cage. Bees should cluster around the queen in the cage, keeping her warm and helping to spread her pheromones throughout the package.
4. Place the frame in the deep, holding the queen cage, with a few bees clustered on top, next to the side frames.
5. Place your entire package in the gap left by removing five frames, with the top opening on its side.
6. Place a pollen patty directly over the queen frame, adding a feeder of sugar syrup.
7. Close up the hive – the bees should migrate out of the package towards the queen.
8. The following day, remove the shipping package and the queen cage, insert the rest of your reserved frames, and continue to feed.
9. After a week, check to see whether the queen is laying eggs.

Things don't always go as planned with this method. The biggest issue is that, if the weather is too cold (under 10 °C / 50 °F), the bees will not vacate the package, leaving the queen to chill and die. Another issue is that the bees sometimes make comb in the package, leaving the brood box in a mess, with honeycomb built everywhere.

INSTALLING A NUC

Installing nuc (nucleus) colonies – frame-sized colonies that include a mated queen and five frames of pollen, honey and brood – is easy and straightforward. If you can't instal the nuc immediately, store it next to its future home in the apiary so that the bees get used to the location. If not installing immediately, remove the cover on the access hole in the front so the bees can go back and forth. Your chances of producing a honey harvest increase greatly when installing a nuc or purchasing a full-sized working colony.

A beekeeper transfers frames from a nuc box to a hive.

Follow these steps:

1. Set your nuc next to the hive deep that will be the bees' future home. Follow steps 1–4 in the 'shake' method.
2. The frames you use in the deep can be brand new, painted with a layer of beeswax or reused from an older hive.
3. You can lightly smoke the bees to calm them or spray them with sugar water.
4. Open up the nuc box and remove each frame, one by one, and slot them into the same configuration that they held in the nuc box, filling up the hive deep from which the old frames have been removed.

5. Space each frame evenly in the deep.
6. Place the almost empty nuc on its side, in front of the hive entrance, for stray bees to move into their new home.
7. Add feeders of sugar syrup.

It is critical to feed all newly installed bees with sugar syrup, until there is adequate forage and good weather. This will take a bit longer for packages than for more established nucs. Protein patties can also be used as supplemental feed to boost the newly installed bees.

MAKING NEW COLONIES

If you have an existing strong colony that is overflowing with worker bees and stored honey, you can expand your colony numbers by dividing or splitting the colony. A smaller version of the original colony, a split can be made any time during the active bee season, though they are easiest to produce when forage is abundant in the spring. Splitting a colony will usually halt any swarm preparations, and using swarm queen cells started by the bees is a great means to produce a queenright split – that is, one with a laying queen present.

To accomplish a split, you should have a purchased queen or queen cell from one of your hives. Follow these steps:

1. Open up the hive of your strong colony to get to the brood boxes and remove two to three brood frames with a clinging worker bee population, plus a frame or two of honey and/or pollen from one of your strong hives. Inspect to make sure the queen isn't present.
2. Set up an empty brood box with a bottom board, hive stand and covers in a different part of the apiary to prevent drifting and robbing.
3. Shake some worker bees from the pulled frames into the new hive body. Alternatively, you can place the split into a 'split box', which is smaller. Slot in the frames that you pulled from your strong colony.
4. Add empty foundation frames (preferably drawn) to fill the new box, adding a newly purchased caged queen or queen cell from your hives. Add a reducer to prevent robbing.
5. Replace the pulled frames from your strong colony with new frames to give them more room.
6. Feed the new split with sugar syrup and protein patties until established – this will take at least a few weeks.

CAPTURING AND INTRODUCING A SWARM

A swarm is a natural way for bees to reproduce and create a new hive. Many beekeepers rely on this method exclusively to populate their hives as they do not want to bear the cost of purchasing new ones. The process of swarming is normal and can be exciting. The original colony replaces the old queen, who leaves the hive with about half of the worker bees and as much honey as her companions can carry. This exodus produces a lot of noise and commotion and is a sight to see! Landing on a nearby structure, the swarm forms a cluster with the queen protected in the centre. From here, scout bees go 'house hunting' and, once they have found some suitable locations, return to perform a 'waggle dance' on the cluster. The bees eliminate the different sites one by one, until they choose one site and suddenly take off and fly towards the preferred site. This process can take up to two or three days while the scouts are searching.

While still in a cluster, you can capture the swarm and bring it back to the apiary and instal it into one of your vacant hives. Bees nearly always swarm in the spring, coinciding with a nectar flow, and since only a strong colony swarms, they usually represent strong local genetics. Swarms are desirable because of this fact and generally thrive better than purchased bees and are more likely to produce a same-season honey harvest.

Any beekeeper can collect swarms by being connected to their local beekeeping community, which maintains 'swarm lists' for retrieval. Swarms are usually very docile and easy to work with, but be careful of any swarms in an Africanized bee area.

Another way to capture swarms is to build a 'swarm trap' or 'bait hive', which is essentially a watertight wooden box with a volume of 40–80 litres (10–18 gal) containing old frames and with a 5-centimetre (2-in) diameter entrance towards the bottom of the box. To bait the trap, use a few drops of lemongrass essential oil or commercially available pheromone lure to attract swarms. Often, swarm traps are placed high in trees, but as long as the box is off the ground, it will become a target for swarms.

According to the British Beekeeper's Association, beekeepers in the UK are insured to move bees and to remove swarms. For more advice on catching swarms, please refer to the following pages.

CATCHING A SWARM

Swarms don't travel far from the mother hive when swarming. Gathering on a tree limb or any structure like a hockey or football net, fence or grill, bees will clump together from a few hours to up to a few days. Once your neighbours and friends know you are a beekeeper, they will probably call you to remove them from the location as soon as possible. Retrieving swarms is a great way to increase your colonies inexpensively. But swarms are very unpredictable and can be difficult to catch and transport. Only if they are located close to the ground and readily accessible is the task an easy one.

Make sure you are ready for that inevitable call to capture a local swarm by having the following equipment ready:

1. Container or box in which to place the bees – usually an empty hive box holding a few old frames, with a bottom and top to secure it. An old window screen is useful for the lid, but make sure it is bee-tight.
2. Ratchet strap or bungee cord to hold the box together.
3. Bee suit, smoker, bee brush.
4. Sugar syrup in a spray bottle.
5. Pruners or loppers to thin brush and perhaps remove the entire branch the cluster is on.
6. Step stool or small ladder – for safety reasons, do not attempt to remove swarms high in a tree!
7. Old white sheet.

If you are on a call list for collecting swarms, you need to ask the right questions before packing up your equipment and arriving at the location. Asking questions will save you a lot of trouble, especially if people want a paper wasp nest to be removed, which they often confuse with a swarm. Most people don't know what a honey bee looks like, so be sure to ask for photos.
Ask the following questions:

1. Is it a honey bee swarm and not that of some other kind of bee?
2. Can you send me a picture of the swarm?
3. How far off the ground is the swarm? If the swarm is high in a tree, inaccessible and away from people, tell them that the bees will leave within a few days. It isn't worth the hazards of climbing a tall ladder.
4. Are the bees a safety hazard and close to an area frequented by people?
5. When did you first notice them?
6. How large is the swarm?

Once you have received that all-important call, follow these steps:

1. Pick early evening if possible.
2. Position your hive box directly under the swarm with the bottom in place on top of the sheet.
3. Spray the swarm with sugar syrup, removing any branches out of the way of the swarm.
4. Grab the branch or item that the swarm is hanging from and shake the entire swarm with a vigorous jerking motion to dislodge it so that it falls into the box.
5. The swarm should drop into the box – with any luck, along with the queen.
6. Most of the bees should follow if the queen has landed in the box. A few strays will fly around and settle on the original swarm location. Wait to see whether they join the queen in the box. If the queen hasn't landed in the box, the bees will follow her to her new location, and you will have to try the procedure again. Only once the queen lands in the box will you be able to retrieve the swarm.
7. Ideally, your bees will be in a cluster on a branch that you can remove and lower the entire swarm into the box.
8. Secure the box, load it into your vehicle and head to your apiary to instal like a bee package.

If you capture a wild swarm of bees, you should instal it exactly like a package into a new 'deep' (the largest brood box of a Langstroth hive) in the apiary (see page 100). The queen should be present – check after about a week by inspecting to make sure the colony is queenright.

If your swarm has landed in a swarm trap, leave them alone for the first week or two. The bees in the swarm box are busy building combs and bringing in nectar, and the queen should be laying eggs. After a fortnight, carefully inspect the inside frames to verify that the colony is queenright. Instal bees from a swarm trap exactly like a nuc, transferring the frames out of the swarm trap into a prepared, empty hive. Be sure to feed both types of swarm until they are fully established.

Maintaining your hive

Maintaining a hive is a continuous operation, year-round, with intense activity in the spring and late summer when you harvest honey. Many novice beekeepers think, once the hive is up and running, they can relax and wait to harvest honey – but that is just the beginning. Monitoring your bee hives is an ongoing job, and the more proactive you are, the healthier and more successful your hives will be.

Inspection

The many threats to honey bee health – parasites, disease, pesticides and inadequate nutrition – mean that bee health must be monitored by regular inspections, and proactive steps taken to protect the bees. By regularly inspecting your colonies, you can be proactive in staving off any problems such as swarming, diseases and pests. More frequent inspections are necessary earlier in the season during the build-up, rather than the later part of the season when the hive is contracting (see *A beekeeper's year*, pages 69–71). There are certain things that you will be looking for each time you open the hive.

Before opening the hive, make sure the weather conditions are favourable – not wet, cold or windy – and in the middle of the day (11 am to 2 pm), when the population is reduced because of foraging bees. Sunny weather is ideal – above 15.5 °C (60 °F). The most important thing to remember is to be calm and methodical when working the bees to avoid startling them and possibly making them aggressive. When you become nervous, bees can sense the pheromones your body gives off and react aggressively. Bees also react negatively to the carbon dioxide we breathe out, so be careful not to breathe on the bees. Move smoothly, without any sudden movements and with purpose.

START WITH THE RIGHT TOOLS

It's a good idea to put together your own hive inspection toolbox. There is nothing more frustrating than opening up your hives, with bees buzzing around, and not having the proper tool for finishing your inspection. Keep these tools at hand for your inspection activities:

- Smoker with fuel;
- Hive tool;
- Bee brush;
- Portable blowtorch for starting the smoker, or matches;
- Marking pens;
- Field notebook;
- Hammer and nails for repairing frames;
- Antihistamines.

READING A FRAME STEP BY STEP

Observing and understanding the nuances of a hive frame is a skill that you will develop and refine over time. Follow these steps:

- Don your bee suit, including gloves, start up your smoker, and have a hive tool handy.
- Observe the front entrance of the hive to see whether bees are flying in and out, bringing in pollen, and whether any dead bees are present.
- Puff some smoke into the front entrance to confuse the guard bees.
- Remove the top cover, using your hive tool, puffing some smoke through the inner cover hole.
- Wait about one minute for the smoke to take effect.

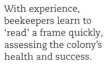

With experience, beekeepers learn to 'read' a frame quickly, assessing the colony's health and success.

- Remove the outer cover and set aside, then smoke again.
- Remove any supers on top of the brood chambers if already in place and set aside, remembering the configuration in which they were placed on the hive. Everything will be stuck together with propolis, and you will need to pry the edges of your hive bodies apart with your hive tool, piece by piece.
- Remove the queen excluder, if using, and smoke lightly again.
- Remove the top deep box and set it aside, smoking lightly as you go.
- One at a time, remove the brood frames in the bottom deep box and gently shake most of the bees back into the hive, at the entrance.
- Holding the frame by the top, inspect the frames, flipping the frame over gently, looking for the queen. Locating the queen can be tough and needs experience, but it is easier if the queen is marked (see page 52). The likely location for the queen will be the edge of a central frame in the brood box. If you can't find the queen, look for evidence of her egg laying by inspecting the cells for eggs, which look like small grains of rice. It is easier to see eggs if you tilt the frame back and forth in the sun or use a magnifying glass. The bottom end of the frame is where you would be more likely

Locating the queen on a brood frame can be challenging, even after most of the bees have been shaken back into the hive.

to spot any eggs. Another clue is the attendants forming a circle around the queen.

- Check for brood to see if larvae and pupae are both present. Take note of the brood pattern. Is it spotty or solid? Do the brood cappings look healthy?
- Is nectar, honey and pollen being stored?
- Look for signs of parasites, tiny mites on the bees or other insects like hive beetles, which will scurry away quickly when exposed to light. If you see any signs of trouble, research the issue and treat the problem if you can.
- Put this frame aside and pull out another frame. Repeat this sequence for every brood frame, slotting each frame back where the previous frame was removed.
- When finished with this box, push the frames together carefully so as not to crush the bees, and place the second deep on top, repeating the process.
- If the bottom deep is empty, the bees have moved upwards into the top deep and you can reverse the deeps so the full one is on the bottom and the empty one on top.
- It is just as important to inspect the honey frames as the brood frames – just take a quick look and see if you need to add another super.
- Replace the supers and queen excluder on top of the second deep in the same order. If you have trouble with bees hanging on the edges as you replace, use a bee brush to gently dislodge them.
- Replace both covers, using the bee brush or smoke to move them out of the way.
- Record all your observations as soon as possible:
  1. Where the queen was located (see page 116).
  2. Whether you observed brood and eggs, and the pattern.
  3. The number and fullness of the honey frames.
  4. Signs of disease or other problems such as swarm or supersedure cells (see page 114).
- Put your smoker in a safe place where the embers can burn out safely.

DIFFERENCE BETWEEN A SWARM CELL
AND SUPERSEDURE CELL

Many beekeepers are confused between a supersedure cell and
a swarm cell, but it is all about location and purpose. In respect
of both types, there will usually be several visible at a time.

Hanging like a large rough peanut on the bottom edge of
a frame, a swarm cell is a cell where the larva develops and
matures into a new queen. Colonies produce swarm cells if they
are planning on swarming – producing a new queen to take the
place of the old one that is preparing to leave the hive.

Supersedure cells are produced by the colony if an ageing
queen isn't producing enough brood to keep the colony viable
or the queen has died. The colony produces an emergency
supersedure cell to replace (or supersede) the absent or ageing
queen. Since a queen might not be available to lay an egg
for a supersedure cell, the workers will search for eggs or the
youngest larvae that are being fed royal jelly, the substance
that allows a growing larvae to fully mature with functioning
reproductive organs, and use this as the replacement queen.
While supersedure cells resemble swarm cells in appearance,
they can appear anywhere on the surface or face of the comb.
The first mature bee to emerge will become the new queen
in most cases, killing by stinging any other emerged or
un-emerged queens.

Think of a supersedure cell as an emergency measure that
bees produce to replace a defective or missing queen, while a
swarm cell is produced purely for swarming and reproduction.

Left and opposite:
Supersedure (queen)
cells hanging from
the bottom of a
frame. The golden,
rough-textured cells
are often compared
to peanut shells.

A queen surrounded by workers as she lays an egg in a cell at the edge of the comb.

FINDING THE QUEEN

Moving around the colony, the queen can be very difficult to spot among thousands of bees, even for an experienced beekeeper. She could literally be anywhere except above the queen excluder, and if you don't use an excluder she could be in your supers or even on the inner cover. Usually, finding the queen takes a bit of work and persistence:

- Open the hive and look for frames with open brood and/or eggs.
- Scan the frame and flip to the other side if you can't find her.
- The queen will move away from the light, so you will need to quickly scan the frames on either side of the one removed.
- Be sure to look at the hive walls and the inner cover.
- Look for a grouping of bees that will include attendants arrayed in a circle facing the queen.
- If you can't find her one day, try the next and instal a queen excluder so that you can limit her movements to the brood boxes only.

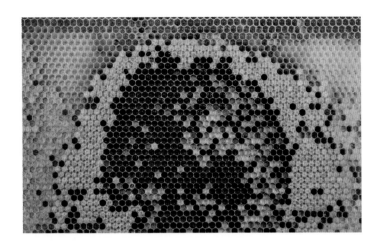

Comb showing a ring of capped brood cells surrounded by cells filled with pollen and honey.

UNDERSTANDING THE BROOD PATTERN

Described as a rainbow, the pattern or configuration of brood, pollen and honey creates bands of areas containing eggs, larvae and capped brood, surrounded by pollen and honey. The brood area should be solidly filled; if it isn't, the brood pattern is described as 'spotty', a potential indication of infection or a failing queen. The capping on the worker bee brood should be smooth, slightly convex and a tan or creamy colour. With drone brood, the capping should be bumpy and dome-like to accommodate the larger male drone bee that grows and extends out of the cell. If the capping of any brood is sunken or a dark colour, this could be a sign of a disease being present and should be investigated.

Always start your inspection with the centre frames as the queen will be more likely to be active here. Usually, a circle of pollen surrounds the brood nest (where the queen is laying eggs) and the adjacent frames will reveal the 'brood pattern'. Starting in the centre of a frame, the queen will work her way outwards, laying eggs in a circular fashion. You should see various stages of brood – from egg, through to developing larvae, to capped brood. After inspecting, note down all of your observations, including the brood pattern and how many frames have brood present.

COVER CLOTHS

Some beekeepers use weighted cotton covers to place on top of a hive while inspecting each frame. This stops bees from flying up and out of the hive while you are inspecting each frame. While the use of cover cloths will slow down your inspection, they can be handy if you have a 'hot' hive, one you know might be aggressive.

Queen health and replacement

BENEFITS OF REQUEENING

As part of any maintenance programme to keep your colony healthy and productive, you must requeen your colonies regularly. Queens live for one to three years, and you should have a maintenance schedule set up for your hives to replace old, substandard or failing queens.

A young queen – one who is two years old or younger – is critical for the vigour of the hive and benefits the hive greatly. Beekeepers often notice that some hives produce more honey than others, and this is usually due to a healthy and young queen. If possible, purchase local queens from a breeder, which will make them more likely to be adapted to local conditions, pests and disease strains. Since such breeders are usually certified, using locally produced queens also avoids introducing new pests or diseases.

REQUEENING AND SUPERSEDURE (INDIRECT AND DIRECT)

Requeening is where the beekeeper replaces the queen with a purchased mated queen (direct), while supersedure is the natural bees' method of replacement without involving the beekeeper (indirect). If you have hives that aren't producing as well as they should, but otherwise healthy, it is more than likely that the queen needs to be replaced, or 'superseded', especially if she is more than two years old. The average colony will supersede or swarm at least once a season. Late summer going into autumn is the best time to replace her with a newly mated queen, so the queen gets settled in going into the winter. Also, if you requeen during September, the brood she lays will become winter bees, which will live longer than other bees because they will ride out the winter in the hive. When spring hits, the queen will be primed to lay eggs and jump-start the season. Also, if you have a 'hot' hive, requeening is necessary for your own wellbeing.

LOSING A QUEEN

New beekeepers will often lose hives over winter, and losing a queen is the most frequent reason. The only bee capable of laying fertilized eggs, the queen is crucial for the colony. Fertilized eggs may become either a worker bee or a queen bee depending on what they are fed initially. Worker bees are fed for the first days of their life with royal jelly and then are switched to pollen and honey. To create another queen within the hive, the workers will feed larvae

A beekeeper places a transported queen cage, with attendant bees, into the beehive.

a diet of royal jelly exclusively. This means that worker bees can potentially create a queen with any worker larvae (known as an 'emergency queen').

Definite behaviours and signs will be exhibited by a queen-less colony. Even if the queen is missing for just an hour, the lack of her pheromonal presence will be detected by the bees and within a day the bees will start making a supersedure cell. Behaviours such as excessive fanning, used to distribute the diminishing chemical signature in the hive, can be quite loud and you will detect the difference as soon as you open the cover. In addition, the guard bees at the entrance will be very defensive and more bees will come out at you from the top. A generally disorganized response is indicative of a queen-less colony. Also, a lack of fresh eggs will tell the beekeeper that something is amiss.

If you catch a queen-less colony early, you are more likely to get it queenright before too much damage is done. The longer you wait, the more likely the colony will perish as the population slowly drops. If the colony is queen-less for too long, it may develop laying workers – workers that lay unfertilized eggs. These unfertilized eggs will hatch and develop into drones, or male bees. Once this happens, it is very difficult to get the colony queenright again. You will know if workers are laying eggs if you see multiple eggs in a cell rather than the single one that a queen lays and lots of drone brood.

QUEEN-LESS TEST

One method to resolve this situation is to put an open brood with eggs from a queenright colony into your queen-less colony. Check back after two to five days to see whether they are making emergency queens on that frame by making queen cells. That is your confirmation that the colony has been queen-less. If you have a caged queen handy, you can also test for queen-lessness. Place the caged queen on top of the frames and watch what happens. If the colony is queenright, they will react aggressively and bite and sting the cage. If the colony is queen-less, the bees will head towards the catch and flit their wings. If you place a queen cage in a queenright colony, she will be killed by the workers very quickly.

INTRODUCING A NEW QUEEN

The introduction of a new queen into the hive is a delicate operation in beekeeping and one that a new beekeeper dreads the most. The proper queen installation ensures that she will be accepted without difficulty and continue the growth and productivity of the hive. Timing and preparation are critical

A beekeeper checks the now empty queen cage to ensure that the new queen has been successfully introduced to the hive. It appears that all is well.

when introducing the queen bee, so that the worker bees don't reject and kill her. Be sure to remove any queen excluders that you have in place before introducing your newly purchased queen so that she can move freely through the hive and lay eggs as needed. Also, check the available food resources to make sure that the colony has the necessary supplies – such as stored honey, pollen and nectar – to support the new queen and her expected brood that will soon populate the hive.

The process of installing a new queen starts with ordering a marked queen from a certified producer, local if possible. Inspect her upon arrival for health and vitality, keeping her in a cool, dark and safe location, dripping a few drops of water onto the mesh of the cage every 12 hours until you are ready for installation, preferably within 48 hours or less.

FINDING THE OLD QUEEN

One of the toughest jobs for any beekeeper, but especially for an inexperienced one, is to find the queen. She is usually found in a frame located near the centre of the hive box that contains newly laid eggs. Look for a bee that has a circle of bees surrounding her. (This is her retinue.) The queen also emits a sound called 'piping', which is a slight, high-pitched buzzing sound. Look for freshly laid eggs, examining uncapped brood cells that look like single grains of rice. Once you locate her, pick her up (she rarely stings) and dispose of her. Wait at least 24 hours before introducing a new queen. Check the hive before introducing a new queen for sealed queen cells, which are peanut-shaped cells. If you find some, you can remove these and introduce them to another hive, as splits, nucs or other queen-less hives, by gently pressing them into the comb of the queen-less hive.

INDIRECT RELEASE VERSUS DIRECT RELEASE
Available from commercial queen rearing operations, or reared by the beekeeper, adult queens can be introduced to queen-less colonies just like you would in a package of bees (indirect release). Look for local producers first to find locally adapted queens. Note that the direct method has a higher chance of rejection.

Direct release:
1. Remove two frames from the centre of the brood box.
2. Sprinkle a little sugar syrup on the caged queen through the screen.
3. Smoke the hive slightly and slowly lower the cage into the hive.
4. Remove the screen from the queen cage with your hive tool and let the queen crawl out onto nearby combs.
5. Replace the frames carefully, making sure you don't crush the queen.
6. Close up the hive.
7. Wait at least a week before opening the hive and check to see whether she is laying eggs.

Indirect release:
1. Follow steps of direct release 1–3.
2. Secure the cage to a frame with the plug facing up between two frames containing brood.
3. Replace any frames and take care not to disturb the queen. The bees will eat through the sugar plug, releasing her.
4. Close up the hive.
5. Wait at least a week before opening the hive and check to see whether the queen is laying eggs.

Careful observation and patience are essential for success in introducing a new queen. Her successful integration in the hive will be indicated by a general sense of hive calmness, with the worker bees feeding and grooming the queen.

SWARM PREVENTION

Bees' natural way to increase their numbers is by reproducing at the colony level. You can take advantage of swarming to increase your colonies but should remember that a colony that has swarmed will greatly impact your honey harvest. When the queen departs with thousands of workers (up to two-thirds of the bee population) and some drones, you can say goodbye to any honey harvest that season. When you inspect your overwintered colonies in the spring, you should be aware of any swarming behaviours and prevent this from happening. Look for:

- plenty of available stored food;
- brood congestion or crowding where the population is rapidly expanding and running out of space;
- a young established queen (one year old);
- peanut-shaped queen cells hanging from the bottom or sides of brood comb (see page 124), which contains a larva that will mature into a virgin queen (unmated). The cell is typically about 25 millimetres (1 in) long and has a rough surface texture resembling a peanut and can be capped or uncapped.

All colonies build emergency queen cups, which are simply empty receptacles ready in case the bees need to rear a new queen. They are commonly observed during a frame inspection. New queens are needed for various reasons – to replace a failing or injured one, an absent queen or in preparation for swarming. When a colony is preparing to swarm, eggs will be laid in the already produced queen cups, which then become queen cells, and the resulting larvae will hatch in three days and start to develop. On the ninth day after the egg is laid, the cell is sealed with wax, and the newly created queen will emerge seven days later, on the sixteenth day. During this process, the old queen will leave with a swarm around the time the queen cells are sealed, resulting in a much-diminished population in the original hive.

If you observe uncapped queen cells, occupied with a developing larvae but not sealed yet, you can make a split of one of your other strong colonies, creating a new one by grafting the newly formed queen cell to a frame in the new colony. If the queen cell is capped, however, the colony is committed to swarming and a warning. It is important to watch your colony with the capped queen cells carefully as you can probably capture the swarm to keep it in the apiary as a new colony. Some beekeepers will remove capped queen cells by scraping them off the frame, aiming to stop the swarming behavior, but by doing this you are just delaying the inevitable. The hive will simply produce more queen cells and swarm anyway.

During this time, it is important to check the brood nest for queen cells with developing larvae, capped and uncapped. If this is done every eight to ten days, necessary steps can be taken to prevent swarming, or – alternatively – to capture the swarm. When colonies are strong and developing rapidly, a period of good weather following bad weather is the most likely time that bees will swarm.

DIFFERENCE BETWEEN HONEYCOMB AND BROOD COMB

Much darker in colour than honeycomb, the brood comb is used by bees to raise their young. It can often be black in colour due to repeated brood cycles, as waste from pupating larvae is left behind sealed within a thin layer of propolis and wax. Any pesticides, chemicals from applications, dirt and spores from different diseases present will be absorbed into the brood wax as well, which is why these combs should be replaced regularly (every three years) to keep the nursery clean. To keep track of when you added your frames, you can note on the frame with permanent marker the date it was first introduced. Never switch frames between the brood box and the honey supers.

The honeycomb present in the supers is used strictly for storing honey and is much lighter in colour than the dark, leathery brood wax. Produced constantly during a nectar flow, this beeswax is a beautiful, light-golden colour, has a wonderful beeswax fragrance and yields a pure, clean-burning wax. Honeycomb frames should also be replaced periodically, but not as often as brood comb.

Few sights can match the bright, golden hue of a honeycomb frame.

Here, faced with a honey-bound hive, a beekeeper removes some of the honey frames and replaces them with new brood frames.

HONEY-BOUND / HIVE-BOUND

When inspecting the brood chamber, be aware that, during a strong nectar flow, bees sometimes prioritize storing food and crowd out the brood nest, leaving the queen no room to lay eggs. This condition is called 'honey-bound' or 'hive-bound'. To solve this, the beekeeper should add another super and then move out two to four honey frames of the brood nest, replacing them with new frames – to make space for new comb to be drawn for the queen to lay in.

REVERSING AS A MANAGEMENT TOOL

The colony will work starting at the bottom brood box and move upwards to the top one, emptying the bottom brood box. During the spring, if you open up your hive and see that the top brood box is almost full, with an empty lower brood box, you should reverse the position of the two brood boxes so that the hive can expand upwards. If you don't provide more room for this upward growth, the hive could feel constrained and swarm. After reversing, the brood nest will expand steadily into the upper brood box.

Reading a hive entrance

Opening a hive can be disruptive and intrusive for the bees. Simply observing the activity outside the hive can give you clues about what is going on inside. Even better is to have an observation cutout, which will provide you with a window into the bees' world. If you don't have this luxury, hive entrances are the next best thing. Entrances, with their landing boards, provide an easy way for bees to get in and out, and there are many things that the traffic can tell you. Bottom entrances, as in a Langstroth hive, typically take up almost the full width of the hive. You can manipulate the size of this space with entrance reducers if needed. Providing full access to the brood nest, the entrance also provides ventilation. This, when combined with a screened bottom board and upper entrances, keeps the hive from overheating and well ventilated from moisture build-up in the winter.

Top entrances can be provided in the honey supers with a small entrance hole or opening, or by a shim or spacer placed between your honey supers and the queen excluder. These top entrances expedite the bees' movement through the hive, so that bees can easily bypass the brood nest and queen excluder. Offering direct access to the supers, upper entrances provide a direct path for foragers to deposit nectar into the supers. One disadvantage to an upper entrance is that it creates another area for guard bees to defend, using more hive resources. But the big advantage to upper entrances is that there is much better ventilation both in the summer and winter. Furthermore, snow, ice and vegetation are less likely to cover these entrances.

HIVE ENTRANCE OBSERVATIONS: LOOK, LISTEN AND SMELL

On any given day, you can check on your hives by standing in front or to the side and take note of what is happening. Notice the following:

- Observe the level of activity of bees coming and going and whether this is in a steady, purposeful way. Are returning bees laden with pollen on their back legs?
- On the landing board, is there a lot of activity among the guard bees or other bees cleaning, fanning and carrying out hive debris?
- Can you hear a slow, steady hum coming out of the hive – even from 1–1.5 metres (4–5 ft) away? If you knock on the side of the hive, does the sound rise for a few seconds and then subside? That is the sound of a happy, working hive. Or is there a higher-pitched buzzing sound, known as 'piping'? This occurs right before swarming.

Careful observation of the traffic of bees, in and out of the hive, can tell the beekeeper a lot about the health of the colony.

- Is the traffic disorganized and haphazard? This could be a sign of a queen-less hive.
- During a nectar flow there will be clouds of bees flying in and out. You will see this especially well by looking at the hive side-on against the sky.
- What smells are you detecting from the hive? Depending on the nectar source, some flowers such as eucalyptus and buckwheat have a distinct aroma. Lots of brood in the spring will have a unique, pleasant aroma as opposed to an unpleasant aroma from an unhealthy brood. When there is a lot of honey in the supers, you will be able to smell the honey, especially on a hot day.
- Are bees smeared across the entire hive front on a hot day in a weird, beard-like shape? It can look as though every bee is outside, hanging on the hive. This is known as 'bearding', when bees make room inside the hive to improve ventilation on a hot summer's day. Many people mistake this behaviour for swarming. You can even look at your bearding bees through a magnifying glass to check for mites. They will be pretty easy to spot.
- Do you see bees fighting on the landing board and hear an agitated buzzing? This could be a sign of robbing – foreign bees trying to steal some easy honey from the hive.
- Do you see a lot of drones being cast out? This is a yearly ritual of bees expelling their male bees or drones for the season, thereby reducing the population going into winter.
- Do you see bees touching, gently exchanging nectar? Forager bees come in loaded with nectar stored in a honey sac, which is transferred to worker bees – who then suck the nectar from the honey sac through their proboscis.

Pesticides

PESTICIDE USE IN THE SURROUNDING AREA

Pesticides pose a major problem to beekeepers when a nearby pesticide application drifts into an apiary. In addition, bees returning to the hive with contaminated food and water can expose the rest of the hive to pesticides. To prevent this, beekeepers should establish an open dialogue with surrounding farmers and growers about limiting pesticide use and using it carefully around an apiary. Register your hives with the proper authorities, so that applicators can locate you before applying pesticides. In the UK, the National Honey Monitoring Scheme works in partnership with UK beekeepers to monitor long-term changes in the condition and health of the UK countryside, including pesticide use, climate change and loss of habitats. Additionally, contact the Apiary Inspection Programme in the UK or your local bee inspector. Remember that your local bee club or association can advocate for you when dealing with farmers.

It is essential to record any irregularities you may observe in and around the entrance to a hive, such as dead or flightless bees and changes in foraging behaviour.

Signs of pesticide poisoning in a hive are:
- an excessive number of dead bees around the hive;
- lack of foraging bees entering and exiting the hive;
- disorientated bees that are unable to fly.

An example of the use of pesticides in beekeeping: a beekeeper applies oxalic acid in water solution to kill the parasitical *Varroa* mites.

HOW TO AVOID EXPOSURE

- Place hives away from farmed fields, introducing a buffer area between the apiary and the fields.
- Register your apiary with local authorities if applicable (such as the National Bee Unit in the UK).
- Paint your hives in a conspicuous colour, so that they are highly visible.
- Report any pesticide incidents that you suspect have harmed your colonies – for example, dead or dying bees.
- Take photographs, if possible, to back up your claims.
- If you are a commercial beekeeper, post your name and contact information in the apiary, and if bees are placed in a field or orchard for pollination services, remove the hives as soon as possible once pollination is complete. Many pesticides are applied after blooming.

PESTICIDE USE BY BEEKEEPER

Unless you maintain your hives organically, you will be applying pesticides regularly for pests and diseases. Be sure to use only pesticides that are labelled for use in the hive and avoid overusing chemicals, as this can have detrimental effects on a colony's health, function and mortality. Beekeepers are legally responsible for following all regulations according to the pesticide's labelling. Read and follow all labels for applications carefully and take safety precautions – such as wearing eye protection, a mask and rubber gloves – when applying. Regularly replace older frames that might be contaminated with lingering amounts of chemical build-up.

Winter preparation

For colonies to survive the winter, you need healthy winter bees. Winter bees are much longer-lived, surviving for weeks (150–200 days) during the winter months, unlike the early summer bees that live on average for just 15–38 days. Colonies raise their winter bees predominantly in August and September. The average winter season losses for managed North American bees were 37 per cent in 2022–23; in England, the figure was much lower, at 16 per cent. This variance is startling – but consideration must be given to the fact that comparing loss rates among different areas of the world is tricky, because of differences in monitoring programmes, conditions and approaches to local reporting.

Your bees should have been stockpiling enough food to last the winter, but if you have taken honey and harvested it, you should check on their winter stores some time in the autumn. Always wear protective gear even when opening the hive during cold weather, as bees will be alerted when you 'crack' the hardened propolis apart with your hive tool.

To prepare for overwintering your bees, start in late August or September:

The beekeeper needs to undertake meticulous preparation to help bee colonies survive during the long, cold winter.

If there is insufficient honey in store for overwintering, the beekeeper must provide extra food, shown here in the form of sugar fondant.

- **Choose local bees adapted to your area** With local genetics, your honey bees are more likely to adapt to the local conditions.
- **Make sure you have completed chemical applications** Monitor and treat for *Varroa* mites before winter begins. All pesticide treatments should be completed at least a few weeks before winter arrives.
- **Put in place pest prevention** Insert mouse guards to prevent mice looking for a warm corner and entering and tearing apart the hive interior to make a nest.
- **Provide adequate food** Make sure the honey stores are sufficient. Count how many frames of honey the bees have available and check with beekeepers in the area whether that amount is enough for local conditions. It is better to err on the side of too much because, if there isn't enough, the bees could starve. The amount of honey needed varies on location depending on the length and severity of the winter season. Experienced beekeepers can simply 'heft' the hives instead of counting and determining from the weight if there is enough stored food. To be on the safe side, leave extra supplies and periodically check on the bees' stores and supplement if necessary. If there isn't enough food, start a feeding regimen. In addition, check the bees' pollen stores, to make sure they have three to six frames of pollen.
- **Reconfigure your hives** Pull off any empty boxes and queen excluders. You want the smallest space possible for the bees to have to expend energy on heating. Honey bees

This overwintering hive has been wrapped with insulating material and secured with straps and an extra weight on top.

are one of the few insects that survive the winter as a colony, and they succeed in doing this by forming a cluster. When temperatures drop below 10–14 °C (50–57 °F), a winter cluster forms and the bees pack loosely around the queen forming an insulating quilt. Worker bees on the outside vibrate wing muscles to generate heat, with the outside bees circulating to the inside and the inside bees taking their place. As temperatures drop outside, the cluster tightens, and the inside cluster temperature must maintain a steady temperature between 34.5–37 °C (94–98 °F). Make sure your honey stores are on top and to either side of the cluster, so that the cluster can move easily in one direction to find the available honey stored in the combs. Screened bottom boards can be swapped for solid ones in order to provide better insulation.

- **Combine weak colonies** Weak colonies have a better chance to survive together rather than apart.
- **Provide insulation** According to the length and severity of your winter, some insulation may be necessary. Place an insulated shallow box with a screened bottom filled with dry organic material, such as wood chips or sawdust, on top of the brood boxes. This will keep the heat in the hive and draw moisture out, preventing condensation and mould in the hive. Many beekeepers wrap their hives with insulating material, such as roofing paper, and there are commercial wraps that you can buy. However, too much wrapping can

often lead to a build-up of excessive moisture and cause the bees to freeze.

- **Secure the hives** Heavy winds could easily topple over a winter hive that is on the light side. Use ratchet straps or place a heavy block on top to avoid this catastrophe.
- **Provide a windbreak** A wind buffer is especially important in the winter, and you can easily provide this by stacking hay bales, creating a wall of evergreen boughs or even by providing a piece of plywood around the windiest side. A favourite method is to place an old Christmas tree against the hive sides.
- **Clear hive entrances** During the winter dead bees can clutter up the entrance, preventing the bees inside from taking their 'cleansing flights' when the weather permits. Check periodically on the hive entrances. The bees will also be taking 'cleansing flights' on warmer winter days (see below).
- **Consider grouping your hives** Some beekeepers like to group their hives back-to-back and wrap the colonies together with insulating material. Be sure to allow bees to enter and exit freely if you do this.
- **Tilt the hives** Make sure the hives are tilted forwards slightly, using a 25–50-millimetre (1–2-in) brick or board underneath the bottom board, so that snow and ice can't collect on the bottom board.
- **Turn over the inner cover** Turn the inner cover over with the notch facing down to provide an upper entrance and ventilation. This will also prevent bees from propolizing the outer cover. The outer cover should be pushed forwards so there's a gap at the front of the outer cover. If your inner cover doesn't have a notch, turn the inner cover over and place a shim, a wedge or a pencil between the inner cover and the top of the super to provide an air space that will allow warm air to escape and avoid a moisture build-up.

CLEANSING FLIGHTS

During winter there are often warmer days (with temperatures above 10 °C / 50 °F) when the bees will emerge from the hive to take 'cleansing flights'. You may notice that there are many dead bees and droppings in front of the hive, often visible against the snow. Bees are performing housekeeping, bringing debris outside the hive and preventing a build-up of unwanted material. Help the bees out by clearing away this debris.

Feeding honey bees

Honey bee nutrition

Many new beekeepers are mystified when they learn that they have to 'feed' their colonies, believing that bees are self-sufficient and make their own food – honey. However, bees, like any other animal, require essential ingredients for their survival. Proper nutrition is essential for a good defense against disease and pests. During a beekeeping year, however, there are inevitably shortages of nectar (the sugar-rich fluid secreted by plants) and pollen grains (the fine, powdery substance produced by most types of flowers) for the foraging bees to collect. This results in the need to 'feed your bees'. Typically, feeding is necessary in the bees' most vulnerable period, in late winter/early spring, to supplement their dwindling resources in the hive, and in the late autumn to boost the bees' stores going into winter.

NECTAR

Nectar is essential to support the energy needs of the colony, such as forager flights and the thermoregulation of the hive. Bees normally convert nectar into honey to be stored in their hive, and if the hive runs out of honey, they will starve.

To produce energy, a healthy bee requires carbohydrates, which are converted to glucose or fructose utilizing enzymes in the bee's stomachs. Nectar is the main source of carbohydrates for honey bees, and the amount that the colony requires depends on how concentrated the sugars are in the nectar, which in turn depends on the floral source and time of year. Bees also require clean water and protein (from pollen). Their floral sources for both pollen and nectar should be diverse so as to provide all essential nutrients. Just as with a human, the more varied the diet, the healthier the honey bee.

Beekeepers must do more to supplement the nutrition in their hives, especially if their apiary is surrounded by fields that are typically farmed monoculturally (that is, with just one crop). The loss of bee forage and habitat – with, for example, the extensive sweetcorn and soybean fields of the United States and Canada having replaced the wild plants that used to provide forage for honey bees – has made it imperative for beekeepers to provide supplemental feeding.

Other floral sources are available to bees, from which they can obtain carbohydrates. Extrafloral nectaries (nectar-secreting plant glands), which are on the outside of the flower, instead of

A bee feeds on honeydew on a fir tree. Aphids secrete honeydew as they feed on plant sap. Honey bees process it into a dark and strong 'forest honey'.

inside where pollen and nectar are usually found, are used by bees frequently. Examples of this are spotted lanternflies (*Lycorma delicatula*), an invasive species in the mid-Atlantic region of the United States, which feeds on sugary plant sap and excretes honeydew, a sugary water that makes leaves look shiny. The fermenting honeydew combined with tree sap creates a substance that bees are attracted to and bring back to the hive. Also, rotting orchard fruit or discarded sugary fluids can be picked up by foragers and taken back to the hive.

POLLEN

In their regular visits to flowers, worker bees come into contact with pollen, collecting grains in their hair. The bees will clean these off and pack them into the pollen baskets on their back legs to carry back to the hive. Pollen gets transferred in this fashion as a bee travels from flower to flower and pollination occurs. Pollen is used to feed larvae, so it is especially important early in the season while the colony is building up its population. Pollen grains are amazing packages of ten essential amino acids, lipids, vitamins, minerals and sterols, as well as the bees' main source of protein.

Once you see visible pollen grains carried into the hives on the legs of bees, you can relax and know that they are bringing in and storing pollen. Pollen is deposited near the brood nest in multi-coloured hues, from yellowish orange to dark brown or even black, according to the type of flower, and the bees pack the pollen in the cells with their heads where it undergoes fermentation in the process of becoming bee bread. A covering of honey and wax protects the bee bread for winter storge. Regarded by some as a superfood because of its many nutrients, bee bread can be harvested from the hive.

As discussed earlier in this chapter, hives going into winter should have at least three to five frames of various pollen sources stored as bee bread. Bee bread is the main source of protein and an essential food source for bees. If pollen isn't available, you should feed your bees pollen substitutes. Many beekeepers give their bees a pollen substitute, 'pollen patties', to supplement their stores at this time of year. Feeding bees with sugar is important when there is a nectar dearth, so it makes sense to feed them pollen patties when pollen is scarce, primarily in late winter when it is still too cold for bees to fly. The need for supplements varies according to location, the season and the colony itself. Observe your bees and then make your decision accordingly.

When visiting flowers to sip nectar, bees also collect pollen in their hair. This shot of bee at a honeysuckle flower shows the cloud of pollen grains thrown up as the bee lands.

Early-spring feeding

Feeding is an ongoing task: by inspecting your hives regularly, you will know when and what to feed your colonies; each colony will be different in strength and feeding needs. However, the most crucial time of year for feeding is early spring, usually March, before floral sources become available and it is still too cold for the bees to fly. Starvation is the most common cause of bee death with over-wintering colonies and also in early spring.

March is well known in the beekeeping world as the 'month of starvation', because bees that clustered during the winter consuming their stored honey have usually depleted their stores and it is too cold (less than 10 °C or 50 °F) for bees to fly to gather new food from the scant flowers available. Bees group together in the hive during winter, with a hive cluster temperature of 35 °C (95 °F), near the bottom of the stored honey reserves. Working their way upwards as a unit, the bees slowly consume their honey stores, eating throughout the winter. When the cluster reaches the top of the hive, food reserves can be depleted – and during cold weather the bees won't move any further upwards, downwards or sideways towards the food reserves, even though these may be present. Since food reserves are depleted, emergency feeding may be necessary. Feeding depends on the weather, as the bees won't take sugar syrup if the outside temperature is too cold (below 10 °C or 50 °F). You will often open up a hive in the spring to find a dead cluster very close to food reserves because it was too cold for the cluster to move.

For emergency feeding, you can add frames of saved honey (having been frozen for later use) or sugar blocks/fondant, placed directly on the cluster with a small spacer. This supplemental feed should continue until natural supplies of nectar become available; otherwise, the bees could starve. For a simpler method, you can sprinkle granulated sugar on top of a piece of newspaper laid on top of the frames, under the top cover of the hive, which the bees can take back to the hive cluster. Bees need water to liquefy the sugar crystals and will use the condensation from inside the hive to accomplish that. Any of these approaches could stave off starvation until the weather turns warmer.

Here, inverted sugar syrup is being readied to ensure the food stores of these European honey bees (*Apis mellifera*) are well supplemented for the winter.

Recommended foods for honey bees

Feeding your bees can be accomplished in various ways according to the time of year, but honey and pollen you have removed from your own disease-free hives are always the best nutrition for honey bees. Feeding bees from another source, such as your neighbours' hives or the supermarket, could introduce disease into your hives.

HONEY FRAMES

Honey and pollen from your hives are always the best nutrition for honey bees – so, if possible, save and freeze frames of honey from your hives to pull out when you need it. Scrape the cappings from the honey first to encourage the bees to use it. Be careful when you do this as the scent of the honey can attract other bees and provoke a robbing frenzy.

SUGAR SYRUP

The food supplement used most frequently by beekeepers is sugar syrup. You should mix sugar syrup at a ratio of 1:1 (equal parts sugar and water, by weight) or 2:1 depending on the time of year. The thinner, 1:1 ratio is used in the spring during population build-up to feed colonies low on reserves and to stimulate brood production. The thicker, 2:1 sugar syrup is used during the population contraction phase in the autumn to ensure colonies have enough stores for the winter. Sugar syrup can turn mouldy after a few days, especially in warm weather, and develop an unpleasant smell. If you wouldn't drink it, don't give it to your bees either. Make up a fresh batch.

Each colony should be fed 18 litres (4 gal) of the thicker sugar syrup in the autumn, starting as soon as the supers are removed, and stopping when it is too cold for the colony to take sugar syrup (below 10 °C or 50 °F). Bees will usually stop taking sugar syrup during a nectar flow, as they prefer to deposit nectar in their hives instead of sugar syrup. Thus, it is important to stop feeding before the start of a nectar flow, as you don't want the sugar water to contaminate the honey crop.

To make larger batches of sugar syrup for multiple hives, you can measure out your ratios and mix in a bucket. The sugar syrup can be stored in the refrigerator, then you can use it as needed. The ratios are approximate only, and measuring sugar and water doesn't have to be precise. You could indicate on the outside of the bucket (using a marker pen) where the approximate mixing levels are for sugar and water.

FONDANT

Fondant is recommended during winter feeding, when the bees are in a cluster, as it is a solid type of sugar. Fondant is made from cooking a mixture of sugar and water. Make this ahead of time and freeze it, so you can pull it out of the freezer when the bees really need it. An easy way to add it to the hive is to place a queen excluder on top of the frames, add a shallow eke (spacer rim), and place the fondant on top of the queen excluder for the bees to access. If the bees need it, they will eat it. Available commercially, it is known as 'baker's fondant'. If you own a lot of hives, buying blocks of this makes good sense.

A beekeeper provides a hive with sugar fondant in spring to stimulate the bees to produce honey earlier in the year.

HOW TO MAKE FONDANT

Fondant should be soft and pliable like dough.

Ingredients and equipment

4.5 kilograms (10 lbs) white granulated sugar
1 litre (2 pts) water
1 tbsp vinegar or lemon juice
Essential oil – lemongrass is the preferred choice (optional)
Large pot
Sugar thermometer
Stand mixer or immersion blender
Moulds (e.g. disposable pie tins, aluminium pans, paper plates, cookie sheets)

Method

1. Have moulds ready, such as disposable pie tins or aluminium pans.
2. Measure the water and vinegar into a large pot and bring to a slow simmer.
3. Pour the sugar in, stirring until completely dissolved.
4. Once dissolved, turn up the heat to medium high and stop stirring and insert your sugar thermometer.
5. Boil until the mixture reaches 113 °C (235 °F). The syrup will foam quite a bit, so keep an eye on it and turn the heat down if the mixture starts to boil over. Remove the pot from the heat and set aside to cool to about 88–93 °C (190–200 °F). Add a few drops of your essential oil at this point, if using.
6. Pour the cooled mixture into a stand mixer bowl with a paddle attachment and beat until the mixture turns white and smooth. Alternatively, you can use an immersion blender and mix the sugar syrup in the pot.
7. Divide the mixture among your moulds and allow it to cool completely.
8. Once cool, break the fondant into pieces and wrap the fondant up in cling film or greaseproof paper and store in the freezer.

POLLEN SUBSTITUTES

Colonies that run out of pollen will slow or cease brood production, which means that the hive's population will decline slowly. Pollen substitutes are used to beef up brood production in the early spring, when the bees would benefit from it most. You can buy commercially available pollen substitutes – based on soy flour, baker's yeasts and natural pollen – in premade slabs, covered in perforated greaseproof paper. Add it to the top bars of the hive when it's needed. Timing is very important, and a rule of thumb is to add pollen patties six weeks before the major honey flow. Avoid adding pollen substitutes in late autumn, when you want brood production to fall.

WINTER PATTIES

Winter patties have a low protein level that will not stimulate brood rearing but provide carbohydrates to keep a colony from starving. It is recommended to place 1–2 patties on top of the bee winter cluster, directly onto the frame tops, early in the winter. Leave the paper covering on, as the bees will nibble through it. They should be stored in the freezer until ready to use.

WATER

Providing a clean source of water is important throughout the year, even in winter – when a heated bird bath is useful.

Bees feeding at a drinking bowl with sweet water in an apiary.

Two methods for
delivering sugar,
using (top) a Mason
jar gravity feeder
and (bottom) a
food storage bag.

Feeding methods

There is a plethora of feeding delivery systems, with beekeepers
recommending different methods according to the region they
are located in:

1. **Entrance feeders** These are advantageous only in warmer
   weather as bees in a cluster won't take the sugar syrup.
   These do not hold much syrup.
2. **Hive-top feeders** Holding large amounts of sugar syrup
   (up to 18 litres / 4 gal), these commercially available feeders
   are placed on top of the hive and bees don't have to leave the
   hive to access them. With large volumes of sugar syrup, you
   have to be careful of mould build-up and drowning bees.
3. **Inverted containers** Perforated Mason jars and baggies
   will hold just under 1 litre (2 pts) of sugar syrup, but you
   can add several of these on top of a hive (see below).
4. **Division board feeders** These hang inside the hive like
   a frame. Bees can use these even in cold weather, but they
   hold less sugar syrup than hive-top feeders.

USING A GLASS JAR GRAVITY FEEDER

1. Fill up a glass jar (such as a Mason jar), with the correct
   quantity of sugar. The jar should be two-thirds full for
   the thicker syrup and one-third full for the thinner.
2. Top up the jar with hot water. Stir to mix and seal with
   the lid.
3. Shake the jar until the sugar dissolves. Leave to settle
   and then shake again if needed to ensure the sugar has
   fully dissolved.
4. Replace the lid with a feeder lid that has six to eight
   punctures – approximately 1–2 millimetres ($\frac{1}{16}$ in) in
   diameter – spread over the lid.
5. Turn the jar over to test the seal and see how fast the
   syrup drips out. After a vacuum forms, the dripping
   should slow, allowing the bees to collect the sugar syrup
   without drowning as it gradually empties into the hive.
6. Set the jar inside the hive on top of the frames, placing
   an empty super around the jar.
7. Replace the inner cover and top cover, covering the notch
   in the inner cover so that robbing bees cannot enter.

You can add more than one glass jar feeder at a time, and it is
helpful to set them up on wooden shims to keep them steady.

USING A FOOD STORAGE BAG FEEDER

This may be a very low-tech feeding method but it is
an effective one.

1. Add enough premixed sugar syrup to fill a 4 litre (1 gal)
   freezer-weight food storage bag about three-quarters full.
2. Squeeze out any air and seal carefully, checking for any
   leaks. If the zip top leaks, add some gaffer tape to
   reinforce it.
3. Instal a wooden shim or strip on top of the frames
   to hold the bag(s) and very carefully place them flat
   side down.
4. Use a sharp knife or razor and make a 7.5–10-cm
   (3–4-in) slit in the top centre of the bag – with smaller,
   parallel ones next to the main slit – so that the bees
   can access the syrup.
5. Place an eke (spacer rim) or a shallow super to make
   space for the bag and replace the inner and outer covers.
6. To refill the bag, use your hive tool to lift up the slit
   openings and carefully add more sugar syrup.
7. Once finished with the feeding, pull out the bags and
   recycle them.

Note: you can add more than one feeding bag (a ten-frame
Langstroth hive, for example, can accommodate two bags).

Harvesting products from the hive

Honey is the obvious product that people think of when keeping bees, but there are several other by-products of the hive that can be gathered and be useful in various ways, including bee pollen, propolis, bee bread, royal jelly and beeswax. Excellent sources of macro and micronutrients that exhibit antimicrobial, antioxidant, and anti-inflammatory effects, these bee products have also attracted the interest of scientists. Numerous studies have found beneficial effects from many of these products.

Some, like beeswax and bee pollen, are bee products of the simplest kind. Many other hive products are mixtures of bee and plant secretions, such as bee bread, which is obtained from the fermentation of bee pollen mixed with bee saliva and flower nectar. Even a honey bee secretion, royal jelly, can be collected by beekeepers with a small syringe – after the removal of the queen larvae – and strained to remove impurities. In this section, we will also touch on harvesting pollen and propolis, the two most commonly harvested products other than honey and beeswax.

Hive products including honey, honeycomb, beeswax, and pollen.

Honey: extraction, bottling and selling

For many people who keep bees, the idea of harvesting honey from your own beehives is the primary reason for becoming a beekeeper. All that hard work of tending your hives, feeding your bees, and worrying over their health and well-being all comes to fruition and you have some excess honey to harvest. And there is nothing better than enjoying a delicious jar of fresh honey from your own beehive. Not every hive will produce harvestable honey every year, so if your main reason for keeping bees is a honey harvest, you should consider having more than one hive. But how do you know when your honey is ready for harvesting?

PACKAGES VERSUS NUCS

If you start beekeeping with a package of bees in the spring (see page 100), you might get a late-summer honey harvest the same season if all conditions are favourable. Usually, a spring-started package colony will produce enough honey to survive one winter only, and you'll need to leave any excess in the hive for the bees' survival. If you decide to remove their stored food, it is likely that your hive will starve in the coming winter. However, once your colony survives the winter, the hive should build up quickly the following spring – and start producing enough excess honey that you can begin to harvest in midsummer.

You are more likely to have a same season honey harvest if you have purchased and installed a nucleus hive, also referred to as a 'nuc' (see page 104), rather than a package. Nucs are a jump start on the beekeeping year, producing quicker population growth, and can result in excess honey stores that you can harvest the same season. Though nucs are generally more expensive than a package, a nuc is a colony in miniature, already doing everything that a larger, full-production colony is doing. The bees have already deposited honey and pollen, the queen is laying eggs, and baby bees are present in various stages of development.

HONEY HARVESTING PREPARATION

The trick to honey harvesting is to remove the bees from the honey as gently and non-invasively as possible. However, before you pull that first capped frame from your hive, there are a number of considerations that you need to take care of first. Remember that honey harvesting can be hot and heavy work, so preparation is key to making the process go more smoothly.

Piled-up supers on hives provide storage space for excess honey, but must be added judiciously.

Adding supers and a queen excluder

Check colonies frequently during a major honey flow to see that you have provided sufficient storage for excess honey. Adding honey supers on top of your brood boxes will ease crowding and allow additional space for the bees to store excess honey. This will also decrease the chances of your colony swarming, as it will prevent the bees from becoming crowded and unhappy.

Adding supers increases the space for bees to allocate additional resources to the new area and makes it more difficult for the honey bees to maintain the hive's humidity and temperature, so beekeepers need to time supering carefully. Before adding honey supers, beekeepers use a rule of thumb known as the $7/10$ rule, meaning the bees should have already drawn comb and deposited nectar in seven out of the ten frames in their current box.

Before adding any supers, consider adding a queen excluder. Adding an excluder under the supers eliminates any chances of the queen travelling up into the supers and laying eggs. You can then pull off your supers to harvest, knowing that there will be no brood present. If you decide to use a queen excluder, it is helpful to add an upper entrance to your super boxes – to allow the bees direct access, instead of their having to squeeze through an excluder in order to get there.

BEEKEEPING TASKS AND EQUIPMENT

147

TIPS FOR SUPERING YOUR HIVES
- Only add one super at a time.
- Add a super that already has drawn comb, if possible, from last year's frames.
- It is better to add supers too early rather than too late.
- The $7/10$ rule applies to adding additional supers.
- Assess the hive's growth pace at least every fortnight during a major honey flow; checking every week is even better as a strong colony can fill a shallow super in seven to fourteen days.
- Your choice of the size of the added super – ten-frame shallow, ten-frame medium, or ten-frame deep – will determine how heavy your hive boxes are when full of bees and honey, so consider this carefully. There are also eight-frame supers that weigh less, thus reducing the risk of injury, and can fit into a smaller parcel of property as the hives take up a smaller footprint.
- If, on inspection, your colony is making queen cells (indicating that the hive is getting ready to swarm), it's probably too late to add supers. If you can remove all the queen cells, it may be possible to curtail, or at least delay, swarming so you can harvest honey.
- Have several supers with frames on hand to add them quickly during a honey flow.

Assessing whether the honey is cured

During the summer build-up, you should be checking periodically on your hives' stored honey, including observing whether your colonies are free of disease. When pulling frames from your supers for inspection, check whether the bees are capping the nectar cells with a thin covering of wax (commonly referred to as 'capped honey' or simply 'cappings'). Ideally, you should only harvest honey that has a wax covering, as this shows that the bees have converted the raw nectar and reduced the water content, producing a thicker, ripe honey that has less than 18 per cent water content (you can check this using a refractometer). A good rule of thumb is that, when the frame contains at least 80 per cent of sealed and capped honey, you can harvest.

Cells that have no wax covering could still contain ripe honey and can be extracted by first checking to see whether the honey is cured. To determine this, flip your frame upside down and give it a shake. If liquid drips out, your nectar isn't yet cured and shouldn't be extracted. The bees will continue to cap honey throughout the summer months.

WARNING:
Using drugs to combat disease during the honey flow can make your honey unsafe for consumption.

How much honey should be removed?
You can expect to pull anywhere from roughly 11 to 45 kilograms (25–100 lbs) of honey from an established hive, with an average of 27 kilograms (60 lbs) per hive. However, you should always leave enough stores for the bees to survive the winter, so you will need to inspect your hives to make sure each has enough. To estimate the weight of a colony's stored honey, a deep frame with fully capped honey contains 2¼–3½ kilograms (5–8 lbs) of honey, while a medium frame has around 1½–2¼ kilograms (3–5 lbs).

The amount of stored food needed by the colony for winter survival varies greatly from one region to another, as well as on other variables – notably the breed, hive health and local climate. In colder regions, colonies need more stored honey than in warmer regions. Ask your neighbouring beekeepers for their experiences in your particular area. Supplemental feeding is possible, but this should be your last resort.

A frame of capped nectar cells: this honey is good and ready to harvest.

The following is the average of ripe sealed stores that each hive
will require to survive winter:

- Southern US and UK – 18 kilograms (40 lbs);
- Central USA – 27 kilograms (60 lbs);
- Northern USA – 36–41 kilograms (80–90 lbs).

If you have a hive with too much honey, and don't harvest it,
a hive can become 'honey bound' or 'hive-bound'. In other words,
the brood nest becomes filled with honey and there is no room
available for the queen to lay eggs. This kind of situation will
almost certainly result in a swarm, so be sure to harvest the
honey when this happens.

Harvesting window
'Harvesting' refers to the selection and collection of the frames
from which you will extract your honey. Understanding your local
conditions will dictate the timing of your honey flows or nectar
flows. When an abundance of nectar-producing plants is in bloom,
it is best to harvest your honey at the conclusion of the final major
honey flow. To maximize your harvest, take the honey later in the
season since a later honey flow also typically occurs in September.
Weather conditions – in particular, the temperature – will dictate
the best time to harvest honey. July to mid-September is the
optimal time for most of the United States and the United
Kingdom. Colder temperatures will prevent you from being able
to harvest as the honey won't flow as easily, making it harder
to extract. The ideal temperature is in the range of 24–27 °C
(75–80 °F). Occasionally, high honey production, which can
occur in warmer climates, allows for an early honey harvest
in addition to a late-season harvest.

Pick a windless sunny day, as the greater population of
worker bees will be out foraging. The smaller the population,
the easier it is to remove bees from the honey.

Have your harvesting equipment ready
Make sure all your equipment is clean and ready to go. Thoroughly
clean the following:

- Protective bee suit and veil, smoker, hive tool, bee brush,
  frame puller;
- Fume board and repellent, or bee escape;
- Extra frames and supers with a bottom lid and cover to
  make it bee-tight, so flying bees cannot get into the honey
  (two covers will work), and some kind of wheeled transport.

The decision when to harvest honey becomes easier with experience.

Where to extract your honey

After removing your honey supers, it is best to leave the apiary and harvest your honey in an enclosed area that is bee-tight, well ventilated and hygienic. Once you start to process your honey, bees will come flocking to your location and can become a nuisance and safety hazard. An enclosed garage or shed with clean, food-safe surfaces, and electrical sockets is ideal. A home kitchen is not recommended unless you cover and protect all your exposed surfaces, as these will quickly become covered in a sticky mess. In any case, there are always straggler bees that come in with the combs taken directly from the hive – and you don't want them in your house.

WARNING:
Never extract honey in an unprotected area outdoors! This risks provoking a robbing frenzy of bees, which can be dangerous.

If you decide to set up a 'honey house' – a small building or room dedicated to the processing of honey – check your national and local government regulations. Your local apiarist (if you have one) may be able to guide you through the relevant regulations.

Three methods for removing honey frames

Before you harvest, maybe the day before, it is very helpful to pop off the cover and examine your frames. You should quickly loosen every frame that you will be removing, breaking up the loose comb, and also loosen the supers with your hive tool, which will make it easier to remove them the following day.

On the day of harvest, check the weather again, consult any neighbours who might be outside, and transport the equipment that you need to the hive location (see previous page). It is handy to take an extra hive tool along, as they are easy to misplace.

There are three main methods for separating bees from honey frames, ready for extraction – either physical or chemical. Note that using bee blowers is not recommended, as it is too stressful for the bees.

1 Shaking method:

The simplest, lowest-tech method is the shaking method. You only need a smoker, bee brush, hive tool and an empty super with a cover and a galvanized tray (or extra cover) to lay underneath the super for catching any honey drips. You want to save every last bit of honey from your bees.

- Smoke the hive entrance and lift off the top cover and vent smoke into the hole of the inner cover. This alert forces the bees further down into the hive.
- Pry up both the inner and outer covers and puff more smoke into the hive.
- Using a hive tool, pry the top frames loose in the super.
- Using either a frame puller or your gloved hands, remove frames of capped honey, one at a time, out of the super and forcefully shake the frame at the front of the hive. Most of the bees will fall off. Remove the rest by brushing them off with the bee brush.
- Put the now bee-free frame into an empty super and cover it over with a piece of plywood (or extra cover) to prevent robbing. Continue (as above) with the rest of the frames.
- Once you have removed all the frames for harvest, leaving any unripe honey, close up the hive, replacing any missing frames with new ones. If you don't replace them, the bees will produce 'burr comb', wax sheets or extra bits of honeycomb that run in different directions in undesirable places. Burr comb is normal on top of frames, but anything extra can make it difficult for the beekeeper to maintain order in the hive.

- Make sure you place the covered super in some kind of wheeled transport, or else you will need to carry it to your honey harvesting station by hand.
- Once in the honey extraction area, remove the cover and brush off any remaining bees with a bee brush. Your frames are now ready for uncapping.

As noted before, full honey supers can be very heavy and hard to handle. The shaking method can be slow and laborious, but it is very effective. Moreover, it employs no chemicals and eliminates a lot of heavy lifting. You will need to wear your bee suit throughout the entire process.

2 Fume board method:

A fume board is a good option if you need to remove your honey cheaply, quickly and efficiently. For these reasons, it is used by many commercial beekeepers, who remove bees by spraying a chemical repellent (usually butyric propionic anhydride or benzaldehyde) onto absorbent fabric fixed to a board, which, attached to the top of the hive, forces the bees to move away from the smell, downwards into the hive. The commercial chemicals used are toxic, flammable and foul-smelling. The hobbyist beekeeper, however, can use natural, essential oil-based products, whose smell – while pleasant to us – can be repellent to bees. These chemicals (available under several brand names) are natural, easy to use and won't taint the wax or the honey.

A commercial beekeeper attaches a fume board to the top of a hive prior to extracting honey.

- Using a repellent chemical or bee-avoidant product, spray the chemical – in the shape of an 'X' or 'S' – onto the felt underside of a fume board. Err on the side of using too little rather than too much. You can always apply more later.
- Remove the top cover and waft some smoke into the inner cover hole. Wait a few seconds, and then remove the inner cover and waft some more smoke across the frame tops.
- Place the soaked fume board on top of your hive, on the upper super, to force the bees out and down into the hive. The chemical products work best in hot, sunny weather (27 °C / 80 °F or higher) and high humidity, as it will vaporize and penetrate the hive more efficiently. Some fume boards have black corrugated tops that work on raising the temperature inside the hive by 5.5–8 °C (10–15 °F), which further accelerates the vaporization.
- Wait at least five minutes for the chemical to work.
- Peek under the fume board to see whether bees are still clinging to the frames. The presence of a few bees is acceptable, but if there are more, apply some additional repellent and wait for another five to ten minutes. Keep doing this until most of the bees have left the supers for the lower part of the hive.
- A few bees will still be clinging to the frames: brush these off with a bee brush as you pull out the frames individually, or in the honey extraction area if you take off the entire super at once. Leave any unripe honey behind.
- Close up the colony.

The disadvantages of this method are: firstly, it is temperature dependent; secondly, the chemicals, if left on for longer than 20 minutes, can impart off-flavours to the wax cappings and/or honey.

.3 Bee escapes:
A bee escape, or escape board, is another physical method of separating bees from honey supers. Bee escapes provide one-way passages so that, once a bee goes through the escape (a board with a triangle-shaped device) and descend into the lower hive at night and in the morning, they are unable to find their way back into the super.
- Start the process 24–48 hours before you plan to harvest any honey.
- Place the bee escape between the upper honey supers and the lower brood boxes, in place of a queen excluder, if you are using one.

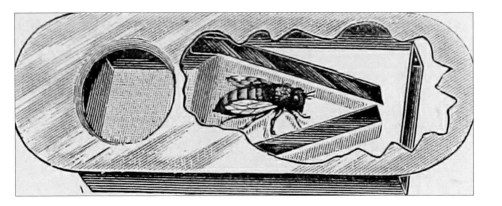

Illustration of a Porter bee escape, with the interior exposed to view. The escape acts as a one-way door that allows bees to leave through the bottom – without letting them back in again.

- Wait for at least 24 hours and check under the covers to see how many bees are present. If more than a few are present, wait a little longer.
- If there is any brood in the supers, the bees will stay with the brood, and you will have to remove the brood with a knife.
- Once most of the bees have exited the supers, you can remove all of the supers at once and take them back to your honey extraction area.

The disadvantage of this method is that, if the escape is left on the hive for more than 48 hours, the bees will eventually find their way back into the supers and start building bridge comb around the board. Moreover, this method is slow and requires more than one visit to the apiary.

EXTRACTION AND PROCESSING
After the hard work of harvesting comes extraction. Although you can remove ripe honey from the hive at any point in the season and go through the extraction process, because this usually involves smaller amounts, most beekeepers like to do their extracting all at once – due to the preparation, work and clean-up involved. Timing the extraction, so that you have as many frames ready as possible, is key to efficiently removing and extracting at one time.

Usually, the best means of doing so is to use an extractor, either manual or motorized: the centrifugal spinning of the frames forces the honey to flow smoothly from the comb, allowing you to collect the honey without damaging the delicate beeswax, which you can reuse for future bee colonies. On page 160, we also describe the purely manual means of extraction – known as the 'crush and strain' method.

The two basic designs
for a honey extractor:
tangential (top) and
radial (bottom). Each
has its advantages
and disadvantages.

Extractor – tangential versus radial

There are two basic designs of extractors – tangential and radial.
A tangential extractor spins the frames horizontally, in a drum-like
metal container, one side of the frames at a time. Then you stop the
extractor and flip the frames over to spin again. A radial extractor
rotates the frames in a circular reel, like the spokes of a wheel,
with the frame's top bars towards the outside of the reel. Honey
is thrown from both sides of the frame at once – with no flipping
necessary. Radial extraction is more efficient because you will
extract more honey more quickly, and it leaves less wax behind in
the honey, which leads to a higher quality of honey. However, radial
extractors tend to cost more – so, if you have a small number of
hives, the tangential extractor might be a better choice.

You can buy either type as a hand crank or motorized version in
different sizes and styles that accommodate varying numbers of
frames. With minimal effort, the motorized extractor does all the
work for you and, while the extractor is spinning, you can focus on
uncapping the next set of frames, thus saving time.

Other equipment you will need to have ready and cleaned:
- Uncapping knife or electric uncapping plane or a sharp
  kitchen knife;
- Uncapping scratcher (to get into tight corners);
- Uncapping tank or bucket with wooden rest to support
  the frames;
- 23 litres (approximately 5 gal) food-grade bucket with
  a honey gate;
- Strainer or sieve that will fit over your bucket;
- Disposable tarpaulin or plastic to cover the honey
  extracting area;
- Clean honey bottles with lids and labels;
- Large bowl of soapy water with a sponge for clean-up
  during and after extraction.

Regardless of your extraction method, all your equipment
should be made out of food-grade stainless-steel, plastic and glass,
and thoroughly cleaned before and after the extraction process.
Arrange all your equipment so that you can move from one task
to another without tripping over leads or bumping into obstacles.
During extraction your hands will be full of dripping honey, so it
is important to streamline your path from one area to another.

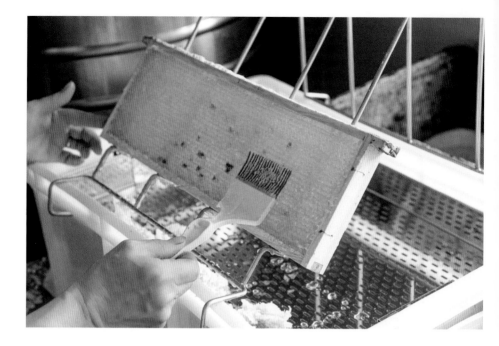

Step-by-step method for extraction

Here we describe the method for extraction when using a tangential extractor. Radial extraction is similar, except you don't have to flip the frames.

- After thoroughly cleaning the area and covering surfaces with tarps or plastic, have all your supers with capped frames ready to hand.
- Select and place your frame sitting vertically across the wooden bar running across your uncapping tank, and tilt the frame over the tank so that your cappings will fall away into the tank.
- Using an uncapping knife (heated or unheated), slice carefully through the wax cappings covering the honey on either side of the frame, flipping after one side is completed. Be sure that the heat setting on the knife isn't set too high or you could scorch your honey and give it an off taste.
- If some of the honey isn't capped, but cured, use an uncapping scratcher or uncapping fork's tines to access odd-shaped areas and corners that can't be reached with a knife, and use it to scratch the cells.
- If you happen to come across any brood on the frame, cut the cells out with a knife.

A beekeeper uses an uncapping scratcher, held above an uncapping tank. Such scratchers are also useful for reaching into awkward corners.

- When finished uncapping both sides of the frame, set the frame across the top of the tank behind the rest bar. Hook the frame's tabs across the tank, so that honey drips into it, then move onto uncapping your next frame.
- Depending on the size of your extractor, uncap the correct amount to load your extractor equally on all sides. For example, if you have a four-rack extractor, which is very common, uncap four frames and load up your extractor with one frame for each basket, so it is balanced. If you have an empty basket, your spinning extractor will be out of balance and won't spin properly. If you end up with an odd number of frames to spin, place an already spun frame into the empty slot to balance it.
- Start spinning your frames slowly for five to ten minutes in one direction, then flip the frames and reverse spin in the other direction for the same amount of time. The warmer the temperature inside your honey extraction area, the quicker the honey will flow from the frames. It is important to start slowly and increase speed as the honey is extracted, as your combs can become damaged. Through the clear lid common on most extractors, you can see the thrown honey from the frames sliding down to the bottom reservoir.
- Some people flip the frames one more time and spin that side again to make sure every last drop of honey is extracted.
- Make sure the extractor is at a full stop before removing the extracted frames. Remove the frames and slot them into a nearby, empty super.

Useful extraction tools include an uncapping knife and scratcher.

Extracting without an extractor – the crush and strain method
As an alternative to mechanical or motorized extraction, honey
can be cut straight from the comb and crushed and then strained.
This is the most straightforward method of extracting: you cut
the entire comb out of the frame, crush it in a bucket, and then
press the crushed comb through a strainer, removing the wax and
other impurities. The resulting extracted honey passes through
the strainer and into a bucket below.

This is a method that works for beekeepers who manage their
bees using wax foundation or foundation-less guide frames,
where the bees build the entire comb without a provided plastic
foundation. Top-bar hive beekeepers also use this type of
extraction as the hanging combs likewise have no foundation.

If you have 'comb' honey – honeycomb that's cut into chunks
and still holds the honey in the wax comb – you don't require
an extractor either. We will discuss the different processes for
harvesting comb honey later in the chapter. Even if you are using
an extractor, there is no greater pleasure than cutting a wax chunk
off of a frame and chewing it to extract every last bit of honey.

TIPS FOR EASIER EXTRACTION
1. Allow plenty of time – extracting honey is an all-day
   affair with prep before and clean-up afterwards.
2. Avoid extraction in your home kitchen – the process
   is very messy and will bring bees into the house!
3. Extract in large batches so you aren't setting up your
   equipment multiple times.
4. If the weather is too cool for extraction, try placing a
   lamp underneath your extractor to warm the honey.
5. Keep a large bowl of soapy water and a towel handy
   so that you can periodically clean up.
6. Recruit help. People are always extremely interested
   in harvesting honey. Take advantage of that interest.
7. If you are a new beekeeper and don't own an extractor,
   your local beekeeping club or association may be able
   to lend you one for a small fee.

COLLECTING AND BOTTLING

Once you have extracted a few frames, the honey will hit the bottom of the extractor basket, filling it up and making it difficult for the extractor to spin. At this point, you need to open the gate on the extractor and drain the honey into a storage bucket.

Have your food-grade storage bucket placed under the gate opening, with a strainer slotted inside the top opening to strain the honey for bee parts, wax, insects and other debris. Use a double-layered metal strainer or, alternatively, a clean 23-litre (5-gal) cloth paint strainer. Strainers can become blocked with debris during extraction, so periodically you need to clean off any debris by scraping and rinsing them off with hot water. The recommended mesh size for strainers is 400 microns, which will filter out debris – but will also ensure that some pollen remains in the honey.

Once your bucket is full, or you have finished extracting, cover the bucket with a lid and leave it for about three days until all the air bubbles and small dirt particles have risen to the surface. Extraction adds a lot of air to the honey.

Run some honey out from the bottom through the gate valve, prior to bottling, to see whether any air bubbles are still in the honey. Use this honey for your own consumption. When you have clear, bubble-free honey coming out, the honey can be bottled, or you can wait until all the honey is extracted and strained in the bucket. When all the honey is extracted, foam will settle on the top and can be skimmed off before bottling.

If you aren't ready for bottling, you can store the honey, covered, in your food-grade bucket. Honey can last for many years in a warm, dark area in an airtight container before crystallizing.

Purchase honey jars from suppliers or use recycled honey jars washed in hot, soapy water and rinsed thoroughly. Dry the jars before filling them. Washing jars and lids in a dishwasher, at a high temperature setting, is recommended.

Before bottling, you need to make sure the honey is warm, so it flows freely into the jars. Doing this on a hot summer day is ideal. If you are bottling on a cold day, you can gently warm the honey by placing it in a warm area for 24 hours.

If selling your honey, make sure the honey is properly weighed to the amount listed on your label. Use a set of digital scales to accurately determine the proper weight.

CLEANING UP

After extraction and bottling have been completed, all surfaces and equipment, including the extractor, should be thoroughly cleaned with hot water and soap. The extractor should also be lubricated with oil and covered in plastic. Before being used again, it will need to be wiped clean with a fibre-free cloth.

All extracted frames – the so-called 'wet frames' – should be placed in empty supers on the remaining colonies for the bees to clean off any lingering honey and deposit it into their winter stores. After several days, when dry, remove the supers and store with a wax moth prevention chemical. The frames can be reused for next year's colonies.

PRODUCING CUT-COMB HONEY

There is an alternative to producing honey in a jar. Cut-comb honey can easily be produced in your hives and is simply the honeycomb cut free from the frame or top bar and then subdivided into smaller pieces. The advantage is you don't need an extractor in order to harvest it. Cut-comb honey simply means that the honey is still enclosed in honeycomb and is ready-to-eat – straight from the hive.

Cut-comb honey is produced in shallow extracting frames provided with a very thin foundation and is the rawest form of honey and as close to how the bees make it as you can get. You only need to make some minor adjustments to your hives to produce cut-comb honey. Think of it as a slab of readily edible honeycomb.

You harvest cut-comb honey by simply cutting the whole honeycomb free from the supporting structure and cutting it into any size or shape. Use a cut-comb knife or a square, stainless-steel comb cutter to cut the honeycomb into chunks or squares ready to be packaged – or to be floated in a jar of runny honey (a beautiful way to present your product). This can be a very messy undertaking, so you'll need to let the honeycomb drain completely before packaging it.

As an alternative way of producing comb honey, you can use special two-piece frames with round sections, available from beekeeping providers, in a specially modified super, with only a single sheet of wax foundation added. When the bees are finished filling the spaces, the supers containing the plastic sections are removed, and what comes out is a perfectly round section of comb honey, created by the bees.

A jar of golden honey with a cut piece of honeycomb suspended inside it.

Wax harvesting and rendering

The construction material of the hive, beeswax, has been used by humans in many ways for thousands of years. Bee colonies draw out combs to create a network for laying eggs and honey production. On the underside of a 12- to 20-day-old worker bee's abdomen are four pairs of wax glands, from which is secreted a liquid wax that hardens as soon as it hits the air and forms a wax scale or flake. Using her mandibles, the bee will build the entire comb structure, cover ripe honey cells, and bridge comb, using the wax flakes.

Beeswax is an incredible substance that can be used in many ways: food preparation, crafts, cosmetics, health products, wood care products, and the waxing and sealing of foodstuffs such as preserves and cheese. Bees work hard at creating all that beeswax, so make use of it! It isn't difficult to clean and render this useful product. 'Rendering' is the term for transforming beeswax from the hive into a clean block of honey.

One important beekeeping use of beeswax is to paint melted wax on your plastic foundation before inserting it into a hive. This simple step will jump-start your colonies into drawing out comb quickly in the spring when you need them to work their hardest to deposit nectar in the honeycomb. The quicker the bees draw out comb, the quicker your honey crop will come in.

A by-product of harvesting your honey, primarily from the wax cappings, beeswax is collected at the same time as the honey. At the conclusion of harvesting your honey, you will be left with a pile of wax cappings dripping with excess honey at the bottom of your uncapping tank on a strainer tray. The best way to clean off all the honey, prior to final cleaning, is to let the bees clean it up and deposit it back into their winter stores.

Beeswax is one of the most valuable hive products, used for thousands of years for a variety of purposes, from producing light to keeping food fresh.

Beeswax has an important use in beekeeping: here, melted wax is being painted onto a new frame as a foundation before being inserted into a hive.

STEP-BY-STEP METHOD FOR CLEANING AND PROCESSING YOUR WAX

A designated old casserole pot or slow cooker and some old kitchen utensils, saved for this purpose, are perfect for slowly melting your beeswax to remove all dirt and impurities from it, so that you end up with a solid block of beeswax, pale yellow to golden in colour.

WARNING:
The cardinal rule for melting any beeswax is never to do this on an open flame.

- To remove remaining honey, place all your wax cappings on top of a grid or screen and place the screen on top of the inner cover of the hive. The bees will be able to access the cappings through the inner cover hole. Placing an empty super on top will keep robbing bees and other insects from accessing the cappings.
- After a few days, you can place the bee-cleaned cappings into a large colander or sieve and rinse thoroughly with a hose outside before processing. Rinsing in a sink can cause pieces of wax to go down the drain and clog up the plumbing. Beeswax can be very dirty, containing dead bees, cocoons, food waste and dirt. If you have only a

small amount, you can save the rinsed wax until you have a larger quantity to process all at once.

- After cleaning, place your wax into a clean mesh bag, such as a paint strainer with a drawstring or an old muslin bag. Place the bag into an old casserole pot or baine marie, lapping the edges around the rim of the pot, and pour clean water into the pot to cover the wax.
- Place the lid on and situate your casserole pot away from anything flammable and where you can watch it, as beeswax can ignite at higher temperatures.
- Turn the heat to low (87–93 °C / 190–200 °F) and let the wax melt for several hours. Keep the heat on low, as any higher temperatures can dilute the quality of your beeswax. Monitor the beeswax and add more water, if needed.
- Once the wax is fully melted, turn off the heat and leave to cool. The water and beeswax will separate, leaving all the dirt and debris in the mesh bag and the beeswax on the bottom of the pot.
- Once the wax is cool, remove the paint strainer mesh bag that contains all the debris and the block of freshly made beeswax from the dirty water. Turn the block over and scrape off any dirty residue.
- If the beeswax is still dirty looking, you can repeat the process until you have a good, golden colour.

ALTERNATIVE – SOLAR WAX MELTER

Harnessing the power of the sun to melt beeswax is an alternative to cleaning and rendering your beeswax on the hob. An insulated wooden (or metal) box, painted black inside and outside, and a sheet of glass that fits tightly over the top are all you need to set up a solar wax melter. Inside the box, place a tubful of your dirty wax (old comb, cappings and other scrapings) and slant the entire box at an angle of 30–35 degrees, orientated towards the sun, covering the top with the glass. As the ambient temperature rises inside the box (to 63 °C / 145 °F), the wax melts and drips off the tray into a collector pan placed below. Be wary of putting plastic frames inside the melter, as the heat can warp the frames. This may be a simple piece of technology, but it is very effective.

Harvesting propolis and pollen

Honey and beeswax are the major products of beekeeping, but there are two other, more minor products that may be of interest, though the harvesting of them can be fiddly.

PROPOLIS

The sticky goo that glues the hive together, propolis is collected by foragers along with nectar, water, and pollen. Many plants exude a sticky resinous substance that covers leaf or flower buds to protect them. A similar response happens when a plant is wounded, and it forms a sticky substance to cover the wound for healing. Collecting this substance, by scraping it off with their mandibles, foragers then take it back to the hive, where it is mixed with beeswax and saliva.

In the hive, the bees use propolis to glue everything together in the hive – frames, boxes, lids, indeed any available surface – to protect themselves against weather. During warm weather, when you are prying apart the things covered in this gooey substance, you can scrape off the propolis and freeze it for safekeeping. During cold weather, the mixture hardens and, when you separate your boxes, there will be a noticeable cracking sound that will alert the bees to your intrusion. For this reason, it's best to scrape off as much propolis as you can during the warmer weather, even though the bees will just add more later.

These bees are using sticky, gooey propolis – the cement of the hive – to hold together the various parts of their hive.

Propolis is another harvestable and highly sought-after product from the hive which contains lots of substances that are reputed to fight infections, heal wounds and treat other ailments. You can even buy propolis traps, so that you can collect it in decent quantities and sell it commercially.

For most beekeepers who don't intend to harvest it, propolis can be an annoyance. The sticky residue will be left all over your clothes and equipment and make it hard to separate your boxes. Use ethyl alcohol to remove propolis from your equipment. It is harder to remove from clothing, but the best way is to scrape it off with your hive tool.

POLLEN

Different pollens are deposited into cells near the brood nest by the worker bees, and are visible in their multi-coloured hues (see below), according to the type of flower and the season. A pollen trap, a device that fits over the hive entrance, contains holes just large enough for a forager to fit through – and in the process the pollen is scraped off the bee's back legs and falls into a collector. The pollen is very perishable and must be collected daily and preserved. Since a beehive needs pollen to survive, traps should be used only on a temporary basis, a few days at a time.

Selling/marketing honey for small-scale beekeepers

In the United Kingdom, contact your local Trading Standards department for specifics on labelling and the relevant honey and health and safety regulations. In the United States, visit the National Honey Board website, your state health department, or your county extension agent, for federal and state labelling guidelines.

Selling at farmers' markets and local shops, or by post or on Facebook Marketplace, are all possibilities for marketing your honey. If you sell online, you'll need to familiarize yourself with the relevant Food Standards Agency regulations.

The honey, once extracted, should be free of mould, insects, debris and any other foreign organic or inorganic substance. Basic labelling requirements are typically the following, though you should always check with local regulations as well:

1. The label must have the word 'honey' on it; if the bees are foraging, you can designate it as 'wildflower' honey.
2. Give the weight of the honey in both ounces and grams.
3. Your name, address, email address and phone number must be listed clearly on the label.
4. If you have added anything to the honey, you must label the honey as 'honey product'.
5. Include a statement that honey shouldn't be given to children under 12 months of age.

In terms of pricing, do your market research by observing the different prices of honey on sale at farmers' markets or local fairs. This will help to determine a fair and competitive price.

Honeycomb cells displaying a range of colourful pollens.

Honey ripening

Collecting nectar is one of the main jobs of forager bees, which is gathered and stored in their 'crop' or honey stomach. Nectar is composed of 80 per cent water and 20 per cent sugar, which can vary according to time of year and floral source. As the forager flies home with her nectar load, she adds an enzyme called invertase to the nectar that starts the ripening process, even before she enters the hive. Once at the hive, the forager regurgitates the nectar to a 'processor' bee at the entrance, which adds additional invertase and takes the nectar to the honeycomb and regurgitates it into one of the cells. The bees will start a process called 'fanning', which involves vibrating their wings, creating a flow of air through the hive that helps water evaporate from the nectar, reducing the water content to 18–19 per cent. At this point, so little water is left that no microbes can grow in it. The bees then cap the cell with an airtight wax covering, so the honey can't absorb any more water. It takes three to ten days for the ripening process to be completed.

Honey pointers/takeaways

- While extracting honey, exercise food safety: always keep both your area and equipment scrupulously clean, as you are producing a foodstuff, potentially for sale.
- Use as little smoke as possible when removing the supers of honey, as the smoke can give both the honey and wax an 'off' taste.
- Don't use chemicals in the hive during honey production as the chemicals could be absorbed in the honey and the wax.
- When moving your honey supers, keep them tightly covered, as bees can start robbing and dirt can get in.
- Store your used and cleaned supers to allow light and air to penetrate, using screens or excluders to keep mice and other rodents out.

Opposite (top and bottom): These marketing images for honey and honeycomb emphasize the natural wonders of the beekeeper's – and their bees' – craft.

RESPONSIBLE
BEEKEEPING

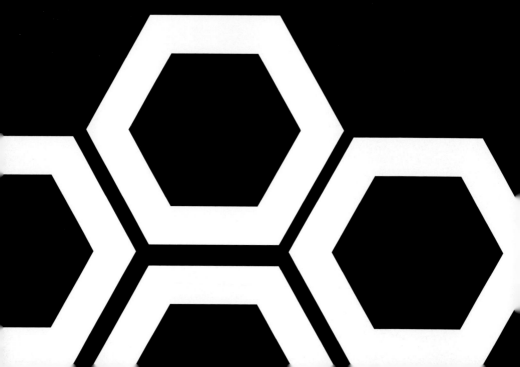

Responsible Beekeeping

Record-keeping

The thing that separates a 'bee-haver' from a beekeeper is data. Attentive beekeepers can tell you what's going on in every one of their hives because they keep careful notes of each colony's activities and progress. Each bee colony has its own distinct personality that requires slight management tweaks to keep it healthy, and a helpful method to remember which colony needs what – and when – is to keep an inspection log for each hive. For beekeepers with multiple bee gardens (apiaries with multiple hives), it's near impossible to remember what the bees are doing in each hive without a record-keeping system (see the *Hive Inspection Sheet*, page 182).

Bee notes are especially crucial in the first few seasons working in a new apiary location because they help the beekeeper learn the seasonality of the nectar flow and how this translates to colony behaviour. Early records establish a baseline for colony growth and swarming tendencies, annual mite build-ups, and harvest yields. Recorded hive histories help the beekeeper to understand the difference between a normal and abnormal year, and when a hive is underperforming in comparison to previous seasons.

Data also make for a more prepared beekeeper. Reviewing notes before hive inspections reminds beekeepers of what actions need to be taken, what new equipment needs to be bought, any problems that need to be checked, and what to expect inside the hive. Notes can be detailed or abbreviated, written as a diary or by checking boxes on a pre-made form, or by entering notes into one of the many customizable mobile apps that automatically input date, time, weather, and latitude/longitude. The US non-profit Bee Informed Partnership has a free BIP ArcIIive mobile app that allows beekeepers to map their bee gardens, track colonies over time, record *Varroa* mite levels, and gauge hive fitness. The data can help the beekeeper to get a visual picture of hive health, and the information is shared as 'citizen science' with the Bee Informed Partnership, which creates annual reports of honey bee health by surveying beekeepers in respect of their management techniques and winter colony losses.

Whichever recording method works best, there are a few essential things that beekeepers should document every time they inspect a hive. Before beginning any such documentation, however, the beekeeper must first decide how to identify individual

Meticulous record-keeping is indispensable in modern beekeeping. Here, the beekeeper uses a tablet to make notes.

colonies. Because of the vagaries of beekeeping, hive boxes are routinely moved within bee gardens and shared with other beekeepers throughout the year, so marking the hive covers, as opposed to the individual hive bodies, is recommended. The simplest way is to paint numbers on the outer covers or paint them with different colours or symbols. That way, if the hive moves to a different garden, its unique marker can go with it. Other beekeepers find it easier to assign a number to the queens rather than the hives, so that, if they divide crowded hives and relocate the queen, her number moves with her. The replacement queen, in the hive she has vacated, gets a new number.

Once the hives are differentiated, you should mark the top of each inspection sheet with the hive ID and a few quick reminders of the colony's origin. Where were the bees purchased, or where was the swarm collected, or was the colony a result of an in-apiary split? Jot down the queen source – was she purchased on her own, or with a package of bees? Did she come with a swarm, or was she reared by the beekeeper? List the breed of bees, if known.

Observational notes
Be sure to record the date, time, weather, and what's in bloom. By keeping a close watch on the synchronicity between flowers and

bees, you'll come to know the cycles of the nectar flow, and when to expect the harvest season to arrive. When certain blooms are on, honey bees can fill their hive in a matter of days, and knowing this gives the beekeeper time to spin surplus honey out of the honeycomb and return the empty honeycomb frames back to the hive so the bees can refill them. Keeping one step ahead of the colony also helps reduce their urge to swarm and look for more space.

Take note of the size and temperament of the hive. A colony's population should be growing in spring and shrinking in autumn. Their mood throughout the year can convey a lot of information. Calm and busy bees are more likely to have everything they need, but honey bees that are fussy, loud, or aggressive can be exhibiting signs of stress.

Record any queen sightings. The queen is elusive and runs from sunlight, so it's not a guarantee she'll make an appearance during a hive inspection. That's why beekeepers often put a dab of paint on her thorax with a queen-marking pen, or affix a tiny marker with a bit of adhesive, to make her easier to find. With a marked queen, it becomes obvious if a new, unmarked queen has emerged and replaced the original monarch. With an unmarked queen, it's harder to notice if she's been replaced when her successor looks identical.

Documenting what you see in the brood nest can give clues about the queen's health if you can't find her during an inspection. If there are eggs in the honeycomb, that's confirmation she was there three days ago or less. After three days, eggs hatch into larvae. The grubs remain in their unsealed cells for six days, receiving food from nurse bees. Once the workers seal the larval cell, it takes another 12 days to pupate and emerge as a fully formed bee. One way to check that the queen is laying eggs at a constant rate is to assess the ratio of eggs, larvae and sealed brood. If there's twice as many larvae as eggs, and twice as much sealed brood as larvae, then she's laying at an even rate. Changes in these ratios can indicate that she's ramping up or slowing down her egg production. Fewer eggs than larvae or sealed brood can also indicate the colony is preparing to swarm.

One way to confirm the hive is in swarm mode is to note if there are any queen cups or sealed queen cells inside the hive. A popular beekeeper tradition is to place a rock on top of the hives that are preparing to swarm. Keeping a good log, and watching the calendar, gives the beekeeper options to manage the impending swarm or to let the colony divide naturally.

Record the amounts of brood, pollen and honey in the hive.

Some colonies hoard pollen over honey, or vice versa. Writing down your observations can help you know if a colony is behaving out of character and needs a food supplement boost.

Note the approximate size of the drone population – are there a lot, some, or no drones present? Too many drones may indicate a worker's ovaries have developed in response to a missing queen, because an unfertilized worker can lay only male bees. Such a hive will die out without intervention.

Jot down any signs of pests or disease. If the brood pattern is spotty instead of uniform and solid, that may mean something is wrong with the queen. It could also be a sign that worker bees are removing larvae or food from the cells because the contents are contaminated somehow. If the brood seals are perforated, the worker bees are sacrificing their larval sisters because they are diseased. *Varroa* mites are visible to the naked eye and look like shiny red-brown dots riding on the bodies of bees. Note any mite sightings. Another dead giveaway of mite infestation is honey bees with wrinkled, deformed wings, caused by a virus passed on by the parasitic *Varroa* mites.

Check the condition of the honeycomb, the wooden frames and hive boxes. Warped, cracked or mouldy hive equipment needs to be replaced, as do any frames with wax that has turned dark with overuse.

At harvest time, you may joyfully record how much honey was extracted. Learning how much the bees can share with the beekeeper is an important lesson in coexistence. Recording the colour, texture and flavour of the honey, along with the seasonal blooms, can help decipher which nectars contributed to the honey.

A queen, surrounded by her attendant workers, has been given a tiny, numbered marker to make her easier to identify.

A row of different-coloured hives in Greece, each carefully numbered. Note, too, how each has been set on top of a tyre, making it more easily accessible to the beekeeper.

Recording interventions

Observational notes are the first step to keeping good data. The second step is recording any actions taken in response to what's going on inside the hive. Ensure that you detail any adjustments made to the colony, to help you assess – at a later date – which interventions worked and which didn't. Knowing the hive history helps to inform better action plans going forward, giving the honey bees a much improved chance of survival.

Record the content and amount of every feeding. Comparing these notes with seasonal bloom notes will start to show a pattern of when honey bees need a 'food assist', and when they're fine to feed on their own – using the local forage.

Note when any new queens are introduced, as well as their origin stories. Keep track of any changes to the hive configuration, such as if any brood boxes or honey supers have been added or removed, and if the frames inside have drawn honeycomb or new, blank sheets of wax foundation. A few seasons of recording this will help beekeepers to anticipate how much equipment they should have on hand for the nectar flow.

It's also important to keep medical records. Keep a list of all mite counts conducted throughout the year. Record the date, time and amount of any natural or chemical treatments used to combat pests and parasites – and report any findings about their efficacy. In some situations, the beekeeper must remove honey supers before applying any treatments.

A civic duty

Besides making you a better beekeeper, keeping good hive notes is a civic duty. An observant beekeeper can address parasites and diseases before they get out of control and spread to neighbouring hives. No one wants a 'hive zero' in their apiary for outbreaks such as American foulbrood, a highly contagious bacterial infection that liquefies bee larvae in the comb. Beekeepers must burn their infected hives in order to eliminate it. While these types of dramatic disease spreads are rare, when they do happen, they are devastating to the beekeeping community.

Responsible beekeepers are careful to keep the peace with their bees, as well as their neighbours. Depending on where you live, beekeeping could be highly regulated, or not at all. Legal requirements differ between countries, states, and even between local neighbourhoods sharing the same postcode. A good place to start looking for information is the nearest beekeeping association, which will be very familiar with local beekeeping ordinances.

In the United States and some European countries, some states and municipalities require beekeepers to register their hives, while others don't, while some localities ban beekeeping entirely. Local zoning codes and animal control ordinances categorize bees as everything from insects to 'livestock' and even 'exotic animals', and sometimes nuisance laws – excessive noise, barking dogs, crowing roosters – apply to keeping bees. Other local rules can regulate the keeping of bees within city limits, on certain-sized properties, within a specified distance of the property boundary, or with neighbour permission. Best practice is to check with a local beekeeping association for all the relevant details.

In the United Kingdom, beekeepers don't need permission to keep hives, but they do need to report any pest control methods they use. UK bees are classified as food-producing animals and, as such, beekeepers are legally required to record any bee medicines they use. Beekeepers must document which medicines they bought, and when, the number of packages and their batch numbers – including the name and address of the supplier, plus the application date and the hive that received the treatment. In addition, as of 2021, UK beekeepers are required to report any *Varroa* mite infestation to the National Bee Unit in England and Wales, and to the Scottish Bee Health Scheme in Scotland.

No matter which beekeeping laws apply to your situation, it's a good idea to talk with your neighbours before getting a beehive to address any concerns they may have in advance, and to make sure residents know how to contact you if a honey bee swarm lands on their property. Inviting neighbours to join the honey harvest is a great way to build support for local beekeeping, as is keeping a few spare bee suits on hand in case anyone wants to join a hive inspection to learn more about honey bees. Observation hives that hold one honeycomb frame safely sealed behind glass give children a safe opportunity to get up close to honey bees.

Not only beekeepers, but also large commercial farmers are starting to be held responsible for honey bee safety in some places. As communities become more aware of the destructive impacts of agrochemicals on pollinators, some local governments require crop farmers to register the dates and times of pesticide sprayings. Beekeepers can sign up for advance notifications, so that they can relocate or cover their hives to protect their bees from toxic exposure.

A beekeeper dressed in a traditional white beekeeping suit, complete with meshed hood and thick gloves. White is used because bees will defend themselves against typically dark-coloured predators such as bears.

Hive Inspection Sheet

HIVE TEMPERAMENT
○ Calm ○ Nervous ○ Aggressive ○ Time to requeen

LOCATED QUEEN ○ NO ○ YES
Marked ○ No ○ Yes
○ Replace queen – Date: _____

LAYING PATTERN
○ Beautiful (solid & uniform)
○ Mediocre (intermittent or random)
○ Poor (spotty)

EGGS PRESENT ○ No ○ Yes
Comments: _____

POPULATION ○ Heavy ○ Moderate ○ Low
○ Added deep body
○ Split hive (new hive): # _____
○ Swarming imminent – needs monitoring

EXCESSIVE DRONE CELLS ○ No ○ Yes
Drone population estimate:
○ Low: 30 ○ Ave.: 30 to 100 ○ High: 100+

QUEEN CELLS ○ No ○ Yes
Along frame bottom: # _____
Converted worker cell: # _____

DISEASE/PESTS ○ No ○ Yes
○ Chalkbrood   ○ Nosema
○ *Varroa* mites   ○ Tracheal mites
○ EFB   ○ AFB
○ Small hive beetle
Other: _____

MEDICATIONS
Added – Date: _____
○ Apistan   ○ Apiguard
○ Mite Away II   ○ Tylan
○ Fumagilin-B   ○ Terramycin™
○ Other: _____

Removed – Date: _____
○ Apistan   ○ Apiguard
○ Mite Away II   ○ Tylan
○ Fumagilin-B   ○ Terramycin™
○ Other: _____

INTEGRATED PEST MANAGEMENT (I P.M.)
○ Screened bottom board
○ Icing sugar mite drop
○ Drone cell foundation
○ Other: _____

EARLY SPRING INSPECTION
○ Reversed brood box(es):
Deep____ Med.____ Shallow____
○ Cleaned bottom board

Spring Feed/Buildup
○ Brood Builder: dry____wet ____ patties_____

○ MegaBee: dry____wet ____ patties _____

○ Fructose: _____
○ Pollen sub: _____
○ Sugar syrup (1/1 ratio): _____
○ Other: _____

SPRING/SUMMER HONEY FLOW PREPARATION
○ Added queen excluder
○ Added super(s):
Deep ____ Med. ____ Shallow ____
○ Added ventilated inner cover
○ Added pollen trap (optional if sufficient stores)

HONEY REMOVAL/EXTRACTION
____ # supers removed
____ kilograms honey extracted
____ kilograms comb honey
○ Remove excluder (if done with honey production)
○ Begin *varroa* control medication: ____

FOOD STORES/WINTER PREPARATION

	Honey	Pollen
High (everywhere)	○	○
Average	○	○
Low	○	○
Near brood	○	○

○ Fed hive
   ○ Sugar Syrup (2/1 ration): ____
   ○ Other: ____
○ Added entrance reducer
○ Colony configuration # ____
   Brood Boxes # ____ Supers

HIVE CONDITION
○ Normal brace comb   ○ Burr comb
○ Excessive propolis   ○ Normal odor
○ Foul odor   ○ Equip. damage
○ Replace equipment – What: ____
○ Other: ____

Type of foundation: ○ Duragilt   ○ Plasticell
○ EZ frame   ○ Wired   ○ Med. brood   ○ Cut comb
Comb condition or age: ____
○ Replace foundation

NOTES: ____

Planting for honey bees

Honey bees do best with good nutrition gleaned from a varied diet. That means they need access to native wildland, where the nectar and pollen offerings are diverse, multi-seasonal, and free of toxic chemicals. Bees derive their protein from pollen, which contains anywhere from 2 to 60 per cent protein. Pollen grains also contain ten essential amino acids, and varying concentrations of carbohydrates, lipids, sterols and other micronutrients. Nectar is the honey bee's main source of carbohydrates, mainly the sugars sucrose, fructose and glucose. Based on flower species and weather, nectar can contain anywhere from 10 to 70 per cent carbohydrates. The remainder is water with low levels of amino acids, lipids, proteins, and various vitamins and minerals.

Honey bees also rely on plants for preventative medicine. They collect medicinal plant oils and resins that they mix with pollen and nectar to create an antimicrobial mix that they feed to larvae and use as a hygienic, waterproof seal for their nests. Conifers and poplars produce a sap for an antimicrobial defence, called propolis, that bees collect to seal cracks and weatherproof their hives. It also serves as a natural protection against bacteria, fungi, and mites.

In the wild, honey bees visit a vast array of native plant species, up to a million blooms, to produce a single kilogram of honey. A bee visits several thousand flowers daily and produces just one-twelfth of a teaspoon of honey in her lifetime. For honey bees to accomplish this incredible feat, they rely on meadows with important native wildflowers and blooming weeds such as knotweeds and smartweeds, dandelions, yucca, asters, goldenrods, mustards, milkweeds, poppies, Spanish needle, knapweed, hyssops, lupines, star thistle, fireweed and yarrow.

However, as monoculture and human development have slowly eaten away at the open space where honey bees forage, it's become vital to help them regain some territory by creating native plant sanctuaries with high-nectar plants, being careful to stagger the bloom. It's especially important to include plants that boom in late autumn, after most natural forage is depleted. When planting for honey bees, think about the area surrounding your beehives as a nectar menu. When the first course is digested, have the next one lined up and ready to serve – that way your bees will have a reliable food source spread throughout the year, allowing ample time for them to store enough food in their pantry to get them through the winter dearth.

Bee-friendly plants can be mighty chestnut trees or delicate herbs and come in every size in between. Any of the cane berry

Bees especially love daisy-like chamomile flowers, seen here growing wild in a meadow.

plants are bee-pleasers – blackberry, raspberry, loganberries – as are perfumy honeysuckles that spread magnificently and require very little care, and farmed crops like rapeseed and buckwheat. With honey bees in mind, let your herb garden flower and go to seed before trimming it back. Bees will thank you for it. Sage, coriander, thyme, marjoram, oregano, rosemary, basil, chive and mint are all loved by bees.

Flower colours are important to consider as well. Honey bee eyesight spans a different colour spectrum from ours; they see a wider range of blue than we do, and many insect-pollinated flowers have evolved to bloom in blues and purples to make themselves more visible to honey bees. Honey bees can't see red, so they are less apt to visit red flowers.

Choosing bee plants that come with additional environmental benefits is a win-win. Bee forage can also feed cattle, produce seeds for resale, be harvested for essential oils and other therapeutics, provide compost for the soil, or be used as 'cover crops' to fix any imbalances in soil composition. In addition, bee forage can provide habitat and refuge for migratory butterflies and other pollinators – such as moths, ladybirds and hummingbirds. Bee-friendly plantings can provide protection and nesting areas for wildlife, which helps with natural pest control. A good example of a pollinator plant multi-tasker is any one of the many annual clovers. Clover affords excellent soil improvement, provides erosion control, is attractive, and provides both food and habitat for bees and other wildlife.

Then, of course, there's the taste of the honey to consider. Like wine, honey reflects terroir – the interplay between the soil, weather and plants grown at a specific time in a specific terrain. Because it's impractical to follow honey bees for miles to see where they are foraging, most beekeepers label their honey 'wildflower honey', since they can't possibly parse out all the different flowers the bees have visited over a season. However, beekeepers who keep a close eye on what's blooming and harvest multiple times a year, in sync with the blooms, can market their honey with more confidence as single-source honey, selling it as one of the popular varietals, such as clover or lavender honey. Beekeepers who transport their hives to pollinate a single crop can also market their honey more specifically, such as orange blossom honey from a hive placed in a commercial orange tree grove in southern states of the USA.

To find out which native bee pollinator plants grow well in your area, start by taking a nature walk. Observe which native plants are thriving, watch where bees land in your neighbourhood, follow buzzing sounds to see which trees attract pollinators, and ask local beekeepers what they know about planting for their bees. Consult the North American Pollinator Protection Campaign (www.pollinator.org) for more comprehensive native plant lists. The international non-profit Xerces Society for Invertebrate Conservation (www.xerces.org) offers regional honey bee plant guides by US state and Canadian province on its website.

A *Planting for Bees* blog on the British Beekeepers Association website (www.bbka.org.uk) offers planting guides for all four seasons. Bees for Development (www.beesfordevelopment.org) in the United Kingdom has excellent lists for tropical and desert plantings. Local garden centre owners will also have plenty of advice. In addition, two American classics, beloved by beekeepers, are still available in reprinted editions: *Honey Plants of North America* (1926) by John H. Lovell; and *American Honey Plants: Together with Those Which Are of Special Value to the Beekeeper as Source of Pollen* (1920) by Frank C. Pellett.

When planning for bees, the Xerces Society recommends starting with a plot of at least 465 square metres (5,000 ft²) in area, if possible, and grouping similar native plants together within it. Its advice for farmers who want to attract wild pollinators for crop production is to preserve anywhere from 10 to 30 per cent of the property as natural habitat. For proper diet diversity, a landscape should feature a minimum of a dozen different flowering plants, with at least three blooming at any given time. Most importantly, pollinator habitat should be protected from areas where agrochemicals are used, surrounded by a safety buffer of at least 30.5 metres (100 ft).

Creating a rich bee buffet follows a simple principle – the more sugar, the better. Bees prefer the plants that produce the most nectar. The list on the following pages is a sampling of honey bee plant favourites – wildflowers, garden ornamentals, trees and farm crops – and are arranged by blooming season, from early to late. These plants grow well in the temperate climates of North America and Europe.

Early spring

Almond trees

One of the first annual blooms in the United States and France is the almond tree. In California's Central Valley every February, just before the white blossoms unfurl to create what looks like snow-covered branches, more than 2 million beehives holding approximately 90 billion honey bees are hauled on semi-trailers to pollinate more than 400,000 hectares (approximately 1 million acres) of almond trees. These pollinators-for-hire have just a two-week blossom window to work, making them vital to California's annual £4 billion ($5 billion) almond industry, which supplies 80 per cent of all almonds consumed worldwide. The honey, however, is regarded as low quality, so it's mostly used in commercial bakeries rather than sold to consumers.

Apple trees

Apple trees are grown worldwide, either as garden favourites or in massive apple orchards, creating another lucrative stop for migratory beekeepers. Apple blossom honey is light amber in colour, granulates quickly, and is one of the sweeter honeys. It has been compared to the flavour of apple pie or candied apples, with hints of cinnamon and apple peel.

Avocado trees

Originally native to Mexico and Central and South America but now found in all parts of the world, avocado trees can reach heights of 18.3 metres (60 ft) and live for more than 400 years, providing honey for generations. Avocado trees cannot bear fruit without honey bees, because the trees come in two flowering types that must be cross-pollinated to produce avocados. Only bees flying between the two types can transfer the pollen. That's why avocado blossoms have evolved to produce copious amounts of nectar to attract bees. A healthy avocado tree can produce more than a million blooms in a season, resulting in up to 200 avocados. The honey is reddish amber, smooth and thick, with a strong, earthy flavour of caramelized molasses or maple syrup.

Cherry trees

Cherry trees are among the first trees to bloom in spring, when almost nothing else is producing, so they are an excellent choice to help bees that are emerging from winter hungry. Pure cherry blossom honey is a little difficult to find, as the cherry blooming season is short and so early in the year that beekeepers tend to wait until more honey from other plants comes in before harvesting. The honey from cherry blossoms is fragrant and sweet, with a tart cherry after-taste.

Citrus trees (orange, lemon, limes, grapefruit)

Citrus trees are reliable sources of honey bee forage, and bloom well in the Mediterranean and warm coastal regions of the United States. The citrus fan favourite is orange blossom honey, a pale, dense honey with distinct fruit notes and a blossomy perfume. Typically, orange blossom honey has small amounts of other citrus honeys blended in, but is labelled as 'pure orange blossom'.

Clovers

A high-value plant for both bees and honey producers, clover is the most common single-source honey found on the grocery shop shelf or at the farmers' market. Its nectar produces a high honey yield with wide commercial appeal. Clover honey is pale and mild, with a slight cinnamon flavour surrounded by warm hints of cooked butter and vanilla. Most clover honeys are a base of sweet white clover with other clovers mixed in, because some varieties can be quite bland on their own. There are nearly 30 types of clover, and they attract all kinds of bees. For the greatest pollinator benefit, plant a variety of species, such as white and yellow sweet clovers, Dutch clover, red clover, ball clover, Persian clover, alsike clover, crimson clover and lespedeza bush clover.

Holly

Abundant in Europe and the United States, holly bushes produce small clusters of white flowers in spring that draw a constant parade of honey, bumble and solitary bees. Then, come winter, the dark, waxy leaves and red berries that have graced many a holiday card are welcomed as food and shelter for hungry birds. Just make sure to plant both a male and female holly plant, otherwise berries won't appear. Holly produces a pale, finely flavoured honey with notes of butterscotch, caramel and brown sugar.

Manuka trees

Sought after for its antibacterial properties, this menthol-tasting honey comes exclusively from New Zealand manuka trees and is the only honey certified for hospital use as a salve in wound dressings. That's because manuka nectar is unique in that it contains a naturally occurring medicinal chemical called methylglyoxal. Manuka is among the most expensive honeys sold, and each bottle is given a Unique Manuka Factor (UMF) rating, a number on the label indicating the amount of active ingredient it contains. Manuka has a medicinal, almost cough drop-type mouthfeel, sometimes with a liquorice or wintergreen ('minty') flavour, and is often added to teas to boost immunity.

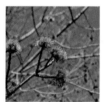

Maple trees

In early spring, maple trees leaf out in brilliant green from the Pacific Northwest in the United States, northwards into Canada, to the mountain maples in the Great Lakes area and the sycamore maples in the United Kingdom, producing tiny, feathery flowers hidden within the foliage. Because there are so many types of maple tree, it's hard to put maple honey into one flavour profile, but typically maple honey is mild, sometimes with a greenish hue, and often has a buttery maple finish – reminiscent of pancakes. Tasters have parsed out flavours of lemon, mint, hazelnut and cinnamon. Maple honey is rare because honey bees collect it so far ahead of the harvest season – so it is not to be passed up by those lucky enough to try it.

Mesquite

Considered both a shrub and a tree that can reach heights of nine metres (30 ft) or more, mesquite produces abundant clusters of yellow blossoms that dangle like slender spikes from its branches. It's found in Mexico and the southern United States, and its nectar produces honey that varies from white to amber, with a smoky scent of molasses or brown sugar that performs well as a meat glaze or when drizzled on hearty bread.

Bottlebrush

Native to Australia, this evergreen tree or shrub has dramatic, drooping branches covered in pipe cleaner-shaped brushes that attract many bees and birds. The brushes are usually siren red, but there are more than 40 bottlebrush species, some that bloom in pink, purple, yellow, white or green. Honey bees are drawn to the creamy white flower nubs close to the stem, hidden within the bristles. Each nub opens to reveal a long stamen tipped with pollen. Bottlebrush honey is very dark and thick, with a strong fruit fragrance and flavours of caramel and molasses, sometimes with hint of bitterness at the finish.

Rosemary

This compact, woody shrub is one of the few bee plants that can bloom year-round, even in the depths of winter. Its small, blue-purple blossoms draw so many honey bees that the bush practically vibrates. Rosemary does double duty as a kitchen ingredient for pastas, sauces and baked goods, and crushing the oils in your palms can help to keep mosquitos away. Its nectar produces a thick, clear honey – with a creamy, floral flavour scented with rosemary.

Thyme

This workhorse herb enjoys the warm, arid climates of the Mediterranean, North America and New Zealand. It's been a source of Greek honey since ancient times and remains a staple in Greek kitchens today. Honey from thyme is light to medium amber in colour, has an intense fresh menthol nose, and delivers a fresh, woody flavour with a tinge of cooked fruit.

White tupelo

This tree grows in the swamplands of Georgia, Florida and South Carolina, where beekeepers position their hives on tall platforms or boats to collect the nectar for two precious weeks in spring when the delicate flowers bloom. They go to all this trouble because tupelo honey commands top dollar as one of the most luxurious honeys on the market, a rare delicacy often referred to as the 'champagne' of honey. It has a green sheen, resists crystallization, and is fruit-forward, with flavours of juicy pear, jasmine, butterscotch and nutmeg.

Late spring/summer

Alfalfa
An excellent cover crop for garden gardeners and the highest-yield hay crop for beef and dairy cattle, sheep and goats, alfalfa has an incredibly deep root system that means it's one of the few forage plants that can withstand seasonal droughts. The pale honey produced from alfalfa is earthy, with a scent of straw, cinnamon or beeswax, and it has a pleasant taste of sweet grass.

Blueberry
The bell-shaped flowers that are white, pink, and sometimes red, need to be buzz-pollinated by bumble bees vibrating their wing muscles to release the pollen. Honey bees, however, have a different technique that requires a little more work. They grab the flower's anther with their legs and kick to release the pollen. They are also known to bite holes at the base of the flowers to create a shortcut to the nectar. Maine, USA, is a common stop for commercial beekeepers who rent their hives to blueberry farmers for pollination. Blueberry blossom honey is dazzling, both in its looks and taste. It's quite thick, is light amber with a violet hue, and tastes as advertised – like blueberries – with a faint, buttery finish. Paired with blueberry muffins, it's nothing short of divine.

Borage
This annual Mediterranean herb has bright blue, star-shaped flowers that turn pink as they age. Both its flowers and leaves are edible, and while it's mostly used as a garden plant, the cosmetics industry has sparked an interest in growing it as a field crop for extracting its medicinal oils. Borage is unique in that it secretes sugar throughout the day, even in cold weather, and the sugar in its nectars has been measured at 52 per cent. The light floral honey from borage is a perfect addition to tea, with its thin texture and hints of lemon and orange flavours.

Inkberry

Also known as gallberry, inkberry is a native perennial evergreen shrub in the holly family. Ornamental gardeners value it for its glossy leaves, explosion of small, white flowers, and berries that turn black and are an important source of winter food for birds. Beekeeper lore is thick with stories about honey bees flying past miles of good forage just to get to a blooming inkberry bush. Inkberry honey is deep crimson, almost opaque, and difficult to find as most of it is sold to the baking industry for breads and sweets. It has a thick mouthfeel and imparts flavours of dried apricots, mango, red berries – and a touch of pine. It is sometimes labelled as 'holly honey'.

Lavender

All kinds of lavender attract all kinds of bees, and the two make a perfect insect-flower pairing. There are nearly 30 lavender species, and not only are they wonderful bee plants, their purple, pink and white blooms are equally famous in cosmetics and in chefs' kitchens. The calm-inducing lavender aroma comes through in the scent and taste of lavender honey. Opening a jar releases a soft floral scent tinged with camphor, almond and vanilla. The honey is transparent to pale gold, with fine granulation and a perfumy note. French patisseries commonly use lavender honey when producing their crêpes and nougats.

Linden trees

Urban beekeepers and city street planners favour linden trees because they are hardy, can grow in almost any location with adequate drainage, and produce copious amounts of nectar. With cooperative weather, bees can turn a linden tree's nectar into 91 kilograms (200 lbs) of honey in just one season. The colour of linden honey has been compared to a chardonnay, a golden harvest hue, and can sometimes taste like the wine – often described as buttery, with hints of kiwi, young bananas or honeydew melons.

Salvia

Salvia is a broad term for a diverse group of annuals and perennials often cultivated as ornamental garden plants, and many are considered important honey bee forage. One in particular, California native black sage, is considered a premium nectar plant. The highly aromatic perennial shrub, with tall stalks of purple pompoms, has long been used medicinally by indigenous tribes and grows only in the dry, rocky, coastal hills of California.

Once the blossoms have been fertilized, they remain on the stem and slowly turn black, giving the plant its name. Black sage honey is highly prized by honey connoisseurs, for it produces a top-quality 'water white' clear honey that almost never granulates. The honey produced from sage has an aroma of balsamic and resin, and the layered flavours contain smoky, candied fruit and butterscotch – with a mentholated kick.

Wild lilac

Also referred to by its genus name, *Ceanothus*, wild lilac bushes come in more than 50 species and produce explosions of fragrant blossoms in white, pink, purple or electric blue. It's a popular choice in showstopper gardens and farm hedgerows. An enormous diversity of bees, caterpillars and other pollinators visit wild lilac, as do wild deer, who like to snack on the leathery leaves. Wild lilac flowers are edible and can be found on wedding cakes. They are often infused whole into honey to impart a lilac flavour – but pure honey from wild lilac has a graceful floral taste all on its own.

Late summer/autumn

Buckwheat

Wild buckwheat is a late-blooming annual, one of the last plants producing nectar when honey bees are storing up food in the lead-up to winter. It's considered an essential plant in pollinator gardens because it's an abundant self-seeder, it flowers prolifically, and the sugar concentration of its nectar has been reported as high as 58 per cent. Not only do honey bees rely on it, but a parade of caterpillars, butterflies and native bees are also drawn to its reliable buffet. Buckwheat is also grown as a commercial crop for its seeds, which are ground into flour. Farmers also use it as a cover crop, and then plough it under as a soil amendment. Buckwheat honey is thick and looks somewhat alarmingly like motor oil. But the aroma is more like a malty beer, and it has indulgent flavours of chocolate malt balls, dark red cherries or toasted coffee.

Fuchsia

The beautiful red-and-purple hanging blooms look like dancing ladies, and their 'skirts' protect the nectar from washing out during rainfall, making this ornamental plant a bee and gardener favourite. However, the honey from fuchsia is rarely harvested because it is rather thin and lacklustre.

Goldenrod

A late-bloomer perennial that bees have come to rely on to get them through winter, goldenrod is one of the last plants of the season offering nectar and pollen. There is a vast number of species, living in all types of habitats from swamps to high deserts. The blooms span the yellow spectrum from a light cream to a striking neon yellow and are often found along roadsides. Goldenrod honey is silky and transparent straight from the honeycomb, but quickly crystallizes into a thick, opaque paste. Some people prefer this kind of honey, which spreads like butter; others reheat it in a pan of water to return it to a liquid state. It has a honeysuckle flavour, with a strong and spicy finish.

Ling heather

This is a hardy perennial associated with the Irish and Scottish countryside that flourishes in dry, sandy soil. Ling heather can withstand extreme temperatures and strong winds, and can live for up to 50 years. It grows several feet tall, is often used as shelter by wildlife, and it's grazed by cattle. Ling honey is unusual because it coagulates into a jelly in the jar but returns to liquid when stirred. Beekeepers often hand-press ling honey from the wax honeycomb to create air bubbles in it, or they will often sell it in the comb. Ling honey is dark amber and chewy with an intense, earthy flavour somewhat like smoked toffee. It can be bitter and tends to be one of those love-it-or-hate-it flavours that honey lovers are fond of debating.

Ivy

A fast-growing climber that gardeners are more apt to rip out than plant, flowering ivy is an important source of late-season food for honey bees. Its strong-smelling, yellow-green flowers are also a refuge for late-flying butterflies, wasps, bumble bees, and a specific solitary bee found in the United Kingdom called the ivy bee. The honey solidifies quickly and can become as hard as concrete in the honeycomb, so it's more often left in the hive as bee food instead of harvested. There is, however, a growing market for ivy honey because some say it has healing properties, like manuka honey, and predict it will become just as important to the medical industry. Beekeepers sometimes cut the honey comb and melt it in warming buckets to extract the ivy honey from the wax. Ivy honey is greyish-white, quite sharp, and what some would call an acquired taste. Fans describe it as like a sharp cheese, with kicks of liquorice or resin; detractors place it closer to bitter cough syrup.

Sunflowers

The universal symbol of cheeriness is the sunflower, and honey bees like it for its wide landing pad on stalks that can reach almost 2.5 metres (8 ft) tall. Sunflowers are the gathering places for insect socials, attracting not only honey bees but also wasps, flies, butterflies and pollen-feeding soldier beetles. Just be sure to avoid the 'pollenless' or double-petalled ornamental varieties. Sunflowers are among the most diverse of pollinator plants, growing in all climates and soils. They are great for hedgerows and for bringing joyful pops of colour to gardens. Sunflower honey is a great starter honey because it's gentle on the tongue. It is light amber with a soft floral flavour, mixed with subtle citrus undertones and hints of butterscotch.

Gardeners everywhere now tend to be much more 'bee-aware,' planting bee-attracting plants such as the ivy and sunflowers here.

Hygiene and safety

The possibility of getting stung is always there when beekeeping, but there are things beekeepers can do to minimize the risk. The most obvious safety precaution is to wear a full bee suit and veil, making sure that the cuffs are tucked into white cotton socks; to wear closed-toe shoes or, better yet, boots and elbow-length leather gloves that are pulled over the bee suit sleeves. Duct tape over the bee suit zips can ensure they don't wriggle loose and create a gap where a bee could slip through. Honey bees can sting through a suit, but it's much harder for their stingers to pierce two layers of clothing to reach skin. Furthermore, there's a good reason why beekeeping suits are white. Dark clothing gives the beekeeper the appearance of one of the honey bee's worst enemies – the bear. The same goes for woollen socks – anything that resembles animal hair is not a good choice for your beekeeping attire.

How not to irritate bees

Honey bees react to sudden changes in air pressure, light intrusion, and unfamiliar scents. So the best approach when opening a hive is to move slowly, making no sudden movements. Just as we don't like to be startled, neither do they. Carefully lifting frames and hive boxes in slow, tai chi-like motion gives the bees time to move out of the way and adjust to what's happening, making them less likely to feel under attack and rush out of the hive defensively. Using puffs of smoke or a feather to gently brush bees aside, so you can manipulate the frames without squishing bees, goes a long way to keeping the peace. Honey bees can become visibly disturbed when one of their sisters is suddenly killed inside the hive; they rush to her aid to inspect the damage. Another calming technique is to put a rag or dish towel over the exposed hive box to block sunlight, peeling it back to lift out only one frame at a time. Just be sure to use a smooth cloth, because honey bees can get their legs entangled in a fluffy, 'terry cloth' fabric.

Because so much of honey bee communication is through scent, beekeeping is not the time to put on perfume or moisturize with fragrant lotions. There are two reasons for this: you want to avoid luring the bees to inspect your body for nectar and, on the other hand, if they find the fragrance repellent, you might put them on high alert that something is interfering with their in-house pheromonal communication system. Eating a banana while beekeeping is also a terrible idea, as the scent mimics the alarm pheromone honey bees use to summon each other to defend the hive. Some beekeepers believe bees are put off by body odour, and

Keep bees as calm and placid as possible by using gentle movements and sparing puffs of smoke.

therefore make sure they are showered and their teeth are brushed before inspecting their hives.

Bee handling rules of behaviour boil down to this: do everything you can to avoid irritating the colony. There are certain things that honey bees really don't like, and beekeepers know to respect that. First and foremost, foul weather puts honey bees in a foul mood. It's never a good idea to open a hive in rain, high winds, the dark, or chilly temperatures. Opening the hive will release all the heat they've worked so hard to generate, setting them back and putting them in danger of freezing. A damp hive can turn mouldy and spread illness.

Another no-no is standing directly in front of the hive entrance, blocking the foraging bees' flight path. Within minutes, a traffic back-up of bees will collect in an impatient cloud behind the beekeeper. The bees will only wait so long before they'll have to get more forceful to make the beekeeper move out of the way.

Removing frames from a hive box can accidentally roll and smash bees, so there are tricks to avoid upsetting them this way. A common method is to use a frame hanger to suspend one or two frames outside the hive, giving the beekeeper room in the hive box to gently pry apart and manipulate the remaining frames. When examining honeycomb, beekeepers hold the wooden frames vertically like a window – and not horizontally like a tray. Holding frames flat, like a tray, can cause the nectar to spill out, which

A flat, metal hive tool may be used to scrape excess wax from the frames of the hive; afterwards, a good scrub using hot water will keep the frames clean and free of deposits. Dry them outside before replacing the frames.

will distress the bees that worked so hard to store it. A seasoned beekeeper also knows to hold frames over the exposed hive when inspecting them, so that the queen does not fall off. A sure-fire way to anger bees is to remove their queen.

Returning the frames to the hive also comes with some bee-calming best practices. Make sure the frames are returned in the exact order and orientation they were found in, and that they are fitted snugly against one another, ensuring the correct bee space to allow safe passage – but not so much room that the bees will start building wax bridges between frames. If there is misplaced or protruding wax on the frames, beekeepers should remove it before returning frames to the hive, to ensure they slide back in smoothly and don't entrap any of the honey bees.

Sometimes gentle handling is all that's needed while working with bees, but every hive is different and some colonies require smoke to get the bees to settle down. A good rule of thumb is to always have a lit smoker within reach, in a fire-safe metal bucket, in case it's needed. A small chef's blowtorch with a safety valve is also handy for quickly relighting the smoker if it goes out. When you've finished inspecting your hives, be sure to stuff a cork or a wad of green grass into the smoker spout, to snuff it out, and return the smoker to the metal bucket. Close the bucket with its metal lid, to prevent the smoker from starting a fire.

During hive inspections, a colony's tolerance for intrusion will start to wane, the longer the hive is open. Respecting the bees' wishes is a safety precaution that beekeepers learn with experience.

How to treat and guard against bee stings

When honey bees have had enough, they will give several warnings before stinging. They will first raise the volume of their collective buzz when they are starting to run out of patience. If that doesn't get the beekeeper's attention, guard bees will take a few buzz-flights near the beekeeper's head as a warning shot. If they need to up the ante, they will hurl themselves head-first into beekeeper's veil, as a sort of 'headbutt' to physically get the beekeeper to move away. Their last resort is to sacrifice themselves by stinging. They will aim for the mouth, nose and head, bending their abdomens into stinging position, emitting a high-pitched buzz of fury as they bury their barbed stingers and release venom from their poison glands. When the honey bee leaves its stinger behind, the tiny, white venom sack remains, pumping venom and plunging the stinger in further.

The main compound in honey bee venom is melittin, a peptide that kills tissue cells and causes pain at the sting site. In general, people who are not allergic to bees can tolerate 15 or fewer bee stings per kilogram of body weight. Quick napkin maths shows that a healthy 65 kilogram (143 lb) adult could safely withstand up to 975 stings. More than 1,500 stings, however, like the tragedies associated with Africanized honey bee attacks, can lead to death from liver and kidney failure.

If you are stung, smoke the sting site. Each time a bee stings, it deposits a bit of the alarm pheromone that smells like a ripe banana and informs other bees where to sting. Smoke, if applied quickly enough, can disrupt this pheromone signal.

Most of the bee's venom enters its victim within 20 seconds, so try to remove the stinger as quickly as possible to lessen the amount. But don't pinch it with your fingers because you'll only force more venom into the wound. Instead, carefully scrape it out sideways with a hive tool, credit card, the edge of a knife or a fingernail. Typically, the pain of a sting will lessen after a few minutes. It's not uncommon for the sting site to become itchy within a few hours and last a day or two. Some common kitchen remedies to reduce swelling are ice cubes or applying a poultice of mud or toothpaste. Kawakawa, an anti-inflammatory plant-based salve from New Zealand, is also soothing. Over-the-counter antihistamines in chewable tablets or liquid form can also help.

Localized swelling after a bee sting can look alarming and is sometimes confused with an allergic reaction. A sting on the wrist could cause a red and painful forearm that swells to the shape of a rugby ball. However, this kind of swelling at the sting site is considered a large local reaction, not a life-threatening allergy.

If, however, within minutes of being stung, areas of the body other than the sting site start reacting, this indicates the first signs of anaphylactic shock. If you have difficulty breathing, a sudden drop in blood pressure, or experience vertigo, blurry vision, hives, swollen lips or tongue, itchy palms or scalp, stomach cramps or diarrhoea, seek medical assistance immediately from trained professionals. Medical studies suggest that less than 2 per cent of adults and less than 1 per cent of children are allergic to honey bees, yet up to 14 per cent of beekeepers develop an extreme honey bee allergy due to their more frequent exposure to honey bee venom.

All beekeepers, whether they have been tested for honey bee allergy or not, should carry an EpiPen, or a similar emergency kit, containing injectable epinephrine – along with an antihistamine in either tablet or liquid form. Honey bee allergies can appear suddenly after years of beekeeping without any problems, and carrying these emergency supplies, along with a mobile phone, can protect not only the beekeeper but anyone who may come near to the hives. If someone is going into shock after a sting, administer an EpiPen injection to the person's thigh and call an ambulance. Injectors are now being developed with audible, step-by-step instructions for the person giving the emergency care, like the recorded instructions built into emergency defibrillators for cardiac arrest. An epinephrine injection may last only 15 minutes, so it's important to get to an accident and emergency department as quickly as possible, rather than waiting to see if the symptoms subside on their own. Most epinephrine injectors are sold in packages of two, in case a second dose is needed.

Hornet, wasp and bee stings account for about 70 deaths in the United States each year, according to the Centers for Disease Control, of which about 18 are thought to be caused by honey bees. Data is difficult to gather because it's often not known what type of stinging insect caused the fatality, and not all sting-related deaths are reported. A 2022 study, of sting-related deaths over a 23-year period in 32 European countries, found that fewer than two Europeans per million die annually of insect stings. The study did not differentiate between honey bees and other stinging insects.

For the rare few who do have a true honey bee allergy, there is no need to live in constant fear. Through a process called venom immunotherapy, allergists can desensitize patients to honey bee venom, preventing systemic reactions in nearly all patients. The procedure begins with injections of very low doses of venom that are gradually increased over two to six months until the dose matches the amount in a honey bee sting, approximately

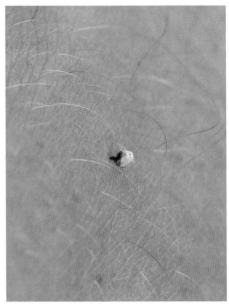

Top left: Bees sting only as a final defence, as stinging leads to their swift demise.

Top right: A bee sting leaves behind a tiny white venom sac, which should be removed from the skin as quickly and carefully as possible.

one-tenth of a gram. Venom immunotherapy stabilizes antibodies to honey bee venom in the patient's body, thereby protecting the person from going into anaphylactic shock. Once the patient can withstand the equivalent of a honey bee sting, they are switched to maintenance venom injections every four weeks. Each year, an additional week can be added between 'maintenance jabs' if the patient hasn't suffered any systemic reactions to a sting.

It's important to stick to the venom immunotherapy maintenance schedule, because people who have gone into anaphylactic shock from a bee sting have a much higher probability of a second occurrence if they do nothing – as high as 60 per cent. Just one missed venom allergy injection requires the allergist to start the desensitization procedure all over again, returning the patient to months of weekly, low-dose jabs until they build back up to 'full-sting-volume' venom tolerance.

Venom immunotherapy treatment has been shown to be highly effective, with an approximate 98 per cent success rate. While patients often stop maintenance therapy after five years, beekeepers are advised to continue routine immunotherapy visits for as long as they are in regular contact with honey bees. Allergists also encourage patients, who have completed venom desensitization treatment, to return every couple of years for skin tests – to make sure their honey bee allergy tests remain negative.

The business of beekeeping

There are up to 125,000 known beekeepers in the United States, and approximately 615,000 in Europe. The official tallies have always been rough estimates, though, because a good number of beekeepers intentionally stay under the radar, either for reasons of personal freedom or for keeping the peace in their communities.

Hobbyists, sideliners, and commercial beekeepers

By and large, more than 80 per cent of beekeepers are keen hobbyists – the garden and rooftop enthusiasts who keep beehives at home for the sheer joy of it. Typically, a hobbyist is someone who maintains a handful of hives for personal use; any money they make from honey or wax goes back into buying more equipment for their bees. A beekeeper can have up to 30 hives and still be considered a hobbyist.

Beekeepers who take it to the next level and supplement their income through beekeeping are considered 'sideliners' or 'part-time' beekeepers. They keep their day jobs, but make money on the side by selling honey, bees, queens and/or renting out their hives for pollination services. If they like public speaking, some

Here, a beekeeper has set up his apiary in their orchard – clearly as a sideline rather than as a full-scale commercial concern.

of them collect fees for hosting beekeeping workshops or speaking to companies and schools. There is also money to be made by collecting swarms from people's gardens or cutting them out of walls. Sideliners manage up to several hundred hives and make up roughly 13 per cent of all beekeepers.

Commercial beekeepers make a living from honey bees, running full-time beekeeping operations with at least 300 hives, and often with several thousand bee colonies. Only about 5 per cent of beekeepers are full-timers; they earn their money in more or less the same way that sideliners do, but on a much larger scale. Their main source of income is renting their beehives to farmers for pollination services, charging anywhere from £40 to £200 ($50 to $250) per hive, depending on the crop. Commercial beekeepers must spend a lot of time transporting their bees across vast distances in the middle of the night, traversing the country during the blooming season. Farmers rent the hives for several weeks at a time. Then, when one crop has finished blooming, the beekeeper moves their hives to the next farm in bloom. A full-time, migratory beekeeper can easily spend half the year on the road, hauling their bees from place to place.

In the United States, the journey typically starts in February at the orange groves in Florida or during the almond bloom in California's Central Valley. The bees then travel according to the blooming season, commuting between apple orchards, berry patches and clover fields. On the European continent, honey bee hives are transported to bright yellow rapeseed fields in April, then to acacia and lime orchards, and by the end of the summer they are making their last stops in fields of buckwheat and heather.

Commercial beekeepers invest in industrial honey-processing facilities, and much of the harvest and wax rendering is done by machines. Some common practices commercial beekeepers use to streamline their business include artificial feeding, artificial queen insemination, the use of antibiotics, and clipping the queen's wings to prevent swarming. Some industrial beekeepers, in areas with freezing temperatures, relocate their bees to warmer regions for the overwintering period. Some build warming huts or storage sheds for their bees, while others will cull their hives because it's cheaper to buy new bees in the spring than to feed their colonies throughout the cold season.

Finding the right land

Beekeeping can be a big business or a cottage kitchen industry. It all depends on what you want to do. Whether you plan to sell wax to artists, sell packages of bees or get your honey into the supermarkets, the one thing every beekeeper needs – in order to take their hobby up to the next level – is land with good, reliable foraging potential.

The first thing you will need to consider is where you'll keep a large apiary. A hive needs access to at least an acre of blooming plants in order to survive. The land will need a water source for the bees. If you are in a cold climate, how will you keep the bees warm? Will you be able to wrap the hives in blankets, do you have access to a warmer location, or will you need to build indoor storage?

If you own large swaths of unfettered open space, problems solved. If not, your choices are to buy, rent or barter for access to land with at least 2.6 square kilometres (1 mile²) of good bee forage, and preferably 13 square kilometres (5 miles²) or more.

One mutually beneficial arrangement in beekeeping is to rent cropland from an organic farmer to pollinate plants that support bees, which then can be harvested for cash. Beekeepers move their bees to the farm and plant what's needed to ensure year-long forage. The landowners, meanwhile, benefit from soil improvement, harvestable crops, free pollination services, and potential income if it's a crop that the government pays farmers to grow. The beekeeper has a safe, chemical-free place to keep all their beehives together, and which they can control for varietal and artisan honey crops that garner a higher retail price.

Another, more informal, method is to use 'outyards' – to keep bees in other people's gardens, undeveloped land, allotments or on their rooftops, often in exchange for jars of honey supplied to the property owner. The beekeeper is given access to the locations and drives to the various outyards on their own schedule to check the bees. The beekeeper has less control over what their bees are foraging, so it's important to inspect the outyard carefully before committing, to make sure there is enough for the bees to eat, that neighbours aren't using pesticides, that the area gets enough sun and that there's a viable means for removing heavy honey supers for harvesting – such as a lift, if the outyard is on a rooftop.

Some popular places for outyards are community gardens, parks and in the gardens of bee-friendly gardeners who are looking for a pollination boost. In urban areas, hidden outyards are commonly found in rooftop gardens atop hotels, museums, churches, restaurants and organic supermarkets.

Ultimately, depending on what you plan to do with your honey bees – sell honey, or pollen, propolis or the bees themselves – it matters which type of bees you select. Make sure you choose a bee strain that is known for focusing on the same product you wish to sell. The crowd-pleaser, however, has always been honey.

Growing your business

A good way to start selling honey is to set up a table at farmers' markets, food festivals or holiday fairs, after obtaining the required local permits. Especially at the beginning of a fledgeling business venture, this is a great way for beekeepers to meet potential customers and develop a marketing list.

As you grow your bee operation, there's always a tribe of mentors at the ready should you need advice. Joining a local beekeeping association is a great way to meet other beekeepers who have lots of ideas and experience in the beekeeping business. They share their knowledge at monthly bee club meetings, and some might even be willing to let you shadow them at work or act as an apprentice for a season as you think about your next steps.

A regional beekeeping club will also be up-to-date on the local and national legal requirements for starting a bee business. Be sure to consult not only with peers, but also with legal advisers and tax accountants when researching all the proper laws for creating a small business, limited (Ltd) company, non-profit or other business entity. Most beekeeping companies are required to hold a business licence, and many also require permits to keep bees, transport bees, sell honey and other hive products, and/or permits to rent land for the purposes of beekeeping. Beekeeping businesses should also acquire liability insurance to protect the company and its employees from any potential legal claims or damages. The insurance should cover the beekeeper, the bees and any property that may be damaged by bees.

Roadside honey stalls are a time-honoured way of selling hive produce.

DISEASES, PARASITES, PESTS AND PREDATORS

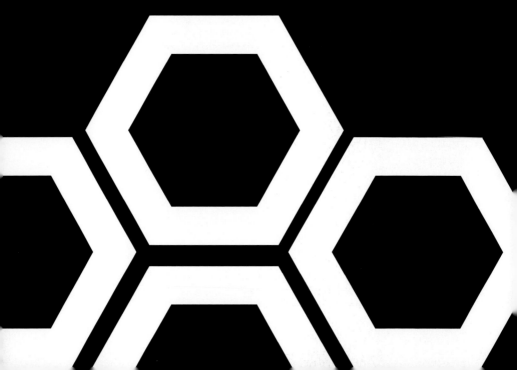

Diseases, Parasites, Pests and Predators

Beekeepers are taught and encouraged to undertake at least two full disease and pest inspections each year: one as the first spring inspection and the second after the summer honey has been removed. There are two notifiable diseases, American foulbrood (AFB) and European foulbrood (EFB), and two notifiable pests, *Aethina tumida* – the small hive beetle (SHB) – and the *Tropilaelaps* mite species.

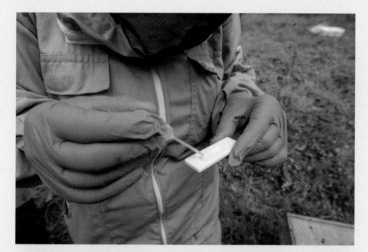

Previous page: An Apiary Inspector removes larvae to check for the presence of foulbrood.

Left: An Apiary Inspector carrying out a lateral flow test (top) and other checks for notifiable diseases (bottom) such as European and American foulbrood.

DISEASE MONITORING AND INSPECTION

While the US Department of Agriculture (USDA) conducts monitoring and research to help protect bees, the United States does not have a federally directed bee disease monitoring and inspection programme. Instead, this is the responsibility of the individual states, so official programmes vary considerably: some states have highly developed bee monitoring systems in place, with teams of Apiary Inspectors, while others have much more patchy programmes. In some states, it can even be down to local beekeeping associations, and their volunteers, to respond to local outbreaks of disease and other bee-related incidents. Pressure is mounting for a nationwide programme or collaborative network of programmes. Several bee diseases are reportable/notifiable (see the following pages), either to state programmes or to the USDA.

In the UK, the Department of Environment, Farming and Rural Affairs (Defra) established, some time ago, the National Bee Unit (NBU), of which the aim is to ensure the health of honey bees and thus successful pollination of crops. The NBU has Regional Bee Inspectors (RBIs) in each region of England and Wales (Scotland makes its own arrangements). Each RBI manages a small team of Seasonal Bee Inspectors who work throughout the active beekeeping season. The Bee Inspector's role is to inspect colonies of honey bees for notifiable pests and diseases, and they carry a warrant and have absolute authority to inspect any colonies.

There is no compulsory national register of beekeepers in the UK. However, the NBU operate a website, BeeBase (www.nationalbeeunit.com), which is free to all and contains a good deal of useful information as well as training materials. To use BeeBase you have to register. So, in reality, most beekeepers are registered, and hence this acts in lieu of a national register.

Diseases

American foulbrood

WHAT IS AMERICAN FOULBROOD?
American foulbrood (AFB) is a disease of capped brood caused by a Gram-positive spore-forming species of bacteria, *Paenibacillus larvae*. Despite its name, it is found globally and is a notifiable disease that must be reported to neighbouring beekeepers and state monitors in the USA. Not only is AFB highly contagious, but the spores remain viable on beekeeping equipment for many years and are present in much of the honey on supermarket shelves. Beekeepers are encouraged to burn any second-hand frames they are given and to thoroughly blowtorch second-hand wooden hive boxes.

Conservative estimates suggest that fewer than one per cent of honey bee colonies in the United States are infected with AFB. Nevertheless, the disease causes more than £4 million ($5 million) worth of loss to the US economy, and when a beekeeper suspects that it is present in one of their colonies, there is a strict protocol that must be followed.

IDENTIFYING AMERICAN FOULBROOD
When inspecting for AFB, beekeepers are looking at sealed brood that may be sunken or greasy, or have perforated cappings. The perforations will be off centre and are a sign the workers are aware from the pheromonal signature that something is wrong in the cell. They attempt to open the cell to inspect the pupa or remove it. The adults will eat a melted-down pupa, thus ensuring the disease is further transmitted.

AFB invades the larva after capping and attacks all of the internal organs, and the pupa then dies from something akin to sepsis. An affected pupa will change from pearly white to light brown and will slowly darken. It appears melted, and in the early stages the remains will 'rope' if a matchstick is inserted halfway down the cell and lifted about 1 cm (½ in) or so straight up. In later stages, the pupal remains reduce, harden, and turn to a blackish scale that cannot be removed. These scales will catch the light and can often be seen in the gravity bottom of the cells.

The spores of *Paenibacillus larvae* are fed to developing larvae by the nurse bees. They pass immediately to the gut where they germinate rapidly. The larvae die and nurse bees ingest the spores when they clean out the cells. The honey stores in an infected colony become contaminated and, as the colony weakens, the honey can be robbed by nearby, strong colonies. In this way, the disease can spread throughout an apiary.

Sometimes beekeepers feed infected honey to their colonies, inadvertently transmitting AFB. The simple rule is never to feed honey to the bees unless it came from that colony. Swarms from a colony with an early infection can arrive in an apiary and begin a cycle of infection. Swarms need to be kept in an isolation apiary until their health status has been confirmed.

HOW TO TREAT AMERICAN FOULBROOD

This disease is prevalent across many countries and is disastrous for the beekeeper concerned. Left alone, it will kill the colony but also infect nearby colonies through drifting and robbing. As the colony weakens, neighbours will take advantage of the situation and rob, thus infecting themselves.

In the United States, treatment with oxytetracycline is legal and practised widely. This suppresses the disease but does not cure it, and some beekeepers are finding that colonies are becoming resistant to the antibiotic. Guidance in the United States is to treat hives with three applications of powdered oxytetracycline five days apart in the spring and autumn. Colonies are treated prophylactically, but success depends on the level of infection of the colony and the mortality rate of the bees due to the suppression of the gut microbiome. Oxytetracycline is sold as Terramycin™ soluble powder – specifically as a control for AFB. It is advertised as preventing AFB, rather than curing it.

A brood comb infected with American foulbrood.

In some US states and Canadian provinces, there is a requirement that infected hives be incinerated. Should this become necessary, please use the following method:

1. Close the hive so that the bees cannot escape.
2. Dig a fire hole and start a small fire.
3. Put in the hive, together with any associated tools, clothing, and so on.
4. Once the fire has died out, bury the ashes and the honey (which won't burn).

In the UK, the beekeeper must immediately impose a voluntary standstill on their affected apiary, so nothing can be removed from any hive in that apiary. AFB is usually identified in the colony by contacting a Bee Inspector, because very few beekeepers have seen it in their colonies. If the signs are those of AFB, the Bee Inspector uses a lateral flow device to confirm the disease. If the disease is confirmed by the Bee Inspector, they will impose a statutory standstill, which is effective for six weeks. After six weeks, all colonies in the apiary are reinspected and, if no disease is found, the standstill order is lifted. Once AFB has been found, the Bee Inspector, using the information on BeeBase, will notify all beekeepers in a five-kilometre (3-mile) radius and inspect each colony within that area.

The Bee Inspector will kill the bees using petrol and the frames will be burned in a pit. The boxes will be thoroughly scorched to make sure bacteria do not remain in the corners and crevices. If the hives are polystyrene, they will be cleaned using a bleach containing ammonia. The beekeeper has no choice regarding the destruction and scorching as the legislation is strictly enforced. It is because of this that AFB is still relatively rare in the UK.

All beginner beekeepers are taught how to recognize healthy brood and what to do if they suspect their brood is diseased.

Note: the above protocol is the same if small hive beetles or *Tropilaelaps* were to be found.

European foulbrood

WHAT IS EUROPEAN FOULBROOD?

European foulbrood (EFB) is notifiable in the United States, the UK and Australia, although not in many European countries. The causative organism of EFB is *Melissococcus plutonius*, a non-spore-forming bacterium that attacks young larvae in the early stages. It is an interesting bacterium because it lodges in the gut of the bee and competes with the bee for food.

European foulbrood is often found in spring. In early spring, the colony is building up after the winter and many of the older winter bees have died. The queen is laying well, and the workers are bringing in whatever is available in the way of nectar or pollen as well as feeding the queen and the larvae. At this time of year, there is more brood than adult bees and food is still scarce, so, in most colonies, the larvae get just enough to eat. The bacteria that are in the gut get preference and take the food. The larvae die of starvation. The workers are too busy to carry out undertaking duties, so the dead and diseased larvae can be found in the cells.

However, in late spring and summer, there may be an abundance of nectar and many young bees in the colony for feeding the developing larvae. In this situation, there may be

A brood comb showing dead larvae following infection with European foulbrood.

enough food for the larvae and the bacteria so the larvae will survive and develop into adult workers. The colony will have plentiful workers to carry out all of the necessary work and undertaking duties will be done. The beekeeper may well see a diseased larva one day only for it to have disappeared the next. The undertakers will have removed it. For this reason, it is easier to find EFB in the early spring than in a full colony in summer.

The adults that were infected with EFB bacteria as larvae will be carrying the disease and will pass it on to young larvae when they feed them. Colonies with EFB will have dead larvae that have lost their striations and are dull white. They will have died at peculiar angles in their cells, because they have tried moving around looking for food. They will look melted and be 'lying ill at ease' in their cells.

EFB is notifiable, and the beekeeper must instigate a voluntary standstill if it is suspected and must notify the Aviary/Bee Inspector immediately. However, the treatment can be very different than that for AFB because there are options depending on the degree of infection and the time of year, and to some extent on the wishes of the beekeeper.

In spring, if the colony is large and the degree of infection small, then the Apiary/Bee Inspector may suggest carrying out a shook swarm, which involves shaking all of the bees onto clean, sterilized comb, with clean hive parts, and the destruction of the old comb. The colony is then reinspected six weeks later to check for the disease. If the beekeeper agrees to this, it is carried out by the Apiary/Bee Inspector. The beekeeper can, however, opt for destruction. If the colony is small or badly infected, or if it is late in the beekeeping calendar, then the Inspector, too, may opt for destruction. The beekeeper must comply, and the same procedure as for AFB (above) must be followed.

Legally, the antibiotic oxytetracycline can be used with the shook swarm. This is used regularly in the United States, but in the UK the National Bee Unit (NBU) has decided not to use it because it suppresses the disease rather than cures it. So, although it is legal in the UK, it is either rarely or never used.

Above: Terramycin™ is an antibiotic powder used (when mixed with sugar) to prevent both American and European foulbrood.

Below: An Inspector extracts larvae for use with a diagnostic kit.

Chalkbrood

Chalkbrood is a fungal disease of sealed brood whose causative organism is *Ascophaera apis*. It is generally considered to be a minor brood disease and is thought to be in every colony. Although the fungal spores are present, the signs usually show only when the colony is under stress. In times of inclement weather or when there are insufficient worker bees to feed the larvae well, then signs of the disease may be present. What is clear is that there are no hard-and-fast rules because we are not always aware that a colony is stressed.

It has been suggested that the fungal spores enter three- or four-day-old larvae via their food or through the infected mouthparts of the nurse bees. The spores thrive in temperatures of 30 °C (86 °F) and high levels of carbon dioxide. Growth begins in the hind gut where long, thread-like strands of the vegetive phase eventually break out.

A small occurrence of chalkbrood is easy to miss, as the early signs will be no more than a tiny, off-centre perforation in the capping. The diseased pupa is emitting the wrong pheromones and the workers realize there is a problem and attempt to open the capping and remove the diseased pupa. The infected pupa will die,

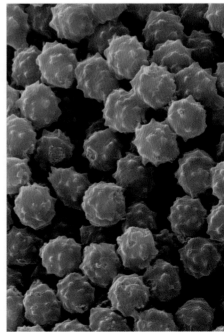

and initially the remains will resemble a dried-out, slightly fluffy piece of white chalk. The pupa has died with its head against the capping and the mouthparts can be clearly seen as yellow against the white background. The whole thing resembles a poached egg.

The fungus produces spores that eventually cause the remains to harden and turn from white to grey and then black. These hard, black pellets resemble mummies, can be removed by the bees and are often found on the floor of the hive.

There is currently no treatment for chalkbrood, but beekeepers are encouraged to practise good apiary hygiene, avoid situations and manipulations that stress the bees, use dry apiary sites and change old combs at least every three years. Queens should never be bred from colonies showing signs of chalkbrood.

Stonebrood

Stonebrood is a rare disease that can affect both adults and larvae and is caused by the fungi *Aspergillus flavus* or *Aspergillus fumigatus*. Affected larvae turn into stone-like mummies that are either pale yellow or green, whereas the abdomens of affected adults can become mummified.

Nosemosis

Nosema is a single-celled, parasitic, microsporidian fungal pathogen that attacks the epithelial lining (thin outer layer) of the gut of the bee. The two variants, *Nosema ceranae* and *Nosema apis*, operate in a similar fashion in that they both invade the cells lining the midgut and are both resistant to changes in temperature and humidity. The signs of infection are quite different for each, but both are potentially fatal pathogens and will, if left untreated, eventually destroy the colony. The infection is called either nosema disease or nosemosis.

The dormant *Nosema* spores invade the epithelial cells lining in the midgut and multiply rapidly. These epithelial cells usually produce the enzymes that digest proteins – so, because spores prevent enzyme production, infected bees are unable to digest the pollen that is necessary for the production of brood food. Bees infected with *Nosema* will therefore only be of use to the colony if they become foragers early. This leads to a shortage of house bees to feed both the queen and the larvae. At the height of the season, the queen can lay her own weight in eggs each day, but only if she is constantly fed easily digestible royal jelly. If the queen is fed less, she will lay fewer eggs. Nosemosis also represents a waste of resources for the colony and leads to an imbalance between house bees and foragers.

Far left: The hard, black, 'mummified' remains of pupae infected with foulbrood are often discarded by the bees on the hive floor.

Near left: Close-up of spores of the *Aspergillus* fungi.

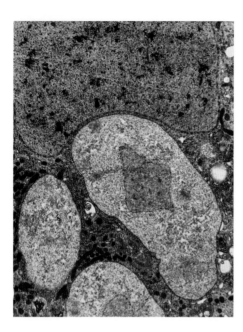

Transmission electron micrograph of *Nosema apis* intracellularly in contact with the nucleus of its bee host.

Within a few days of infection, each affected epithelial cell will rupture and release over 30 million *Nosema* spores into the excretory system to be shed in the faeces. Newly emerged workers will not be infected and within hours will be actively cleaning cells. These young bees on cleaning duties ingest the spores in the faeces and are immediately infected. The spores now germinate, produce spores, and the cycle continues.

Infections of *Nosema ceranae* and *Nosema apis* present differently and usually at different times of the year. *Nosema apis* is usually found at an early spring inspection. The colony often has tell-tale signs of dysentery because the bees' rectums have been unable to hold the loose faeces caused by all of the ruptured cells, and defecation inside the hive has been the only option during winter confinement. The colony fails to build up at the same rate as others in the apiary and appears to be short of house bees. It appears to play a role in colony collapse disorder (CCD). At this stage, the colony will be weak and likely to be robbed by foragers from stronger colonies, thus enabling the disease to be transferred to the robbing colony. A single spore is sufficient to cause infection, and within days it will have multiplied to several million spores in the gut of the bee.

A *Nosema ceranae* infection mainly affects Asian honey bees, but it has been found in the United States as well as in Europe.

The infection rarely causes dysentery, however it is a contributing factor in colony depopulation.

It is thought that the *Nosema ceranae* pathogen is more virulent and outcompetes *Nosema apis*. However, it remains impossible to distinguish between the variants other than by using complex equipment unavailable to beekeepers. Research suggests that in most colonies with nosemosis the dominant organism is now *Nosema ceranae*.

An infection with *Nosema ceranae* can appear to be asymptomatic, although the colony will have a declining population and, as a result, less nectar being collected. The colony can suddenly succumb in the summer months at the height of the season.

The only treatment for nosemosis is Fumidil-B™, a proprietary medicine containing the antibiotic fumagillin. This effective remedy is no longer available in the UK as it has not been approved by the Veterinary Medicines Directorate. It is, however, still available and widely used in the United States where it is sold as a feeding supplement to be added to a syrup feed. One level teaspoon of Fumidil-B™ added to 17 litres (4.5 gal) of strong sugar solution and fed prophylactically in the autumn is said to prevent nosemosis.

In the UK, the recommended treatment for nosemosis is to transfer the colony to clean comb as gently as possible. Honey bee pathologist Leslie Bailey designed a system that involves allowing the infected bees to move up into a new brood box containing clean, sterilized comb at their own pace. The bees cannot be shaken as in a shook swarm, as this would cause them to empty their infected rectal contents onto the new comb.

Dead bees covered with dust and mites, following a *Nosema* infection.

Parasites

Varroa destructor

The *Varroa* mite was first detected in the United States in 1987, in the UK in 1992, and Australia in 2022, although it is likely to have been present for some time in these countries by these dates.

The *Varroa* mite is a parasitic mite that can reproduce only in honey bee brood and has a preference for drone brood because their development period is longer than that of workers. It developed along with the Asian honey bee (*Apis ceranae*), and they have coadapted. The pupae of the Asian honey bee have a shorter period of development so that the mite does not have time to produce more than one mated female mite from each worker cell. Also, the Asian honey bee has greater grooming and mite removal behaviour. The Western honey bee (*Apis mellifera*) has no such defences and subsequently its colonies succumb to mite infestations and the associated viruses. Some beekeepers attempting to breed for hygienic behaviour in bees are having some success, but are losing many colonies to parasitic mite syndrome (see below) in the meantime. Hygienic bees will detect and remove infested pupae and the associated mites.

The mite feeds on the fat body of the bee and, in doing so, transmits viruses. A colony badly infected with *Varroa* and the associated viruses is said to have varroosis, or parasitic mite syndrome (PMS), which usually leads to the death of the colony. Signs of PMS are worker bees dying as they are emerging from their cells. They are often seen with their proboscis protruding.

Because the larvae of honey bees are entirely dependent upon the adult workers, they produce a number and range of pheromones indicating their age and nutritional requirements to enable the workers to attend to their needs. These brood ester pheromones (BEP) consist of ten fatty acid esters, four of which are used to inform the workers when the larva is ready to pupate and must therefore be capped. A combination of methyl palmitate, methyl oleate and methyl linoleate increases in quantity when the larva is ready to be capped. The problem arises because at slightly lower levels these same esters signal to the *Varroa* mite that it is time to enter the cell and hide underneath the food store until capping is complete.

Foundress mites (pregnant females) lay several eggs but the first is always a male. Subsequent eggs are female. The mites pass quickly through several nymph stages and, when mature, the male mates with his sisters and dies. The male *Varroa* mite thus spends

A bee researcher removes a *Varroa destructor* mite from a bee.

A reddish-brown female *Varroa* mite on an infested bee.

his entire life inside a sealed cell. The adult female mite is reddish brown, flat and roughly oval in shape. It is, on average, approximately 1–2 millimetres ($\frac{1}{16}$ in) long and 1–2 millimetres ($\frac{1}{16}$ in) wide. Males are smaller, white and spend their entire life inside the brood cell.

The foundress mite prefers to enter drone cells rather than worker cells because the drone larvae is capped for ten days, thus giving additional time for the new female mites to mature and mate with their brother. The recently mated females attach themselves to the emerging bee as she leaves her cell and immediately start feeding on her fat body.

During feeding the mites transmit several damaging viruses. Thus, the damage is twofold: a depletion in sustenance because of the direct feeding, and a transmission of several damaging viruses. The *Varroa* mite is now endemic in the United States and the UK. The NBU assumes that all colonies are infested with the mite and beekeepers are asked to opt out on BeeBase if their colonies are mite free.

Beekeeping authorities and organizations issue copious advice to beekeepers about treatments for *Varroa*. They strongly advise a system of integrated pest management whereby the mite infestation is measured and various treatments are given depending on the time of year, the size of the colony, and whether or not honey is present. Integrated pest management combines biotechnical methods with approved veterinary medicines in the hope of keeping mite levels below the economic injury level.

It is now recognized that it is more or less impossible to rid a colony of *Varroa* mites. The western honey bee, *Apis mellifera*, did not develop along with the mites and has no natural methods of defence. The recommendation is that beekeepers attempt to keep the number of mites below the economic injury level, which for the average colony is thought to be 1,000 mites.

This, however, does not take account of the damage done by viruses (see page 227), the effects of which are aggravated by the presence of *Varroa* mites.

The acarine mite

The acarine or tracheal mite, *Acarapis woodi*, is a parasite of adult bees that causes the disease acarosis. The mite invades the first thoracic spiracle of an adult bee and lodges in the attached tracheal breathing tube. This is the largest spiracle and has a cap that does not completely close. Female mites lay six or seven eggs in the trachea, which take about 14 days to hatch. The young mites exit the trachea via the spiracle and hang on to a nearby hair on the bee's thorax. Bees are often congested within the hive and pass each other closely and frequently. The young mites easily transfer to the spiracle of an adjacent bee less than ten days old. They are attracted by the breathing movements and enter the trachea through the open first spiracle. The mites appear unable to enter bees older than ten days.

There appear to be no outward signs of acarosis, although it shortens the life of the bee and can reduce colony build-up in the spring.

Colour-enhanced scanning electron micrograph of an acarine mite (*Acarapis woodi*).

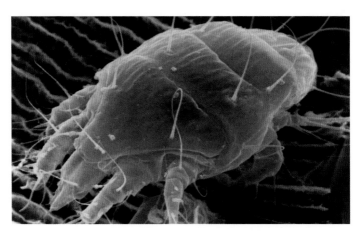

Acarine mites can only be detected by removing the head of a dead bee and dissecting out the two thoracic trachea using a dissecting microscope. If the mites are present, the trachea will appear stained with small brown or black spots. A healthy trachea will be pearly white throughout.

Infestations of acarine mites are now quite rare because of the use of medicines for the *Varroa* mites. The same integrated pest management system used against *Varroa* has successfully killed these mites. However, there is an increasing number of beekeepers wishing to rear hygienic bees and avoid the use of varroacides. In some of these colonies, infestations of acarine mites are returning.

Tropilaelaps mite species

Native to Asia, *Tropilaelaps* mite species are parasites of the giant honey bees of Southeast Asia. There are two species (*Tropilaelaps clareae* and *Tropilaelaps mercedesae*) that can also parasitize European honey bees (*Apis mellifera*) and reproduce on their brood, posing a serious threat to honey bee health. As yet, however, the mites have not been detected in Europe, the United States, Australia or New Zealand. Accidental introduction is an ever-present possibility and vigilance is required. The presence of *Tropilaelaps* mite species is notifiable.

Tropilaelaps mites are visible to the naked eye on both brood and adult bees: busy, reddish brown mites around 1–2 millimetres (1⁄16 in) long and 0.5–1 millimetres (less than 1⁄16 in) wide. Adult mites lay eggs in the brood cells of developing larvae that hatch and feed on developing honey bees. As with *Varroa,* the presence of *Tropilaelaps* mites exacerbates the transmission of honey bee viruses (see page 227), causing irregular brood, deformed honey bees, and, eventually, colony decline.

Light micrograph of the parasitic mite *Tropilaelaps*.

Viruses

A bee showing the distinctive signs of deformed wing virus, often carried by *Varroa* mites.

Viruses are small pieces of genetic material and proteins that cannot exist outside of the cells of their host. They can reproduce using only the organisms and structures inside these cells. They can adapt quickly to changing conditions and produce variants. Viruses are present naturally in all living things, including honey bees. Most viruses cause no visible signs under normal conditions, but stressful situations such as congestion, damp, significant temperature or weather variations, or an additional parasite may cause the adverse effect.

Some of the most common viruses of honey bees have been present in colonies for many years without causing major problems. However, these viruses have become more virulent with the spread of the *Varroa* mite, and it is certainly possible that the deformed wing virus (DWV) replicates in the mites. If DWV has evolved a mechanism for reproducing in *Varroa* mites, then this implies that each mite can act as a reservoir for the virus.

Before *Varroa*, the virus could be transmitted only vertically from adult worker to larvae or through the queen to the egg. With the arrival of the mites, the virus can now be transmitted horizontally between hosts separated by time and space. In other words, the virus can now spread easily between individual adult bees and between colonies. This has allowed the virus to extend its reach.

It is definitely the case that, since the arrival of *Varroa*, more honey bees have presented with the outward signs of viruses such as DWV and chronic bee paralysis virus (CBPV), and it is firmly believed that the increased incidence and virulence are vectored by the mites.

Deformed wing virus (DWV)

Deformed wings and shrunken abdomens are often seen in newly emerged workers or drones when the colony has a high *Varroa* load. It is caused by an RNA virus whose main vector is the *Varroa* mite. Obviously, the bees cannot fly or contribute to the colony in any way and will die within a few days. This not only represents a waste of resources but it also leaves the colony with fewer bees.

In serious infestations, the *Varroa* mites can be seen on the backs of bees or walking from bee to bee. At this point, immediate intervention is required if the colony is to survive. The beekeeper should check the daily mite drop – that is, how many mites fall naturally to the floor each day.

The smaller bee at the centre of this image has a shorter, shrunken abdomen. This indicates the presence of *Varroa* mites in the colony.

Chronic bee paralysis virus (CBPV)

CBPV is found in every continent where honey bees are present and is not thought to be spread by *Varroa* mites. It was first identified by Leslie Bailey at the Rothamsted Experimental Station (now Rothamsted Research), UK, in the 1960s. It is a disease of all stages in the life cycle of the bee, but the signs are found only in adults. Dr Bailey identified two types or syndromes:

Type one CBPV is characterized by: trembling in adult bees, an inability to fly, extended abdomens and dislocated wings (K wing). Infected bees are frequently found on the top bars of a hive where they do not respond to smoke, or in front of the hive climbing up grass stems.

Type two CBPV, known as black hairless syndrome in the United States, produces 'little black robbers' – infected bees that have been attacked by nest mates and have had their hairs bitten off. These bees are unacceptable to their nest mates because they are producing the 'wrong' pheromones. The bees appear smaller than their peers because of their lack of hair and their shiny and greasy appearance. If they try to return to the hive, they are attacked by the guard bees and hence zigzag in flight in an attempt to gain entrance. They behave as robber bees.

It is now recognized that both syndromes are caused by the same CBPV and that signs of both can appear together in the same colony. There is therefore no longer any point in differentiating between type one and type two.

In recent years, CBPV has become a major threat to honey bee colonies globally. In severe infections, piles of dead and crawling bees, sometimes inches thick, can be found outside the hive entrance. It is clear that the bees have died at or near the same time, so this is not a situation of natural losses.

When a bee is first infected with CBPV, the virus lodges within the brain and uses the brain for its own reproductive purposes. It is this loss of brain use that causes the shaking and paralysis. An infected and paralyzed bee can harbour several trillion virus particles in its brain within a very short time after infection.

CBPV is transmitted horizontally from bee to bee, either by bees brushing against each other or by faecal transfer during cleaning duties. Thus, large, populous colonies contained by winter or a long period of summer rain can rapidly succumb. In its early stages, CBPV can also be transferred from colony to colony by drifting or robbing.

Sometimes, the colony can recover from the viral infection, but the loss of so many adult bees means that the colony is no longer viable and will be lost. Currently, there is no known treatment other than caging the queen and shaking the bees out so that only the flying bees can return to the colony.

Acute bee paralysis virus (ABPV)

Like CBPV, acute bee paralysis virus (ABPV) is associated with the *Varroa* mite. ABPV is distinguished from CBPV by the length of time it takes to kill the infected bee as this virus can kill in less than five days. As usual, the larvae ingest the virus when fed by an infected nurse bee. A high dose of the virus will kill the bee, but if only a small amount is transferred then the larva will survive to adulthood and continue the cycle of infection while carrying out its feeding duties.

Israeli acute paralysis virus is related to ABPV and was implicated in colony collapse disorder (CCD) in the United States in 2007. A further paralysis virus has been named slow bee paralysis virus (SBPV) because it kills the bees slowly, taking about two weeks.

Sacbrood virus

Sacbrood is caused by a virus in the *Iflavirus* genus, which is thought to be present in most colonies. US bacteriologist G. F. White inoculated larvae with extracts from diseased larvae in 1917 and identified that the disease was caused by a virus. It was present in many countries but thought to be absent in the UK. It was not absent, but simply called by the name of addled brood. In 1964, Leslie Bailey at the Rothamsted Research Centre in England identified the sacbrood virus.

Sacbrood is a larval disease that prevents the final pupal moult. The final pupal skin remains intact and forms a fluid-filled sac containing the dead pupa, the ecdysial (moulting) fluid and millions of the virus. The dead pupa is lying on its back with its head nearest to the capping. It gives the appearance of a Chinese slipper. Usually, the capping will have been pierced by the workers because it is emitting the wrong pheromone. The virus does not remain active for long once the pupa has died, but very young adult bees cleaning the cells ingest some of the infected ecdysial fluid and the virus multiplies in the hypopharyngeal, or brood food, glands in their head.

The disease can appear to die out in the winter because the dead pupae have been removed and there are few, if any, young larvae to be fed. However, the virus remains active in the hypopharyngeal

Dead larvae infected with the sacbrood virus. The virus remains infectious to worker bees for a few days after the larvae's death.

glands of the adult bees, and in spring is transferred to the larvae as they are fed. The adults show no signs of the disease, and it can seem to the beekeeper that sacbrood has only just appeared.

Infected adult bees that forage for pollen add secretions to their pollen loads. When this pollen is then used as a component of brood food, it passes the virus to the larvae. Most infected adults, however, stop eating pollen and become foragers early, thus representing a loss to the colony. Their shortened lives help to contain the disease.

Sacbrood is usually found in the spring when the remaining winter bees are carrying out whatever needs doing in the colony. When tested, most colonies carry the virus even if the signs of the disease are absent. After a few days, the virus in the dead larvae becomes inactive – but early in their life the worker bees clean cells and thus ingest the still-infected fluid.

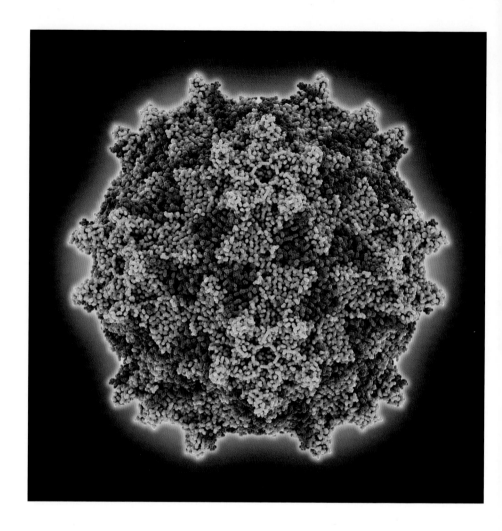

Black queen cell virus (BQCV)

Black queen cell virus (BQCV) is associated with both variants of *Nosema*, although the path of transmission is not known. But nosemosis affects the gut of the bee, and it has been suggested that a damaged gut lining may allow the virus to enter more easily. A colony may be asymptomatic for nosemosis, but the virus will show as a slightly shrivelled and black queen cell. BQCV occurs most frequently when queen rearing is carried out early in the season and larvae have been transferred to cell cups by grafting. The virus is clearly present and has been passed to the queen larva.

Molecular model of the black queen cell virus.

Pests and predators

There are many pests and predators of honey bee colonies, although they may differ across the globe because of the climate, terrain and available species.

Wax moths

In both the United States and UK, there are two species of wax moths that infest honey bee colonies – the greater and the lesser wax moth. The life cycle of each is similar in that they progress through egg, larva, pupa and adult, although the damage caused by the two species varies enormously. In nature, the greater and the lesser wax moths perform a valuable cleaning service, clearing out diseased and damaged combs from dead or abandoned hives and nests.

GREATER WAX MOTH

The greater wax moth (*Galleria mellonella*) is the more destructive but can usually attack only weak or diseased colonies or stored comb. A strong colony can and will destroy the adult moths and their larvae.

The female wax moth will fly into a beehive at night and lay hundreds of eggs in crevices and corners, where they remain unnoticed by the house bees. When the egg hatches, the larva immediately travels to an area of wax to feed on the wax and any impurities in it, such as larval skins. At this stage, they are easily distinguished from the larvae of the small hive beetle (*Aethina tumida*) by the absence of spines along their back. After about three days, their abdominal legs appear and they continue to grow

A greater wax moth (*Galleria mellonella*) at rest on a piece of bark.

The devastating
effects of the larvae of
the greater wax moth
on a comb are all too
plain to see.

and develop. The interesting thing about wax moth larvae is that their rate of development is dependent on their environment. The availability of food is an obvious determinant, but so is temperature and humidity. If food is plentiful and the temperature ideal, the larva can double in weight every day in the first ten days.

Unfortunately, conditions inside a beehive are ideal for wax moth larval development, enabling all seven moults to occur in about seven weeks. At this point, the larva will be approximately two centimetres (¾ in) long and light grey in colour. Larvae of the greater wax moth burrow underneath the wax cappings, causing the developing honey bee pupae to be exposed. These straight lines of exposed pupae are known as bald brood. But the damage does not stop there. The discarded skins, silk pupal cases and the faeces of the wax moth destroy the comb, leaving a nasty layer of debris.

As the greater wax moth larva reaches maturity, it causes further damage by burrowing into the walls of the hive, leaving a characteristic boat-shaped indentation. The larva then pupates in the burrow. This is unsightly in a wooden hive but can destroy a polystyrene hive because the burrowing can go completely through the wall.

The pupal stage can last from a week to 50 days depending on the conditions within the hive. The adult moth when it emerges is just over 1.5 centimetres (½ in) long and light grey in colour. The adult will leave the hive in order to mate and the process is repeated.

Greater wax moth larvae do not like the light and will move quickly to hide if the hive is opened. However, if the hive tool is tapped on the comb, the larvae will pop out of any cells they are occupying. They can then be destroyed.

LESSER WAX MOTH

The lesser wax moth (*Achroia grisella*) is smaller than its cousin the greater wax moth and will not be tolerated in most colonies. It causes much less damage within a hive but can devastate stored comb.

Deterrence and treatment

Beekeepers can deter wax moths by general apiary hygiene. Discarded brace or burr comb and wax scrapings from the crown board or floor should be placed in a sealed container and removed from the apiary. Combs should never be left out in the apiary as, apart from robbing, they will immediately attract any moths in the area. Colonies that have died should be sealed and removed as soon as possible. Good apiary hygiene and keeping strong, healthy colonies is usually enough to keep the moths at bay.

Most beekeepers treat their stored brood and super combs with 80 per cent ethanoic (acetic) acid over the winter period, which will kill all stages of wax moth; however, ethanoic acid is not approved for wax moth control in the United States, where paradichlorobenzene (PDB) and aluminium phosphide (Phostoxin) are used instead. PDB is registered for use in protecting stored comb, but it cannot be used for wax moth control in live bee colonies, nor is it approved for the protection of comb honey. There are restrictions on the use of PDB in certain US states, however. In 2022, the EPA approved the use of a biological wax moth treatment called Certan, which uses *Bacillus thuringiensis* (Bt), a bacterium commonly found in nature that selectively kills wax moths at the larval stage.

The small hive beetle (SHB) – *Aethina tumida*. The beetle is a recent and as yet rare interloper in the hives of Europe and the United States but can seriously weaken colonies.

Small hive beetle (SHB)

The small hive beetle – *Aethina tumida* – is native to southern Africa where it is well established and causes little harm. African bees migrate, leaving comb, brood, and pests in the hive, thus partially alleviating the problem. Observations of *Apis scutellata* colonies in Kenya show little disturbance to egg laying or foraging despite the presence of numerous beetles in each hive.

The situation with western honey bees is very different because *Apis mellifera* is unused to dealing with such disturbance and they have no habit of migration. It has recently spread and now poses a significant threat to honey bee colonies in North America, though it has yet to reach the UK. It is now a problem in many US states, including Florida, South Carolina, Georgia and Utah, since it was first found in several areas of the southwestern region in 1996. The SHB was found in Calabria in southern Italy in 2014, although the Italian government immediately instigated a largely successful identification and eradication programme. While the beetle has yet to arrive in the UK, the beekeeping community is expecting it and is prepared. As in the United States, it is listed as one of the statutory notifiable pests that must be reported to the authorities if it is suspected or found in a colony.

One of the problems with eradication is the pupation stage in the soil. Even if the adult beetles and larvae can be removed from the hive, the surrounding soil needs to be sprayed with an insecticide to kill the pupae.

Female beetles locate honey bee colonies by scent and are able to fly up to five kilometres (3 miles) to a colony. Once inside, the beetle lays a large number of eggs in crevices away from the brood nest, usually in places where the bees are unlikely to go. Sometimes, however, the eggs are laid directly on the brood

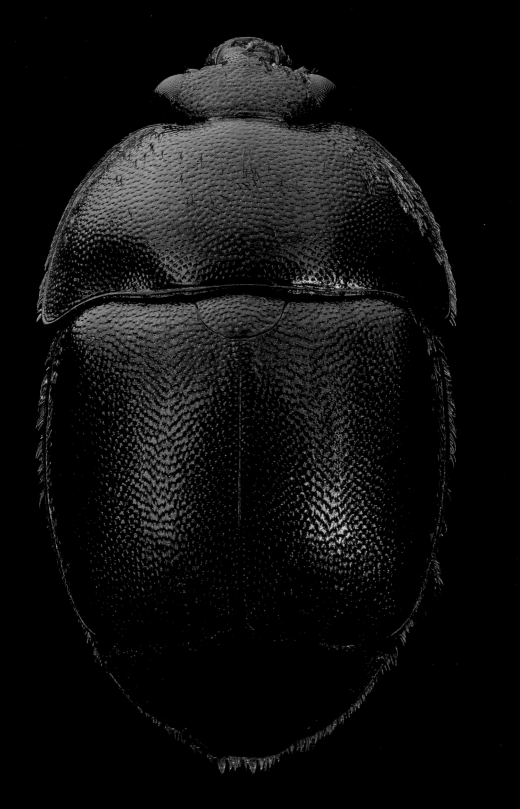

combs or pollen cells. The eggs hatch within a few days and the larvae move quickly to start feeding on honey bee eggs, larvae, pollen and honey; anything, really, that is in the hive and edible. The larval stage lasts for between seven and ten days and is temperature dependent. On completion of their development, the mature larvae enter the wandering phase and exit the colony in large numbers at night and disperse up to 20 metres (65 ft) from the hive. They burrow into the top ten centimetres (4 in) of soil to pupate, which again is temperature and humidity dependent. Pupation can take between three and six weeks during which time complete metamorphosis takes place. Adult beetles mate, locate a colony to infest, and the cycle continues.

Problems present at the larval stage for several reasons. Multiple SHB larvae can congregate in each cell and devour the eggs and larvae, thus reducing the space for the queen to lay and the number of bees in the colony. Colonies are weakened and less able to protect themselves. The most serious problem, however, is that their feeding causes fermentation of the honey, turning it into a foul-smelling, runny mess.

Asian hornet (yellow-legged hornet)

It is thought that Asian hornets, also known as yellow-legged hornets (*Vespa velutina nigrithorax*), first reached France in 2004 when a mated queen arrived from China in pottery. France proved an ideal environment for the hornets, which spread rapidly across the whole of France and adjacent European countries. The hornet was seen in Tetbury in Gloucestershire in 2016, where a single nest was found and destroyed by Bee Inspectors. By the end of 2023, more than 70 nests had been found across England, and it is now thought that this invasive insect is in the UK to stay. In August 2023, an individual yellow-legged hornet was found in Savannah, in the US state of Georgia.

Once mated, an Asian hornet queen collects wood pulp and builds a small spherical nest. She lays a few worker eggs, which she tends herself. As soon as the workers emerge, they perform the housekeeping, nest building and nursing duties. The queen now lays eggs and nothing more. This is the primary nest.

Usually, as the nest expands the workers relocate to a new, larger, secondary nest, which is often – but not always – high in a tree. The secondary nest can measure up to 40–50 centimetres (16–20 in) across and be home to over 60,000 worker hornets.

Towards the end of the season, the queen stops laying worker eggs and lays males and queens. The queens mate and hibernate during the winter, the males and workers die. In spring, the queens

The Asian hornet, while not native to either Europe or the Americas, is a recent invasive species in these regions and a fearsome predator of beehives.

emerge from hibernation and start collecting wood pulp.

Unlike bee larvae, Asian hornet larvae are carnivorous. The worker hornets predate on all insects, which they take back to the nest to feed their larvae – and this includes many pollinating insects whose populations are being seriously reduced.

When the hornets find a colony of honey bees, they hover outside, facing inwards towards the colony. The returning foragers are caught in large numbers and the colony becomes quiescent and remains in the hive. It is not unusual for there to be large numbers of hornets attacking each hive. Many colonies have been lost, and many beekeepers have given up.

Asian hornets are difficult to deal with because they can be very aggressive to humans if they consider their nest is being attacked. Destroying a large nest requires full hazard gear and must be done at night.

As of 2023, the UK government, through the NBU, are still at the stage where they believe eradication of the hornets is possible. There is a national contingency plan involving both local and national organizations, but if eradication proves not to be possible then the next stage is containment. Containment has failed in every other European country where the hornets have spread. The United States has, so far, been able to contain the hornets found in Georgia. In 2016, the UK did not consider containment because the first nest was found and destroyed. The Asian hornet problem is not easily solved.

A green woodpecker
feeding at the side of
a beehive: the damage
comes less from the
loss of scavenged
bees than from the
loss of heat and
watertightness
due to multiple
pecked-out holes.

Woodpeckers

Woodpeckers of varying species can be a voracious pest during a
hard winter. Woodpeckers usually feed on insects from trees or in
the soil. However, if the ground is frozen, they will look elsewhere.
Honey bee colonies provide easily available ready meals, and both
adult bees and any brood will be taken. Serious damage can be
caused to hives as multiple holes allow damp and cold to enter.
Polystyrene hives are the most vulnerable. Woodpeckers seem to
have the ability to alert their companions to the location of these
tasty meals, so attacks by several woodpeckers are normal. The
solution lies in covering each hive with chicken wire, so if the birds
do get a foothold they cannot reach the hive with their beak.

Mice

Mice cause a nuisance to beehives in the winter. A clustering
colony of honey bees represents a warm, dry, safe space for a
mouse to spend the winter. A mouse can enter a hive any time
from when the cluster forms and predate the bees whenever it is
hungry. The main problem arises because mice have no bladder
and continually urinate, which causes a foul smell unacceptable to
the bees. To prevent mice from entering, most beekeepers reduce
their hive entrance and place a mouse guard across it.

Mouse guards are long metal strips with two rows of holes, each
with a diameter of 10 millimetres (¾ in). A mouse's skull is wider
than it is high, so the mouse is unable to pass through these holes.

Other mammals

Many mammals of different sizes predate honey bee colonies
as they provide an easy source of food and shelter. Bears are
present in many US states and have been listed as the most
serious vertebrate predator of honey bee colonies. In some areas,
persistent bear attacks have limited beekeeping development.
They can readily destroy a hive if they get a taste for either the
honey or the bees. Honey badgers and monkeys, baboons and
chimpanzees predate in Africa, whereas mice, voles and rats
attack colonies in the UK. Racoons, weasels, polecats and ferrets
can all be occasional predators of honey bee colonies, although
none are listed as serious pests.

TROUBLESHOOTING

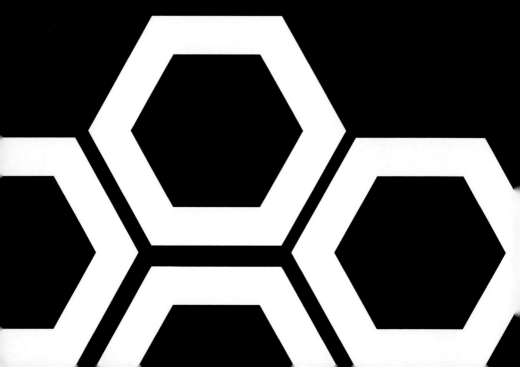

Troubleshooting

'Bad' bee behaviour

Some beekeepers talk about their bees being vicious or highly aggressive – or even go so far as to suggest that the hive needs to be dowsed in petrol and exterminated. However, there are no such things as 'bad' bees, or even bad bee behaviours, which are usually interpreted as aggressive actions towards humans. There are several possible reasons for this aggressive, or – to be more accurate – 'defensive' conduct. Like most other living creatures, bees have two types of behaviours: they have *intrinsic* behaviours such as flying, foraging or feeding their young; and they also exhibit *learned* behaviours such as locating their home and determining which flowers yield nectar at specific times. Both of these types of behaviours benefit the superorganism that is the colony of bees. In fact, in all cases, the behaviour of a bee, or the bee population as a whole, is to the advantage of the colony.

Previous page: A beehive wrecked and shredded by mice. Simple preventive measures should minimize such problems.

Below: At a hive entrance, a worker bee fends off an encroaching bee from another colony.

Chasing

Problem: Bees are chasing you back to the house or to your vehicle.
Solution: One quick, short-term solution is to walk into a darker area such as under trees and stand still: the bees will often fly round and then return to their hives. However, you should check whether the hive is queenless, and if so requeen or combine the colony with a queenright colony immediately. If there is a queen, replace her with a queen of gentler stock.

Fighting

Problem: Worker bees fighting at the hive entrance, wrestling one another, tearing wings and legs off. (If it's autumn and the workers are fighting with drones, this is a typical seasonal 'drone purge' and nothing to be worried about.)
Solution: Reduce the entrance to the width of a single bee, so the colony has a better chance of defending itself against robber bees. Screen ventilation holes. Consolidate hive to smallest configuration of boxes possible to eliminate unused space. If possible, relocate hive to an area without other hives nearby.

Robbing

Problem: Bees from one hive are flying into another, stealing its honey.
Solution: Feed colonies in the evening and, where possible, feed all the colonies at the same time. Add frames of honey to the robbing hive so that they have their own ample food supply. Feed sugar water and pollen patties to divert their attention. If possible, relocate the robbing hive to an area away from other hives.

Absconding

Problem: Colony repeatedly swarms.
Solution: Check whether the hive is overcrowded and, if so, add more brood and honey boxes, preferably with empty frames of drawn comb, so that the queen has more room to lay eggs and the workers have more room to store honey and pollen. Make the colony more comfortable by ensuring that the hive is facing the morning sun, has ventilation to prevent condensation, and that there is plenty of forage in the surrounding area. Swarm guards over the entrance can help, but must be used carefully to prevent killing too many drones that can't pass through them.

Rogue comb building
Problem: Bees build 'Gaudí-esque' sculptures on the hive's interior walls, inner cover and floor. They build wax bridges gluing the frames together.
Solution: Check that the bee space is correct; push frames together that are too far apart; add frames or follower boards if the gaps between frames and walls are too large. Scrape sculptural wax off the inner cover and ensure the lid is fitting securely.

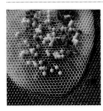

Drone-laying
Problem: Large, bullet-shaped drone cells protruding from the nest where worker bee larvae should be.
Solution: This is a sign that a worker bee's ovaries have developed in response to lack of a queen, but because the worker isn't mated, she can produce only unfertilized male bees. Instal a new queen or combine the hive with a strong hive. Remove the drone larvae if the hive is battling a *Varroa* mite infestation.

Two queens in one hive
Problem: While rare, this is not a problem and a fortunate event when two queens get along and share space. Lucky you.
Solution: Leave them be. Or, split the hive in two – with one queen apiece – and plenty of brood, honey, and pollen per hive.

Honey bees invade a wild hive, intent on ripping open the capped cells – fighting off the resident bees in the process. Once they have filled their honey stomachs, they'll ferry the stolen cargo back to the home hive.

Diseases

Diseased bees often exhibit behaviours such as being unable to fly or are black and shiny where their hair has been chewed away. They may be refused entry into their hive or be driven or dragged out. Guard bees will prevent bees from entering their own colony if they sense they are carrying some viruses.

Close observation, careful maintenance, and stringent, preventive measures (such as the application of Terramycin™ against foulbroods, shown here) are key to troubleshooting in beekeeping.

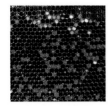

American foulbrood

Problem: Brood nest has a foul smell, larvae has liquified behind punctured, sunken wax cappings into a brown, glue-like consistency inside the cells.

Solution: Burn all infected colonies and contaminated equipment, because American foulbrood is highly contagious. Like both foulbrood diseases, it is notifiable under the law. In the United States, state apiary inspection services or the Beltsville Bee Lab in Maryland will confirm American foulbrood contamination from a posted-in sample. This is free of charge. In the UK, if you suspect American foulbrood is present in your colonies, you must inform the NBU immediately.

European foulbrood

Problem: Young, two to four-day-old diseased larvae in open cells. Larvae is grey or splotchy instead of the normal pearly white.

Solution: Requeen with a young, vibrant queen. In advanced cases, an antibiotic such as oxytetracycline powder treatment can be fed to the bees, if the honey supers are removed first. It is a notifiable disease (see the notes on American foulbrood, above).

Chalkbrood

Problem: Dead, chalky-white mummified larvae encased in a cottony fluff, often found at the entrance where nurse bees have discarded them.

Solution: Requeen with a young queen. Throw out infected combs. Going forward, replace brood combs regularly to keep spores to a minimum. Keep hive stress low by providing lots of food, a warm location and assistance with keeping the colony population high.

Sacbrood

Problem: Scattershot brood pattern with shrunken, perforated cappings throughout the brood nest.

Solution: Bees can usually control this short-living virus by removing diseased brood, but the colony will have a harder time if the hive is already stressed. Requeen, remove infected combs and store them for at least two months to eliminate the virus. As an on-going precaution for all viruses, honeycomb frames should be replaced every three to four years or as soon as the wax darkens.

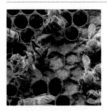

Nosemosis

Problem: Faecal staining on the outside of the hive, near to the entrance.

Solution: Provide plenty of honey to over-wintering hives. Feed fumagillin-medicated syrup.

Paralysis

Problem: Greasy, hairless bees that tremble and are unable to fly, crawling up the sides of the hive or on blades of grass near the hive.

Solution: Add a few frames of sealed brood from a healthy colony. If the problem persists, requeen with a queen from a different strain of bees.

A hive with listless bees unable to fly can be pepped up with frames of sealed brood from a healthy colony.

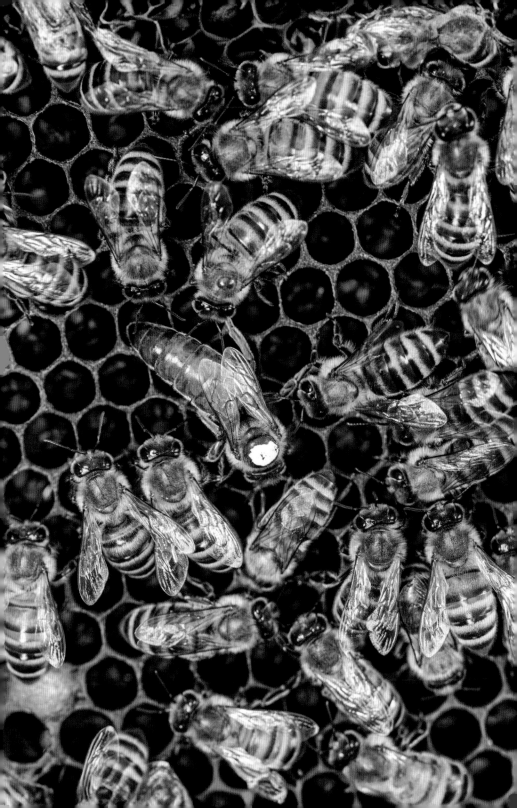

Parasites, pests and predators

Parasites such as *Varroa* will undermine the health of the colony from within while pests and predators – from wasps to bears – threaten the colony from without, robbing the hive of honey and, in the process, killing bees and compromising or destroying the hive infrastructure.

Formic acid is one of the treatments recommended for the control of *Varroa* mites. It can be applied as biodegradable gel strips, designed to be laid across the top bars of the brood nest.

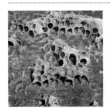

***Varroa destructor* mite**

Problem: Visible rust-red shiny mites attached to bee bodies and bee larvae. Bees' wings are deformed, leaving them unable to fly.

Nonchemical solutions:
Create sacrificial drone comb by placing short honey super frames into the brood box. The bees will create drone cells suspended from the underside of the honey frame. Monitor and then, as soon as the drone cells are capped, remove them. Mites prefer drone larvae, and this baiting method helps reduce their numbers in the hive. The capped brood can be fed to chickens; they are impervious to the mites and enjoy pecking for the larvae.

Cage the queen for one to two weeks to interrupt her laying and provide a brood break, creating a period when there are no capped cells in which mites can multiply.

There are many natural and chemical treatments available for *Varroa*:
- Essential oils–Apiguard® or Thymovar®
- Formic acids–Mite-Away Quick Strips®, Formic Pro®, Oxalic Acid/Api Bioxal®, HopGuard®
- Synthetic chemicals–Apivar®, Apistan®, CheckMite+®

The Honey Bee Health Coalition
(provides an excellent guide to *Varroa* management):
https://honeybeehealthcoalition.org/wp-content/uploads/2022/08/HBHC-Guide_Varroa-Mgmt_8thEd-082422.pdf

Prevention measures:
Mite test monthly with either an isopropyl alcohol wash or icing sugar shake. Put half a cup (for approximately every 300 bees) in a glass jar with screened lid, and swirl in alcohol or roll in sugar (the alcohol kills the mites, but the sugar doesn't). Shake alcohol or sugar into a large bowl with water and count how many mites are floating. Use the following equation:

The number of mites: 300 × 5 (to account for mites trapped in brood cells) = infestation rate

A healthy hive is considered anything below 4 per cent infested. Use a screened bottom board so that the mites fall out of the hive when hygienic bees clean one another of mites.

Tracheal mite
Problem: Large numbers of bees crawling out of the hive, unable to fly. Disjointed wings are in a 'K' position.
Solution: Treat with menthol pellets or grease patties (vegetable suet plus sugar).

Small hive beetle (SHB)
Problem: Shiny, round black beetles crawling over honeycomb. Slimy honey that smells like rotten oranges.
Solution: Use oil traps or beetle towels, or treat with CheckMite+®.

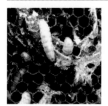

Wax moth
Problem: White grubs carving silken tunnels through honeycomb. White papery cocoons attached to wooden frames.
Solution: Remove destroyed frames. Store honey supers and empty combs in cold environments such as a freezer or outdoors covered in mice-proof mesh and tarps. If this is impractical, keep unused equipment aerated, in a ventilated room, with boxes on their sides open on top and bottom holding just a handful of frames. Or place moth ball crystals (paradichlorobenzene) on a piece of paper between every fifth box in a stored stack of unused bee equipment.

Ants
Problem: Trail of ants from ground, up hive stand, and into hive.
Solution: Remove brush, grass, weeds, and rotten wood from around the colonies. Ring the ground around the hive in ground cinnamon. Create ant traps by placing hive stand legs in containers of waste cooking or motor oil.

Mice
Problem: Nests in back corners of bottom hive box; chew holes in honeycomb.
Solution: Cover the hive entrance with metal 'mouse guards'. These have small holes (a little larger than the width of a bee) that allow only the bees to pass through.

Wasps

Problem: Wasps dive-bombing the entrance, especially in autumn.
Solution: Make sure the hive cover fits securely. Screen all ventilation holes. Reduce the hive entrance to allow just one bee to pass through, making it easier for the colony to defend the front door. Wasp traps found in DIY stores can also help.

Woodpeckers (and other birds)

Problem: Hives being robbed by woodpeckers.
Solution: Use a wire-mesh fence to keep woodpeckers away, although, if it is too close, it may become a convenient perch. The strong, black material weed suppressant used in gardens can work well. It can be stapled to the hive and the woodpeckers cannot get a grip to attack the hive.

Skunks

Problem: Scratches at the entrance of the hive where a skunk has disturbed the bees, so they come out to investigate and get eaten. Scat with honey bee exoskeletons near the entrance.
Solution: Raise the hive higher than the skunk can reach. Stacked breeze blocks work well.

Bears and badgers

Problem: Knocked-over and smashed hives; bees and honeycomb eaten.
Solution: Enclose the apiary with an electric fence, away from trees that bears can climb. Instal motion lights (with lights facing away from hives). All hives should be on a strong stand that is level and should be securely strapped onto the stand. This is especially important in winter. Put a heavy weight on the roof to help with stability. Large plastic bee food containers filled with water are very useful for this purpose. Hives may be dislodged or knocked over, but if they are securely strapped together and to the stand they usually survive.

TROUBLESHOOTING

Birds and mammals, such as hungry woodpeckers and bears, are perennial threats to hives, but basic measures can help guard against these predators.

Other problems

Poorly sited hives

The hives may be in a frost pocket, not level, or are in the damp or dark at the bottom of a slope. The site may have looked suitable in the summer when the sun was high in the sky, but in winter when the sun is lower, it may leave the bees in dark shade for most of the time. It is important to visualize the area intended as an apiary in the winter and, if possible, seek local opinion about whether the area floods or frosts linger in the area.

Bees can also be upset if the hive is sited under trees and rain drips the on roof. This can lead to defensive behaviour when the colony is inspected, or the colony can struggle and remain small. The hive will probably need to be placed in a different position in the apiary.

Especially careful thought needs to be given when siting hives near rivers and streams or on flood plains, and to possible precautions. When the Somerset Levels flooded, many hives were swept away but there was one beekeeper who used polystyrene hives and had strapped them onto a wooden board. This acted like a raft and the hives were seen floating downstream. Fortunately, when the beekeeper retrieved his hives, he found that the bees had survived and were still in residence.

Another siting problem is where the apiary has been positioned too near a footpath, playground, or pond where children are playing. The bees may be viewed as a threat and sting when disturbed or attempts are made to swat them or chase them away.

The experienced beekeeper learns to use smoke judiciously during inspections and harvesting.

The bees have been subjected to excessive smoking
Smoke needs to be used to maintain control and keep the bees inside the box that is being examined. Ideally, however, smoking should be used only occasionally during inspection.

The colony is too small
As winter approaches, the beekeeper needs to assess the size of colonies, as small colonies may be particularly challenged over winter. First, check the bees in the colony are healthy and have food and have a small entrance so that the hive can be defended against bees from other colonies or wasps. One answer to a small colony is to put it into a nucleus or to combine it with another colony. Combining two different colonies is not difficult but they must have only one queen.

Poor choice of equipment or equipment in need of repair
This will often mean the bees have to defend several entrances where the equipment doesn't quite fit together or has a small gap where the woodwork has been damaged. This will leave the hive open to robbing by other colonies or wasps.

Hives do need maintenance and should be checked to ensure they are sound before they are used. The winter is a good time to repair hives and repaint those that need work. Keep an eye out for sales. Beekeeping equipment manufacturers often hold sales during the winter or early spring, providing an opportunity to renew old boxes.

Excessive rain
This may not lead to flooding (see opposite) but it can cause the hive stand to sink into the ground. If only one or two legs sink, the stand may become unstable and topple over. Placing the stand on a flagstone may help, but it is essential to ensure colonies are securely strapped onto their stands.

Wind and wind direction

Winds are also a potential hazard, as they may cause bees to be blown into other hives or, if the wind is from one direction, this could result in unequal numbers in the hives, especially if the hives are sited in a straight line. Consider the prevailing wind direction when siting hives; it may also help if they are arranged in a semi-circle or a square formation.

Fire

Bees are likely to abscond if the colony is subjected regularly to a lot of smoke, possibly sited too close to where garden waste is burned. If the grass is short around the apiary and the hive stands are on flagstones, there is a chance they may survive a local grass fire. A small fire may not affect them and will leave them unscathed, but a major heathland or forest fire will have a devastating effect.

Lack of forage

Bees will not be badly affected if they are placed on the roof of a tall block of flats or in a field in the countryside, but wherever they are located they do need forage. Flowers in window boxes, pots and tubs will help, especially bulbs such as crocuses and snowdrops in the early spring.

Bees are resilient, but will rely on the beekeeper if they have been placed in areas that do not provide sufficient food for them to store for the winter. If there is no food in the area, move the bees elsewhere. Bees need to be inspected regularly and fed when necessary.

If an apiary has been plagued by a serious epidemic, it may be necessary to conduct a safe, hygienic burning of the hives and tools that came into contact with the unhealthy bees.

Overleaf: An idyllic siting for both bees and beekeeper – an apiary in a lush wildflower meadow.

Beekeeping myths debunked

Beekeeping is expensive
It's not – if you build your own equipment. Beekeepers are friendly and often share or donate equipment to one another. Also, honey sales can offset material costs.

Beekeepers can make money through selling honey
The cost of maintaining the colonies needs to be reflected in the price of a 450 gram (1 lb) jar of honey. Unfortunately, something called honey can be bought in a supermarket for less than a quarter of this cost. This is often imported honey that has been adulterated in the country of origin by adding such things as rice or corn syrup or chemicals to achieve a product looking similar to honey. This is a worldwide problem that is driving the price of genuine honey (a substance produced solely by honey bees) lower. Many beekeepers have decided to give up beekeeping as a means to support their families because it is so hard to sell their own honey at a realistic price.

A honey bee visits lavender flowers.

Bees are prone to aggression

Bees sting only if they feel they must defend their colony. A bee knows it will die if it stings; its stinger will come out and disembowel the bee. So they will give plenty of warnings first. Bees will ignore you if you respect them and take the right precautions and handle them gently.

Bees won't find enough forage in a city

Urban bees have a wealth of resources because of all the imported plants that bloom year-round in urban and suburban gardens, as opposed to the country where they all must compete for seasonal blooms. Also there is lots of water available in fountains and gutters, as well as from lawn sprinklers.

Neighbours will not want to be close to hives

The best way to alleviate fear is to invite the neighbours in. Show them the hive, invite them to a honey harvest, and share the bounty. Hives often go unnoticed under the watch of a careful beekeeper who can prevent swarming. This is especially true for urban rooftop hives, which are completely out of sight.

Beekeeping is easy because the bees take care of themselves

Keeping bees in manufactured hives is putting them in an unnatural environment, so they need extra support to stay healthy. Just like a pet dog, they need a water source, regular feeding and a home that is warm and dry with enough room to move around. Expect to be very busy in spring and summer as colonies expand and produce honey. Have a beekeeper on back-up who can step in if you need to leave for an extended period during the honey flow.

Beekeeping is hard because you must know science, botany and entomology

There are so many wonderful websites, books and beekeeping clubs everywhere, created by beekeepers who love to share their love of bees, that anyone can become a beekeeper. The best way to see whether it's a good fit for you is to spend a beekeeping year under the mentorship of another beekeeper.

There will be too much honey to harvest and process

Bees need at least a full year before they start producing
enough honey to share with the keeper. Even then, the harvest is
dependent on the weather, the health of the bees and the skills of
the beekeeper. Some years will be productive; other years will be a
'honey pass'. Like everything in nature, the honey flow is variable
and unpredictable, and the bees' honey needs always come before
the keeper's. You can keep your day job.

Swarming means the beekeeper has done something wrong

Honey bees have a natural instinct to swarm because this is how
they replicate in the wild: swarming is thus usually a sign of a
healthy expanding colony. A good, experienced beekeeper can
direct and control swarming on most occasions, although there are
bees that are just determined to swarm because of their inherited
genetics. Despite the best efforts of even the most seasoned
beekeepers, some colonies are 'swarmier' than others and will
divide themselves multiple times in a season.

Hives need managing by a skilled beekeeper or the bees may
decide to swarm and find homes that are suitable for bees such as
a roof space or chimney but which may upset the owners, who will
not appreciate the damage that could be caused. The bees may not
cause a problem initially, but as the colony expands, their honey
could seep through the walls or ceilings and mean expensive
repairs, or the bees may become a nuisance within the house.
It is important to check a colony carefully to ensure there is not
a high *Varroa* load or disease that has caused the colony to
swarm or abscond.

In an expanding
colony, the hive
may become
overcrowded –
prompting honey
bees to swarm and
split into two or more
groups. While one
group remains in the
hive, others may find
alternative spaces in
which to settle.

Drones don't contribute to the hive

In fact, drones are important for the balance of the colony: it is the workers that build the drone cells and dictate the number of drones in the hive, unless there is a problem with the queen. If drone brood is removed, more will be built, but it does take resources from the workers to replace drone brood. Research has shown that drones can help to keep the brood warm by occupying cells next to the brood if temperatures fall in the summer. Drones also help in fanning the currents of air through the colony when the weather is exceptionally hot. Drone brood is sometimes removed as a *Varroa* control, but this should not be performed often as it will interfere with the balance of the colony. If the colony is suffering because they do not have sufficient food, some of the drone larvae may be consumed, acting as an emergency supply of food for the workers.

Bees like bananas

It's true that if you put an over-ripe banana in a hive, the bees will eat it, and lots of beekeepers have been trying this as a sugar feed ever since reports widely shared on the Internet claim vitamins in the bananas are helping bees to ward off infections. However, push-back is mounting from entomologists who say it's unnatural for bees to eat bananas, and that it disrupts their delicate systems. Debate is ongoing, but the safest bet is to feed bees what they already eat in the wild.

BEEKEEPING FOLKLORE
In folk belief, bees have often been considered to be a link between the living world and the spirit world. So, if there was any message that someone wished to pass to someone who was dead, they 'told the bees' and the bees would pass along the message. 'Telling the bees' was a widely reported practice in Europe – and also in the United States, where European settlers are thought to have introduced the practice along with beekeeping.

The death of loved ones

Some superstitions relate to the importance of accepting the bees as a part of the family and keeping them informed of any news in the household. Marriages, new births and especially deaths were marked by decorating the hive and telling the bees what had happened. One of the most familiar customs, still practised today, is telling the bees of the death of a loved one. Imparting the news of a death to the bees is done on a hive-by-hive basis. The beekeeper first knocks on the hive before giving the occupants notice of the death. The hive may also be covered by a black cloth, or a similar piece of material, for the period of mourning.

Shortly after Queen Elizabeth II died in 2022, the Royal Beekeeper performed a ritual in the Buckingham Palace gardens. In his white beekeeping suit he crossed to the small island in the garden lake, where he tended five beehives on behalf of the Royal Family. Over the top of each hive he draped a black sash. Then he gave a gentle rap on each hive's side, as though calling the residents' attention, and told the bees of the Queen's death.

According to tradition, bees that are 'put into mourning' help shepherd the dead into the afterlife, as well as compensating their 'family' with a generous honey harvest. Bees that are not properly informed, on the other hand, are said to cease producing honey or to abscond from the hive.

Another custom relating to a death of a family member is moving the hives to show that a change has taken place. In some cases, they are moved to the right; in others, they are turned to face the door of the family home. This ritual is known as 'ricking'.

This late nineteenth-century painting by Charles Napier Hemy (1841–1917) depicts a widow and her son informing the bees, in their garden apiary, of a recent death in the family.

For centuries, European beekeepers treated their bees as members of an extended family, addressing them in calm tones – and without harsh words – to avoid upsetting the hive.

A new beginning

The death of the beekeeper requires the new beekeeper to introduce themselves formally as the bees' new owner and ask for acceptance as their new master/mistress. It was said that not doing this would encourage the bees to desert the hive or the colony to stop producing honey – or even die. This is a tradition that is often shared with new beekeepers to encourage them to continue talking to their bees. Talking to bees can be very calming and stress-relieving for the beekeeper, the good news being that the bees listen but don't talk back! This is actually good advice, as it connects new beekeepers to their bees and encourages an atmosphere of calm and respect.

Clockwise from top left: Bright blossoms attract a harvesting bee; an Indian honey bee investigates a bidens flower; the distinctive tawny mining bee collects nectar and pollen from the blossoms.

Clockwise from top: Close-up, macro shot of a Northern white-tailed bumble bee on a lantana flower; identified by its pure-black head, a female carpenter bee is seen feeding; this leaf-cutting bee harvests scraps of leaves, which it will use to construct cells within its nest.

REFERENCE
SECTION

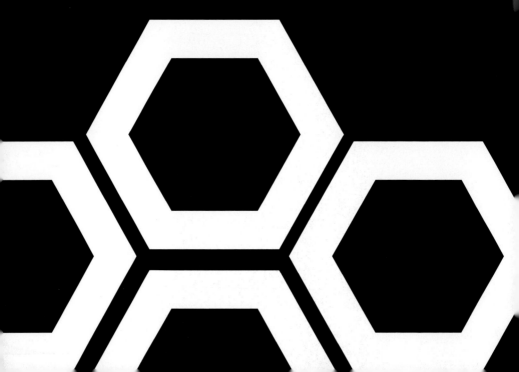

Glossary

Apiary Area where bee hives are located.

Bait Hive Box with old combs for attracting and holding a swarm of bees.

Bee Bread Mixture of pollen and honey used as food for bees.

Bee Package Screened cage that holds a varying amount of bees and a caged queen with sugar syrup. Can be posted to beekeepers.

Bee Space Area between ten millimetres (⅜ in) and six millimetres (¼ in) that separates hive components for bees to move around in.

Brood Immature stages of bees: egg, larvae and pupae.

Brood Comb Type of beeswax that is used by bees to raise their young. It is much darker than regular honeycomb for supers.

Brood Pattern Arrangement of brood, pollen and honey on a frame.

Burr Comb Extra honeycomb produced by bees to fill a space to join two parts of a hive.

Capped Brood Pupae whose cells have been sealed up.

Capped Honey Ripe honey with a wax topping (cappings).

Cappings The wax seal covering ripe honey, which is removed when harvesting honey.

Cleansing Flights When bees emerge from the hive during warmer weather in the winter to remove debris from the hive and defecate.

Cluster Group of bees clumped together for warmth, such as in winter.

Cut Comb Honey Honeycomb full of honey, cut to fit into a container.

Dearth Time when pollen and nectar is scarce or not available.

Deep Largest box of a Langstroth hive, usually used for raising brood.

Dividing Splitting a colony from two or more bee colonies.

Drawn Comb Honeycomb built upon a foundation, on a frame.

Drifting When honey bees 'drift' or move from one colony to another, particularly when hives are placed in straight lines and painted the same colour. This is a vector for disease spread.

Drone Male honey bee.

Eke Very shallow super that creates space in the beehive. Usually 5–7.5 centimetres (2–3 in) tall.

Entrance Reducer Device that fits across the entrance of a hive to reduce the ingress and egress of bees, primarily used to stop robbing.

Fanning Movement of a bee's wings used to regulate temperature in the hive and to ripen nectar.

Festooning The practice of bees joining up and linking their legs together to form a single line, or chain.

Forager Worker bee that collects pollen and/or nectar from a floral source and returns back to the hive.

Frame Structural element that holds the honeycomb within the hive.

Fume Board Lid with a flannel interior to soak up a bee repellent chemical to repel bees for honey harvesting.

Guard Bees Bees that keep intruders from entering the hive.

Inner Cover Lightweight cover that is placed under the outer telescoping cover.

Langstroth Hive Traditional hive system in use for over 100 years with stackable and expandable units with hanging frames.

Marked Queen Queen painted with a mark of paint on top of her thorax to clearly identify her as the queen.

Nectar Flow Time of abundant nectar and pollen available for bees to produce excess honey.

Nuc Miniature hive, usually consisting of five frames with a laying queen, brood (in various stages), capped honey and pollen.

Piping Acoustic sound emitted by young queens during the process of swarming.

Pollen Male reproductive cells produced by flowers.

Pollen Basket 'Saddlebag' located on the hind legs of bees to carry pollen back to the hive.

Pollen Trap Device that will scrape off pollen grains from the back legs of worker bees carrying pollen.

Propolis Sticky, glue-like substance produced by bees.

Queen Cell Larva developed inside a cell that matures into new queens.

Queen Excluder Screen designed with openings to allow smaller worker bees through, but are too big for the larger queen and drones to fit through.

Queenless Colony without a viable queen.

Queenright Colony that contains a healthy, egg-laying queen.

Rendering Turning dirty wax cappings and burr comb into clean wax slabs.

Requeening Replacing an old queen with a new one.

Reversing Spring management practice to switch the position of the hive bodies, so that you can move the brood box to the lowest point in the hive.

Robbing The practice of bees stealing honey from weaker hives.

Royal Jelly Nutritious glandular secretion to feed young bees and developing queens.

Scout Bees Bees searching for a new home, pollen or nectar sources.

Stinging Pheromones Produced by the sting glands of the honey bee, which coordinate defensive behaviour.

Super Hive box for storing honey, placed above a brood box.

Supersedure Replacement of a failing or absent queen in a hive.

Swarm Queen that leaves the parent colony with drones and half of the workers to find a replacement home.

Swarm Management Management practices used throughout the year to keep a colony from swarming.

Uncapping Knife Sharp tool that is usually heated to remove the wax coverings of ripe honey for harvesting.

Wax Moth Larvae and adults of *Galleria mellonella*, which can destroy brood combs.

Index

Page references in *italics* indicate images.

A

absconding behaviour 245
acarine mite 225–6, *225*
acute bee paralysis virus (ABPV) 230
African honey bee 27–8, *27*, 236
Africanized honey bee 27, 30, *30*, 75, 86, 107, 201
aggression, bees and 265
Ah-Muzen-Cab 9, *9*
alfalfa 36, 40, 192
allergies 72–3, *73*, 201, 202–3
almond trees 38, 188, *188*, 193, 205
American foulbrood 75, 179, 210, *210*, 212–14, *213*, 216, *217*, 249, *249*
ants 254
apiary 274
Apiary Inspector *209*, 210, *210*, 211
  protecting 89
  sites 85
  starting 85–9, *87*, *88*, *89*
Apidae 21
Apis genus 22, 25
Apis nuluensis 31
apple trees 188, *188*
Asian honey bee 24, 25, 31–2, *31*, 220–1, 223
Asian hornet (yellow-legged hornets) (*Vespa velutina nigrithorax*) 31, 238–9, *239*
avocado trees 188, *188*

B

'bad' bee behaviour 244–7, *244*, *245*, *246*, *247*
badgers 89
bait hive box 107, 274
Bailey, Leslie 221
bananas 267
bears 89, 180, 241, 255
BeeBase 211
bee bread 44, 136, 145, 274

bee density 86–7, *87*
bee hotels 40, 41, *41*
Bee Inspector 86, 211, 214, 216, 238
beekeeping
  association or club 16, 84, 179, 207, 211
  becoming a beekeeper 82–3
  business of 204–7
  commercial 14, 28, 51, 129, 153, *153*, 192, 204–5
  course 16, *16*, 84
  history of 7, 8–17, *9*, *15*
  myths 264–7, *264*, *266*
  year *68*, 69–71, 110
bee package 82, 97, 100, 109, 274
bee space 14, 90, 97, 200, 247, 274
bidens flower 270, *270*
black queen cell virus (BQCV) 232, *232*
blossoms 21, 26, 33, 74, *74*, 186, 188, *188*, 189, 190, 191, 192, 194, 270
blueberry 192
borage 192
bottlebrush 191, *191*
brood 274
brood comb 75, 123, 124, *213*, *215*, 236, 249, 274, 275
brood pattern or configuration 70, 113, 117, *117*, 177, 250, 274
Buckfast bee 28, *28*
bumble bee 21–2, 24, 33, 34–5, *34*, 36, 39, 60, *60*, 192, 196
burr comb 152, 183, 235, 274

C

calmness/gentleness around the hive 79, *79*
capped brood 117, 121, 212, 253, 274
capped honey 148–9, 152, 274
Carniolan bee 26, *26*, 29, 74
carpenter bee 36–7, *37*, 271, *271*
Carr, William Broughton 15
Caucasian bee *26*, 26–7, 29, 74

chalkbrood 182, 218–19, *218*, 249, *249*
chasing behaviour 245
cherry trees 189, *189*
Chittka, Lars: *The Mind of a Bee* 60, 61
chronic bee paralysis virus (CBPV) 228, 229–30
citrus trees 189, *189*
city, foraging in a 265
clean-up 162
cleansings flights 133
clothing
  hygiene 78
  protective 77–8
clovers 189, *189*
cluster 29, 31, 43, 44, 56, 58, 63, 100, 103, 107, 108, 109, 132, 137, 141, 143, 189, 190, 241, 274
colonies
  new 105
  sharing 88–9
  size 259
  starting or replacing 99–100, *99*
  temper 74
commercial beekeepers 14, 28, 51, 129, 153, *153*, 192, 204–5
Cordovan bee 29, *29*
costs 83, 264
cover cloths 117
crush and strain method 93, 155, 160
cuckoo bee 39–40, *39*
Cuevas de la Araña, Spain 8, 9, *9*
cut-comb honey 97, 162

D

Dadant, Charles 15
dearth 29, 78, 136, 185, 274
death
  of loved ones 268, *268*
  of the beekeeper 269
deformed wing virus (DWV) 227, *227*, 228, *228*
direct release 122

Resources and Supplies

BEEKEEPING BOOKS

Beekeeping for dummies, 5th edition
Howland Blackiston
For Dummies/John Wiley & Sons

The Backyard Beekeeper, 4th edition
Kim Flottum
Quarry Books

The Beekeeper's Handbook
Diana Sammataro, Alphonse Avitabile, Dewey
M. Caron (Foreword)
Comstock Publishing Associates

Hive Management: A seasonal guide
for beekeepers
Richard E. Bonney
Storey Publishing, LLC

The Beekeeper's Problem Solver: 100 common
problems explored and explained
James E. Tew
Quarry Books

US edition: *The Beekeeper's Bible: Bees, honey,*
recipes & other home uses
UK edition: *Collins Beekeeper's Bible: Bees,*
honey, recipes & other home uses
Richard A. Jones and Sharon Sweeney-Lynch
Abrams Books / HarperCollins*Publishers* UK

INDUSTRY MAGAZINES

US
American Bee Journal
Dadant & Sons
www.dadant.com

Bee Culture, The Magazine
of American Beekeeping
A.I. Root Company
www.beeculture.com

UK
BeeCraft
Bee Craft Ltd
www.bee-craft.com

BEEKEEPING SUPPLIES & EQUIPMENT

US
Mann Lake, Ltd.
www.mannlakeltd.com

Dadant & Sons
www.dadant.com

Blue Sky Bee Supply
www.blueskybeesupply.com

Betterbee, Inc.
www.betterbee.com

Olivarez Honey Bees
www.ohbees.com

UK
EH Thorne (Beehives) Ltd
www.thorne.co.uk

Maisemore Apiaries
www.bees-online.co.uk

ABELO
www.abelo.co.uk

National Bee Supplies Ltd
www.beekeeping.co.uk

HONEY BEE RESEARCH & EDUCATION SOURCES

US
Penn State Extension
Beekeeping 101
Online course
www.extension.psu.edu/beekeeping-101

Bee Informed Partnership
www.beeinformed.org

Honey Bee Health Coalition
www.honeybeehealthcoalition.org

Best Bees Company
www.bestbees.com

Project *Apis m.*
www.projectapism.org

American Beekeeping Federation
www.abfnet.org

UK
APHA–National Bee Unit BeeBase
www.nationalbeeunit.com

The British Beekeepers Association
www.bbka.org.uk

Northern Bee Books
www.northernbeebooks.co.uk

Picture Credits

About the Authors

MEREDITH MAY
Meredith is the author of *The Honey Bus*, the best-selling memoir of her beekeeping childhood with her grandfather in Big Sur, California. She is a fifth-generation beekeeper and a former award-winning reporter for the *San Francisco Chronicle*. Her latest work is an illustrated children's book: *My Hive: A Girl, Her Grandpa, and Their Honeybee Family.*

CLAIRE JONES
A beekeeper for over 25 years in her Maryland meadow, Claire is an award-winning garden designer, garden communicator, and travel organizer of garden-centric trips around the world. Writing about gardening and beekeeping on her blog, *The Garden Diaries*, Claire has also decorated the White House in the United States on many occasions. Her greatest pleasure is smearing fresh-from-the-hive honey on her breakfast toast while watching her 'girls' collecting nectar and pollen from her meadow.

ANNE ROWBERRY

Anne has been keeping bees for around 20 years after purchasing two beehives, joining a club, and increasing her knowledge through the British Beekeepers Association (BBKA) modules and Microscopy and Husbandry examinations, eventually achieving a Master Beekeepers' Certificate. As President of the BBKA, she lectures nationally and internationally on bee-related subjects. She is committed to developing beekeeping in the UK, improving bee husbandry, and enjoying her bees. As part of this goal she is also an assessor for the BBKA Examinations.

Previously, Anne also trained as a teacher, and gained an MEd (Management) and a Diploma in Counselling. As such, she has worked for many institutions, from the UK's National Outdoor Pursuits Centre and Avon County Executive Committee, to the United World College of South East Asia and a charity focused on sustainable agriculture in Africa, setting up and managing their first digital image bank.

MARGARET MURDIN

Margaret has been keeping bees for more than 20 years and has recently downsized from managing over 40 colonies to just 6 colonies. She is a Master Beekeeper, has won the prestigious Wax Chandlers' Award, and gained the National Diploma in Beekeeping (NDB).

Margaret is a Past President of the British Beekeepers Association (BBKA) and sits on the Examination Board as Assistant Moderator. She is a Correspondence Course Tutor and an Assessor for all BBKA examinations and assessments.

Previously, Margaret was the Principal of a large Further and Higher Education College, a Chief Examiner for Teacher Education, and a tutor and examiner for the Open University. She has sat on several UK Government Committees advising on further, higher, and special education.